Detection, Detention, Deportation

Detection, Detention, Deportation

Criminal justice and migration control through the lens of crimmigration

Jelmer Brouwer

Boom juridisch
Den Haag
2020

Omslagontwerp: Primo!Studio, Delft
Opmaak binnenwerk: Anne-Marie Krens – Tekstbeeld – Oegstgeest

ISBN 978-94-6236-988-7
ISBN 978-94-6094-445-1 (e-book)
NUR 820

www.boomjuridisch.nl

Table of contents

1 Introduction

1 Introduction

1.1 Finding the border in a time of globalisation

Driven by a range of different processes commonly placed together under the broad banner of globalisation, borders have undergone significant changes (Gready, 2004). Whereas the 1990s saw widespread optimism about a borderless world, the terrorist attacks of September 11, 2001 are generally seen as ushering in a period of renewed attempts by many countries to strengthen control over their borders in response to transnational threats (Diener & Hagen, 2009). States have sought ways to appear to be in control of these various risks and threats emanating from an increasingly globalising world, intending to address public concerns and fears (Aas, 2007). As Gready (2004, p. 350) notes, "globalisation erases certain borders while entrenching, establishing and redrawing others." We are thus witnessing simultaneously a process of 'debordering' and a process of 'rebordering' (Melin, 2016). Much has been written about the securitisation and criminalisation of migration that has been a result of this (Bosworth & Guild, 2008; Huysmans, 2007).

Security and protection are not the only, or even primary, reasons for this renewed focus on borders. Loader and Sparks (2002) claim that people's sense of place and differences between 'us' and 'them' are particularly salient in times of big transformations. For many people, the transformations associated with globalisation – increased migration, transnational cultures, multiculturalism, and neoliberal economies – are deeply threatening to their sense of national identity, security and belonging (Aas, 2007; Bloemraad, 2015; van Houtum & van Naerssen, 2002). Borders are by their very nature tools for symbolic processes of inclusion and exclusion: they are a crucial instrument in shaping national identity and defining who belongs to the polity and who does not (Diener & Hagen, 2009; Weber, 2006). Bosworth and Guild (2008) therefore claim that migration control is a way for states to at least symbolically manifest their sovereignty at a time when state sovereignty and the relevance of national territory appears to be in decline (see also Weber & Bowling, 2004). Besides reaffirming sovereignty, border control is equally aimed at establishing the boundaries of belonging and creating a coherent sense of national identity (Momen, 2005).

Whereas borders were long seen as "the physical and highly visible lines of separation between political, social and economic spaces (Newman, 2006, p. 144)", more recently scholars have started to reconceptualise borders, focussing instead on the more dynamic concept of *bordering practices* (Browne, 2006; Cote-Boucher, Infantino, & Salter, 2014; Moffette, 2018; Pratt & Thompson, 2008; Salter, 2008). For example, Motomura (1993, p. 712) already defined the border as "not a fixed location but rather where the government performs border functions." In this dissertation, bordering practices are defined as all measures taken by a state to regulate and enforce its borders in order to determine who has the right to stay within its territory; this can be both at the external border and inside the national territory.

Geddes (2008), quoted in Weber (2019), makes a distinction between three types of borders. Territorial borders are the traditional physical demarcations between nation states. Yet, as Fabini (2019, p. 2) argues, "borders exist not only between states, but also within nation-states." Geddes therefore identifies two other types of borders. Organisational borders are more bureaucratic bordering practices occurring inside national territories, such as denying migrants access to basic services. Conceptual borders, which Fassin (2011) refers to as boundaries, are manifestations of perceptions about who belongs or not and do not necessarily lead to formal exclusion. Weber (2018, p. 2) accordingly argues that "borders do not operate solely through territorial exclusion, but instead may create regimes of differential in/exclusion by controlling access to essential resources."

Controlling mobility thus no longer takes the form of controlling every person at a fixed place in between two countries. Instead, facilitated by the rise of identification and surveillance techniques, it occurs at a wide range of different locations and by a wide range of different actors, both at the actual border, at external sites, and inside national territories (Loftus, 2015; Lyon, 2007; Weber & Bowling, 2004). The externalisation of bordering practices can be seen in visa policies, carrier sanctions, and cooperation with third states to prevent would-be immigrants from getting even near the territory of the state or leaving their country altogether. The internalisation of bordering practices manifests itself through migration checks at an increasing number of internal 'border sites' and punitive responses to unauthorised entry or stay, such as detention and deportation (Aas, 2013; Weber & Bowling, 2004). However, it can also manifest itself through socially excluding unauthorised migrants from a range of social services, aimed at achieving 'voluntary' departure (Aliverti, Milivojevic, & Weber, 2019; Bowling & Westenra, 2018; Leerkes, Engbersen, & Van der Leun, 2012).

In recent decades such internal border controls have intensified and diversified throughout the western world (Bowling & Westenra, 2018; Moffette, 2014). These numerous "borders behind the border (Leerkes, Leach, & Bachmeier, 2012)" have led some to argue that "the border is everywhere (Balibar, 2002, p. 80)." Others maintain that even though borders have become deterritorialised, border functions still occur at specific sites (Salter, 2008). As Monforte (2015, p. 6) puts it, "borders become real through check points and barbed wires at the edges of territory. They also become real through police controls and measures of detention and deportation within and across territories." Indeed, what is so particular about these contemporary forms of border control is not that the border is everywhere, but rather that borders manifest themselves in different ways for different groups of people (Weber, 2006). As contemporary bordering practices are increasingly risk-based, they are aimed at facilitating smooth and undisturbed passage to low-risk travellers, while allowing for interventions targeting high-risk individuals. Borders thus no longer apply on the basis of physical presence, but rather on the basis of individual characteristics. It has accordingly become commonplace to point out the paradox of the globalisation process when it comes to global mobility: instead of making everyone a 'global citizen', the world has become divided between a global elite that enjoys nearly unrestricted freedom of movement and an "immobilised global underclass" (Pickering & Weber, 2006, p. 8).

Perhaps nowhere are these transformations in the nature of border control more discernible than in the European Union. On the one hand, internal borders in the Schengen area are no longer supposed to be permanently controlled and all EU citizens – but not third country nationals – in principle enjoy freedom of movement within the continent. For individual Member States this meant a partial loss of sovereignty and reduced opportunities to monitor individuals entering their territory, but this has at least to some extent been replaced by increased migration control measures inside their territory. Moreover, the implementation of the Schengen agreement was matched by some of the most stringent asylum and refugee policies (Benhabib, 2002). As Casella Colombeau (2019, p. 2), "most of the articles adopted with the Convention are conceived as compensatory measures for this free movement (among them reinforcement of external border control, police and judicial cooperation, and common visa and asylum policies)." In recent years many EU Member States have also significantly increased their efforts to return unauthorised migrants to their countries of origin (Weber, 2014). Finally, following an unprecedented influx of migrants during the 2015 refugee crisis and a number of high profile terrorist attacks inside the EU around the same time, many states have sought ways to reinstate some form of control over their territorial borders, either through the reinstalment of temporary border checks or ongoing identity checks in their border areas (Casella Colombeau, 2019). This has led to some scholars even arguing that the Schengen area actually never got rid of its internal borders at all (Barbero, 2018).

While the intra-Schengen borders are no longer supposed to be controlled, the European Union has increasingly strengthened its external borders, set up more sophisticated methods to monitor third country nationals inside the EU, and developed a range of externalisation policies to prevent unwanted third country nationals from coming even near the EU's territory, leading to fierce criticisms about the creation of a 'fortress Europe'. This approach of relaxation of the internal borders while strengthening the external borders has been understood as a fundamental part of creating a common European identity (Green & Grewcock, 2002).

1.1.1 This dissertation

This criminological dissertation aims to provide a better understanding of the nature of contemporary bordering practices in the European Union, through an empirical examination of *how, where,* and *by whom* these practices are carried out in the Netherlands, as well as *who* is subjected to it and how it is experienced (cf. Weber & McCulloch, 2018). As a founding member of both the European Union and the Schengen area, the Netherlands makes for a particularly interesting case study. Long known for its tolerant attitude towards migrants, in recent decades the country has taken a lead in expressing concerns over European integration and asylum and migration issues, to the extent that the Economist referred to the Dutch as "the hipsters of European neurosis".[1] What do such anxieties mean for the nature of bordering practices in the country?

This dissertation is a criminological examination of contemporary bordering practices (Loftus, 2015). For a long time criminological scholarship has concerned itself with the nation state as primary field of reference, assuming sovereign states with a bounded territory and relatively stable community (Aas, 2007). But as globalisation and migration started to pose new challenges to contemporary criminal justice systems, the field has had to adapt to new realities and reidentify some of the core elements of the discipline. As Hogg (2002, p. 195) already asked back in 2002:

> "What happens to the conceptual apparatus of criminology and how salient are its taken-for-granted terms – crime, law, justice, state, sovereignty – at a time when global change and conflict may be eroding some elements at least of the international framework of states it has taken for granted?"

In his introduction to the edited collection 'globalisation and the challenge to criminology', Pakes (2013, p. 6) writes that "it is clear globalisation is forcing a drastic reconceptualisation of places of engagement for criminology." One of those novel places of criminological engagement that has emerged in recent years is the border in its many forms and conceptualisations (Aas and Bosworth, 2013; Kaufman, 2014; Stumpf, 2006). Criminological scholarship has in the last years identified migration control as a central system of global social

1 https://www.economist.com/europe/2016/01/07/early-adopters.

control, next to the criminal justice system (Pickering et al., 2014). It has been observed that responses to unwanted mobility have increasingly employed criminal justice tools, and territorial exclusion has become a common response to criminal behaviour (Aas, 2013). As a result, criminological inquiries have needed to move beyond a narrow understanding of criminological concepts and to sites that are outside the traditional criminal justice system (Aas, 2007; Bosworth, 2012; Pickering et al., 2014; Stumpf, 2006). Recent research has accordingly dealt with criminalising discourse around migrants (Van Berlo, 2015), and administrative practices such as immigration detention and deportation (Bosworth, 2014; Stanley, 2017).

The dissertation builds on a recent surge in criminological literature that concerns itself with "the growing interdependence between criminal justice and migration control" (Bosworth, Aas, & Pickering, 2017, p. 35). It follows Weber and Bowling's (2004) 'sites of enforcement' framework for studying migration control practices, in order to encompass the wide array of enforcement locations and actors involved in bordering practices. In particular, it examines two bordering practices – intra-Schengen migration policing and criminal punishment and deportation – through the lens of *crimmigration*. Crimmigration refers to the growing merger of migration control and the criminal justice system and has proven to be a useful framework for understanding contemporary forms of border control and the various ways it is both shaped by, and shapes the criminal justice system (Pickering et al., 2014; Stumpf, 2006; Van der Woude, Van der Leun, & Nijland, 2014). As Weber & McCulloch (2018, p. 5) highlight in a recent contribution discussing some of the key theoretical developments in the criminology of borders:

> "While the concept of crimmigration does not capture all developments in contemporary border control, particularly outside the US, it provides a powerful and systematic framework for the examination of punitive practices such as criminal deportation, immigration detention and migration policing, and is particularly useful in framing analyses of *how* immigration controls are enforced (emphasis in original)."

The remainder of this introduction consists of three sections. The following paragraph discusses the concept of crimmigration in detail, from its inception more than ten years ago to the current state of play. It starts with a detailed examination of the original publication by Stumpf (2006), followed by an overview of the developments that have taken place in the field since then. This is followed by a description of the criminal justice and migration control systems in the Netherlands, as well as a brief discussion on existing studies on crimmigration in the Netherlands. Finally, paragraph four provides an overview of the different case studies that make up this dissertation.

1.2 Crimmigration

Stumpf (2006) introduced the term crimmigration to refer to the growing merger of criminal law and migration law. Traditionally these are two clearly distinct legal domains, each with their own aims, principles, and protections. Stumpf notes that at first it might seem odd that these two legal systems are becoming increasingly alike, "because criminal law seems a distinct cousin to immigration law" (p. 379). Whereas criminal law deals with harm committed by individuals or groups to other individuals or society in general, migration law deals with the question whether foreigners should be allowed to enter the state's territory and stay there.

At the same time, both legal systems have always shared some similarities – including their distinctive dissimilarity from most other legal domains, namely that they deal with the relationship between individuals and the state. Both legal systems also have a gatekeeper function, dealing with questions about who belongs to society and who does not. As Stumpf (2006, p. 380) notes:

> "Both criminal and immigration law are, at their core, systems of inclusion and exclusion. They are similarly designed to determine whether and how to include individuals as members of society or exclude them from it. Both create insiders and outsiders. Both are designed to create categories of people."

The difference is of course that criminal law deals with internal security and the moral borders of society, while migration law is more focussed on external security and territorial borders (Aas, 2013). Traditionally both legal domains also have fundamentally different outcomes. Criminal enforcement results in the most extreme case in exclusion by means of imprisonment, usually aimed at an eventual return into society. Exclusion through migration law enforcement, on the other hand, usually has a much more permanent character, by denying entry to or removing an individual from the state's territory.

However, these strict boundaries have begun to dissolve, as criminal law has started to adopt elements of migration law and vice versa. Stumpf (2006, p. 376) herself writes that "the merger of the two areas in both substance and procedure has created parallel systems in which immigration law and the criminal justice system are merely nominally separate." This observation in itself was not entirely novel, as various American scholars had already observed and described at least parts of this trend (Kanstroom, 2000; Legomsky, 2005; Welch, 2004). Miller, for example, wrote already in 2003 about a "dynamic process by which both systems converge at points to create a new system of social control that draws from both immigration and criminal justice" (2003, p. 615). However, by coining the term crimmigration for this process, Stumpf managed to draw significant academic attention to this phenomenon and practically started a new field of study.

1.2.1 Crimmigration: a bi-directional process

Stumpf identifies three fronts of crimmigration (p. 381):
1. The substance of immigration and criminal law increasingly overlap;
2. Immigration enforcement has come to resemble criminal law enforcement;
3. The procedural aspects of prosecuting immigration violations has taken on many of the earmarks of criminal procedure.

Regarding the first 'front', she draws attention to the expansion of criminal grounds that are reason to deport non-citizens, the growing number of immigration law violations that have become criminal offenses, and the general trend in immigration enforcement towards detention and deportation of particularly risky individuals. Regarding the second front, she highlights how the two immigration enforcement agencies in the United States have come to resemble criminal law enforcement agencies, both in terms of mandate and enforcement powers. She also notes how police agencies in the country are increasingly involved in enforcing immigration laws. Regarding the third front, she particularly notes the vast differences in procedural protections. While immigration proceedings have become increasingly similar to criminal processes – and detention is now common sanction in immigration enforcement – this has not been matched by a similar transfer of the procedural protections that are an integral part of the criminal justice system.

Stumpf explicitly stated that crimmigration should be understood as a bi-directional process, as "the convergence of immigration and criminal law has been a two-way street" (p. 384). She argues that both domains have a 'gravitational pull' on each other, meaning that the transfer of procedures and substance occurs in both directions. In a later publication she notes more explicitly that crimmigration describes two trends: criminalising migration related activities, such as illegal entry and stay, and an increase in deportations of lawfully residing citizens on the basis of expanding criminal deportability grounds (Stumpf, 2013).

Most attention has generally been paid to the first development captured within crimmigration, the criminalisation of migration. Even Stumpf herself seems to take this as a starting point of the crimmigration trend: "I argue that the trend toward criminalizing immigration law has set us on a path towards establishing irrevocably intertwined systems: immigration and criminal law as doppelgangers" (p. 378). The criminalisation trend has become well established in a range of different academic disciplines, with many scholars highlighting how the language and practices of criminal enforcement are increasingly employed to address migration. Key examples are the criminalisation of various migration law violations, the use of immigration detention for unauthorised migrants, and the involvement of policing and even military actors in controlling migration (Marin & Spena, 2016).

The other crimmigration development, which has generally attracted less attention, is the increase of migration control related consequences for individuals in the criminal justice system (Chacon, 2009). This is what Miller (2003) refers to as the immigrationisation of criminal law. The most important example is the adoption of migration law measures, such as residence permit revocation and deportation, in response to crimes committed by migrants. It involves using criminal law to decide on who has the right to stay (Marin & Spena, 2016). This side of the crimmigration coin neatly fits within the more general trend of using administrative law to address criminal phenomena (Moffette, 2014).

1.2.2 Membership theory

One of the reasons behind the crimmigration trend identified by Stumpf is a change in societal perceptions of immigrants:

> "Public perceptions of immigrants have tended to be more positive than perceptions of criminal offenders. (...) This vision, however, is in transition. Undocumented immigrants are increasingly perceived as criminals, likely to commit future criminal acts because of their history of entering the country unlawfully" (p. 395).

She also notes the increasingly common discursive link between immigrants and terrorism. In seeking to identify the underlying motivations for this change in perceptions, Stumpf turns to membership theory. According to membership theory, only people who are marked as full-fledged members of society are able to claim individual rights and privileges. Individuals who are not members of this social contract between the government and its citizens are exempt from these rights and privileges. Within membership theory the distinction between insiders and outsiders is based on societal beliefs about who belongs and who should be excluded.

Both criminal law and migration law are traditionally concerned with exactly this question of belonging, albeit on different grounds. Criminal law assumes membership, and places the burden on the government to prove that an individual is not worthy of inclusion. On the other hand, migration law assumes non-membership and does not place such a strong burden of proof on the government to deny inclusion to an individual. However, the bottom line is the same: both systems are concerned with making decisions about whether the actions and characteristics of individuals merit their inclusion in the national community (Stumpf, 2006, p. 397).

Stumpf sees membership theory acting in both immigration and criminal law decision making, noting that it is extremely flexible and the application of a whole range of constitutional rights is dependent on notions about who belongs. The state has the possibility to exclude individuals from society either on a temporary or a permanent basis, and both criminal law and migration law offer plenty of opportunities to that end. As Stumpf (p. 402) writes:

> "Government plays the role of a bouncer in the crimmigration context. Upon discovering that an individual either is not a member or has broken the membership's rules, the government has enormous discretion to use persuasion or force to remove the individual from the premises."

Whereas incarceration is the predominant method for temporary exclusion *within* society, deportation leads to a more permanent form of exclusion *from* society. Besides these very explicit forms of exclusion, there is a whole range of less intrusive processes that lead to more limited forms of social exclusion. In this regard, Stumpf mentions revoking the voting rights of ex-offenders, but one can also think of the limited rights that are extended to legal residents without full citizenship status.

Stumpf then continues to explore exactly how membership theory has pushed both legal domains closer to each other and identifies two developments that played a key role in this. The first development is the general development of the criminal justice system from a system based at least partially on the ideals of rehabilitation towards harsher punishments and underlying motives, such as deterrence, incapacitation, and retribution, echoing longstanding criminological discussions about the culture of control and new penology (Feeley & Simon, 1992; Garland, 2001). This includes removing certain rights and privileges associated with citizenship even after an ex-offender is released from prison. Stumpf sees a similar emphasis on harsh responses in immigration law, primarily through the growing use of deportation for both criminal and migration law violations. She argues that these parallel trends are ultimately the outcomes of more exclusionary notions of membership. At the same time, she emphasises the important membership differences between the two groups. Ex-offenders lose some of their privileges, but are still formally citizens, and can therefore better be characterised as pseudo-citizens. Non-citizens, on the other hand, lack membership completely, but in most cases still have membership status in their country of origin.

The second development she identifies is the reliance on sovereign power as a fundament of criminological policymaking. While sovereign power has long been used as a basis for immigration law policies, within the criminal justice field this is relatively novel. In the turn from rehabilitation towards retribution, criminal law also turned to the state's power to impose harsh sanctions and express moral condemnation as the primary response to criminal behaviour. Such a strategy seems to stem from consistently high crime rates in combination with a gradual disbelief in the possibility of rehabilitation (Garland, 2001). The expressive dimension of punishment, with its focus on expressing society's moral condemnation, is similar to the state's expressive role in immigration law, communicating inclusion and exclusion. Under this model, Stumpf (2006, p. 412) asserts, "ex-offenders and immigrants become the 'outsiders' from whom citizens need protection."

Stumpf probes two explanations for this punitive turn. First, the growth of contemporary societies has made traditional sanctions based on public humiliation in front of the community less effective and thus created a need for punishment based on more formal state powers. Second, high rates of crime and unauthorised immigration have created a need for the state to show their citizens they are capable of controlling both crime and migration. Harsh sanctions to express moral outrage are therefore politically attractive, regardless of their actual effectiveness.

1.2.3 More outsiders, less rights

Stumpf warned that the crimmigration trend ultimately leads to an "ever expanding population of outsiders" who nonetheless might have strong connections to the society (p. 479). In the context of crimmigration, the non-citizen becomes a criminal and the criminal becomes a non-citizen. Noting that crimmigration tends to rely only on the harshest elements of both legal systems, she argues that "the undesirable result is an ever-expanding population of the excluded and alienated" (p. 378). Something similar is argued by Marin and Spena (2016, p. 150), who note that "[while] criminal law's legitimacy largely depends on it being inclusive, [...] crimmigration instead is utterly exclusionary." Stumpf also notes that class and race are often important factors defining who falls within the scope of both immigration and criminal law. Whereas in immigration law enforcement this is often explicit and legal, disparate treatment of certain categories of people within the criminal justice system is usually more implicit. For example, the use of race or ethnicity as a factor in deciding who to stop is often allowed during immigration controls, but not during criminal police controls.

This relates to a second problematic aspect of crimmigration: whereas the merger of migration law and criminal procedure leads to a more punitive approach towards migrants, in many cases this is not matched by an equal transfer of procedural and constitutional or human rights protection (Bosworth et al., 2017; Marin & Spena, 2016). Indeed, it has been argued that human rights often have limited legal value in crimmigration settings (Van Berlo, 2017). Legomsky (2007, p. 472) argued in this regard that "immigration law has been absorbing the theories, methods, perceptions, and priorities of the criminal enforcement model while rejecting the criminal adjudication model in favour of a civil regulatory regime." For example, in the case of termination of legal stay and deportation following a criminal conviction, which is legally speaking only an administrative sanction and not a form of punishment, many scholars have argued that for those subjected to this measure, it certainly *feels* like punishment (Bosworth et al., 2017; Turnbull & Hasselberg, 2017). Chacon

(2009), on the other hand, highlights the reversed process, showing how the more relaxed procedural standards of the administrative migration law enforcement system find their way into the criminal enforcement system. Because criminal law enforcement generally comes with more protection, this has severe consequences for the legal position of migrants caught up in this system.

1.2.4 Ad hoc instrumentalism

Stumpf's paper has spurred a range of publications further examining and researching the process of crimmigration, leading to a dynamic and interdisciplinary research field around the themes of criminal justice and border control. Several years after Stumpf's publication, David Sklansky (2012) made a particularly important contribution to the crimmigration literature with the introduction of the concept of 'ad hoc instrumentalism'. Sklansky starts by ascribing to the view of Stumpf that immigration law and criminal law have become increasingly intertwined: "immigration enforcement and criminal justice are now so thoroughly entangled it is impossible to say where one starts and the other leaves off" (p. 159). He then goes on to note that scholars have placed the crimmigration trend within three larger developments, namely nativism, overcriminalisation, and an obsession with security:

> "Although the rise of crimmigration cannot be attributed to a growing problem of crime committed by non-citizens, it plainly *does* have something to do with escalating *concerns* about immigration – and, more specifically, fear of 'criminal aliens'. Those concerns rose sharply after the terrorist attacks of September 11, 2001, but apprehensions about immigration were on the increase even before those attacks (p. 193, emphasis in original)."

Following this assessment, he outlines his aim of adding to the literature a better understanding of why crimmigration came about and how it actually operates at the enforcement level. In order to do so, he connects the rise of crimmigration to what he terms ad hoc instrumentalism – which both explains crimmigration and is an outcome of it.

Sklansky defines ad hoc instrumentalism as "a manner of thinking about law and legal institutions that downplays concerns about consistency and places little stock in formal legal categories, but instead sees legal rules and legal procedures simply as a set of interchangeable tools" (p. 161). Public officials on different levels – including specifically those at street level – can choose in each individual case which enforcement regime, criminal or civil, is most convenient and effective against a problematic individual. Whether that individual is a criminal suspect, an unauthorised migrant, or both is irrelevant, as long as the response is effective against that particular person. Although he highlights the importance of the discretionary decisions made by street-level officials, he also emphasises that this is the result of decisions made at the policy level to equip these street-level officials with both a large amount of discretion and a whole range of different enforcement tools from different legal areas.

Such an instrumentalist approach offers clear benefits to the state, as different legal domains offer different 'advantages'. Administrative enforcement generally means there are less procedural guarantees and rights for the individual, while interventions based on criminal law are generally perceived as more severe and offering better deterrence. Crimmigration thus enables authorities to pick and choose from a whole toolbox of legal instruments to address problematic individuals. Whether these tools stem from criminal law or migration law is of secondary importance; what matters most is that the intended aim is achieved. Sklansky, too, notes these strengths, but also highlights fundamental concerns about the compatibility of ad hoc instrumentalism with the rule of law and accountability. The many different tools that authorities could use in any given situation diminishes the transparency of decisions made by government actors, potentially making it complicated for individuals to understand what certain decisions are based on. He concludes that the best way to address these concerns is to improve the transparency of the system, including the different responsible actors.

1.2.5 From criminal law and migration law to criminal justice and migration control

Initial scholarship on crimmigration consisted almost exclusively of legal analyses focussing on the United States. However, in recent years studies into crimmigration have become ever more diverse, in terms of both geographical scope and disciplinary approach. Two developments stand out in this regard. First, the study of crimmigration has found increasing resonance in other parts of the world, especially Australia (Grewcock, 2011; Stanley, 2017; Weber, 2019) and Europe (Aas, 2011; Van der Woude, Barker, & Van der Leun, 2017). While caution is needed to apply the same conceptual framework to different national socio-political contexts, these studies have made clear that the overarching trend of crimmigration can also be observed outside the United States. This is in part thanks to the second development that has taken place: the study of crimmigration has become increasingly interdisciplinary, especially since criminologists have started incorporating the crimmigration framework in their analyses. This has had an impact on how the term crimmigration itself is seen and understood, as especially European criminologists who have taken up the term have suggested it is necessary to have a much wider perspective on crimmigration than seeing it as merely a legal process (Pakes & Holt, 2017; Van der Leun & Van der Woude, 2012).

Aas (2011) was the first to suggest that the definition of crimmigration needs to be broader than the merger of criminal law and migration law, while

Van der Leun and Van der Woude (2012) make this point more explicitly. They note that European scholars tended to rely on the broader and more abstract framework of securitisation of migration instead of the crimmigration framework. As they see this as the result of the many different specific national contexts in Europe, they suggest there is a need for a broader understanding of the term crimmigration that goes beyond a purely legal merger of criminal law and migration law. They propose to define crimmigration as "the intertwinement of crime control and migration control (Van der Leun & Van der Woude, 2012, p. 43)." In this way, the definition not only encompasses legal signs, but also what they call social signs of crimmigration. One example of such a social sign of crimmigration that they mention is ethnic profiling by law enforcement and other criminal justice actors.

Broadening the definition of crimmigration in this way offers the advantage of enabling more comparative and interdisciplinary research, including empirical studies into specific crimmigration phenomena. Moreover, by connecting the crimmigration trend to specific societal contexts it also becomes possible to start looking into the drivers of crimmigration. Van der Leun and Van der Woude (2012) highlight the question of how issues related to crime and migration are framed and perceived in political and public discourses. They argue that discourses based on fear and security, in which immigrants are framed as dangerous and (potential) criminals, are an important driver for the adoption of crimmigration tools as a form of social control. Pakes and Holt (2017, p. 74) also argue in favour of a broad perspective on crimmigration, "so that we are seeing what we need to see". They point out that the term crimmigration brings together a whole range of processes that can be as much the result of policy changes as it can be the result of legal changes. Whereas formal criminalisation processes are easier to notice, they argue that it is equally important to pay attention to "the administrative, oblique and hidden processes that acquire their potency from the very fact that they evade scrutiny (p. 74)." These do not necessarily need to involve legislation changes, but can be integration of working practices or organisational changes.

Crimmigration can be seen at various levels – discourse, legislation, policy, and enforcement practices – and in various criminal justice contexts and sites, such as policing (Aas, 2011; Parmar, 2019; Weber, 2011), courts (Aliverti, 2012), and prisons (Aas, 2014; Kaufman, 2015; Ugelvik & Damsa, 2018). It can also be observed in sites that are traditionally less familiar to criminologists (Bowling & Westenra, 2018), such as airports (Blackwood, 2015), land borders (Pratt & Thompson, 2008), and immigration detention (Bosworth, 2014; Menjívar, Gómez Cervantes, & Alvord, 2018). Broadening the definition of crimmigration has created possibilities for more empirical studies into crimmigration, something that especially European criminologists have slowly started doing in recent years (Bosworth, Hasselberg, & Turnbull, 2016; Ugelvik & Damsa, 2018; Van der Woude et al., 2017). This has resulted in the emergence of a subfield sometimes referred to as 'border criminology' or the 'criminology of mobility' (Aliverti & Bosworth, 2017; Cote-Boucher, 2011; Pickering et al., 2014). Questions that have been explored are how policing changes when it involves checking people's immigration status, how the nature and aim of criminal punishment are altered when it is applied to non-citizens, and how such forms of social control impact on the lives of migrants (Kaufman, 2014; Ugelvik, 2017).

Besides examining *how* crimmigration influences migration control and the criminal justice system, many of these studies are concerned with the question *who* gets excluded and on what basis (Bosworth et al., 2017). A particular influential account in this regard is offered by Aas (2011), who looks at the nature of surveillance and crime control in the EU from a crimmigration perspective. She argues that besides controlling migration, contemporary surveillance is equally focussed on tackling crime, resulting in exclusionary outcomes that defy simplistic categorisations. Whether the gate opens or closes depends as much on legal citizenship as it does on (alleged) involvement in criminal activities. Aas concludes that "not all European citizens are entitled to the privileges and that, on the other hand, the privileges are extended to a group of bona fide global citizens" (p. 343). This results in four different social groups, depending on their citizenship and moral status. Of course, there is considerable overlap as well as considerable variation within these social groups.

	Citizenship status	*Morally worth*
Citizens (insiders inside)	Yes	Yes
Subcitizens (outsiders inside)	Yes	No
Supracitizens (insiders outside)	No	Yes
Non-citizens (outsiders outside)	No	No

Table 1.1 Insiders and outsiders (based on Aas, 2011)

Aas notes that borders have always been important sites for states to engage in 'social sorting' and distinguish the unwanted from the wanted immigrant. However, in recent times these processes have become globalised, reflecting stark global inequalities (Aas, 2007; Walters, 2002).

Despite these significant developments in the study of crimmigration, the number of studies based on first-hand accounts and fieldwork are still quite limited, not in the least because of the difficulties of gaining access to the sites where bordering practices take place (Bosworth, 2012). Notwithstanding some notable exceptions, most work in this area is still primarily theoretical, often drawing on legal analyses or policy documents (Pickering et al., 2014). Authors from different academic disciplines have therefore called for more empirical examinations of the different enforcement actors involved in the implementation of bordering practices and the impact these have on those who are subjected to them (Bowling & Westenra, 2018; Cote-Boucher et al., 2014; Garip,

Gleeson, & Hall, 2019; Loftus, 2015; Pickering et al., 2014; Vega, 2019). This dissertation, an empirical examination of bordering practices in the Netherlands, can be seen as an answer to that call. Based on various forms of extensive fieldwork at sites where the criminal justice system intersects with migration control, it adds empirical richness to the existing body of literature on crimmigration.

1.3 Crime, migration, and crimmigration in the Netherlands

The Netherlands has long been described as a tolerant and liberal country, open towards foreigners and with a relatively mild criminal justice climate (Van Swaaningen, 2005). However, since the early 2000s various authors have observed increasingly repressive and punitive discourses, followed by matching policy and legislative reforms, both in the field of criminal justice and migration control. Crime and deviance were for a long time hardly considered as problematic. However, starting in the late 1980s a strong law and order discourse emerged in the Netherlands and criminal justice policies increasingly started to emphasise protection of the public (Van der Woude et al., 2014). Various authors have argued that these developments are akin to David Garland's (2001) hugely influential description of the culture of control (Downes & Van Swaaningen, 2007; Pakes, 2004). Moreover, Downes and Van Swaaningen (2007, p. 31) argue that as a result of these developments, "managerial, instrumental, and incapacitative measures took precedence over previous goals of resocialisation and restorative justice." Driven by discourses that fit within Feeley and Simon's (1992) new penology, crime control policies increasingly focus on identifying and targeting specific offender groups (Downes & Van Swaaningen, 2007). Moreover, the main aim of penal interventions has shifted to temporary or permanent exclusion of unwanted individuals, through practices described as "banishment modern style" (Van Swaaningen, 2005, p. 296). Whereas these broad trends have been identified in a number of countries, the discourse in the Netherlands stands out because of the explicit link that is often drawn between crime and ethnic minorities and migrants.

Since the turn of the century, issues of migration and integration have come to dominate political and public discussions (Van der Woude et al., 2014). Particular emphasis has often been placed on the (alleged) over-offending of certain ethnic minority groups. According to Pakes (2004), this is not only seen as a threat to individual and public safety, but also a rejection of the liberal and tolerant values that are characteristic of the 'Dutch way of life'. Van der Leun and Van der Woude (2012, p. 50) accordingly argue that "a key characteristic of the Dutch culture of control – besides concerns about property and petty crime – are growing concerns and negative sentiments about immigration policy and immigrants, both in public and political discourse." They explicitly link this Dutch culture of control to the emergence of different manifestations of crimmigration in the Netherlands.

1.3.1 Crimmigration in the Netherlands?

A limited number of studies have been published in recent years that offer a variety of examples of crimmigration in the Netherlands (Staring, 2012; Van der Leun & Van der Woude, 2012; Van der Leun, Van der Woude, & De Ridder, 2013; Van der Woude et al., 2014). This includes examples of both sides of crimmigration.

Regarding the criminalisation of migration, it has been observed that although illegal stay is formally not criminalised in the Netherlands, repeated apprehensions for illegal stay or a conviction for a criminal offense can result in being declared an undesirable alien. Staying in the Netherlands as an undesirable alien is a criminal offense, thus creating an indirect form of criminalisation of illegal stay (Van der Woude et al., 2014). Moreover, the number of undesirable alien declarations has significantly increased since 2000 (Leerkes & Broeders, 2010). Since the implementation of the EU Returns Directive this has partly been replaced by re-entry bans for third country nationals. Attention has also been repeatedly drawn to the high number of immigration detainees and sober detention circumstances in the Netherlands, which highlights the use of traditional criminal justice tools to control immigration (Nijland, 2012). In this regard Leerkes and Broeders (2010) have argued that while immigration detention still primarily functions to effectuate return, it also serves to deter illegal stay and symbolically assert state control. However, in recent years the number of immigration detainees has considerably decreased.

Regarding the immigrationisation of the criminal justice system, most focus has been placed on the expansion of grounds for deportation of legally residing migrants on the basis of a criminal conviction (Stronks, 2013; Van der Woude et al., 2014); this is discussed in more detail in chapter six and seven of this dissertation. Finally, at the enforcement level it has been observed that the police now routinely checks the immigration status of every arrested suspect (De Vries, 2014). Moreover, it has been highlighted that both the Alien Police and the Royal Netherlands Marechaussee, who are in charge of monitoring and combating illegal stay, also have investigative powers for certain types of crime (Van der Woude et al., 2014). This is further examined in chapter three, four, and five.

Based on these examples it has been argued that "there are clear indications that crimmigration is occurring in the Netherlands (Van der Woude et al., 2014, p. 573)." Despite this handful of studies, empirical examinations of crimmigration in the Netherlands have so far been absent. The aim of this dissertation is to start filling that gap.

1.4 This dissertation

This dissertation studies bordering practices in the Netherlands through a crimmigration lens.

> *To what extent are contemporary bordering practices in the Netherlands characterised by crimmigration, who is targeted by these bordering practices, and how are they experienced and understood by those implementing them and those subjected to them?*

In order to answer that research question, the dissertation follows the approach proposed by Vollmer (2017), who argued that a comprehensive understanding of European bordering requires a combination of discourse analysis, legal and policy analysis, and empirical examinations of specific bordering sites. The dissertation starts with a comprehensive discourse analysis of media coverage of unauthorised migrants, followed by two empirical case studies of selected bordering sites. By taking into account specific local contexts, these case studies provide an in-depth and nuanced understanding of the large-scale patterns and meta-level theoretical work described above.

In the Netherlands, the different steps and associated actors of the criminal justice system are commonly referred to as the 'criminal justice chain'. Similarly, in the migration control system this is commonly referred to as the 'alien chain'. As this term becomes slightly awkward in an English translation, this dissertation will instead refer to the 'migration control chain'. Both chains describe the different steps of the most common process from beginning until the end, as well as the various agencies and other actors responsible for these steps. Figure 1.1 illustrates both chains in a simplified manner.

The criminal justice chain deals with criminal behaviour and starts with arrest by the police of an individual on suspicion of having committed a criminal offense. This is subsequently determined in court and, if found guilty, the individual is then punished. If this punishment entails imprisonment, this is carried out by the Custodial Institutions Agency (DJI). Upon completion of the punishment, an individual is released into society again (notwithstanding sanctions that include placement in a forensic psychiatric centre).

The migration control chain is slightly more complex, due to the many different types of migrants it covers. For example, for an asylum seeker the chain will look completely different than for a foreign drug trafficker who is arrested at the airport. The Immigration and Naturalisation Service (IND) is the agency responsible for deciding on all residence applications in the Netherlands. The chain illustrated above is therefore specifically applicable to migrants who are staying unauthorised in the Netherlands: this can be either because the IND has rejected their asylum or residence application, because their legal stay has expired and they did not leave the Netherlands, because their legal stay has been revoked, or because they never applied for legal stay in the first place.

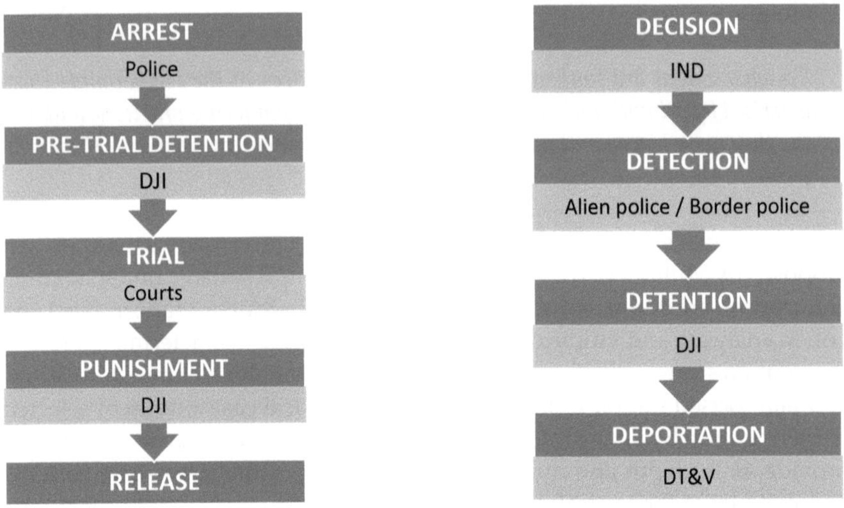

Figure 1.1 Simplified representation of the two chains of social control (source: own)

In this specific chain an unauthorised migrant is first detected at the border by the Royal Netherlands Marechaussee (RNM), the Dutch military and border police agency, or inside the national territory by the specialised immigration policing agency (AVIM). If a migrant is subsequently placed in immigration detention, this is administered by DJI again. Finally, the Repatriation and Departure Service (DT&V), a specialised agency created out of the IND in 2007, is responsible for organising the departure of unauthorised migrants from the Netherlands.

Traditionally the two different chains are part of two distinct policy fields, each with their own actors, aims, and logic. One of the aims of this dissertation is to see whether the two chains increasingly intersect and what this means for the individuals within one of these chains. The core of this dissertation therefore consists of three different case studies dealing with crime, migration, and borders. All of these are based on extensive and unique empirical data. A strong focus is placed on those actors at the front line: enforcement staff carrying out bordering practices and the individuals subjected to them. Front-line officers operate in all domains of the social control system. They are the police officers, prison guards, and immigration officers that deal directly with the public on a daily basis. They are responsible for implementing the official policies, but also enjoy varying degrees of discretionary freedom. It was Lipsky (1980) who therefore famously argued that these street-level bureaucrats are actually the real policy makers. At the same time, their work and decisions cannot be understood without taking into account the wider social surroundings and policy frameworks they operate in. The dissertation therefore covers the various levels – discourse, law, policy, and enforcement – that are of relevance for understanding crimmigration and bordering.

The first chapter after this introduction focusses on the media and the public discourse around unauthorised migrants, providing a broad picture of the public discourse around crime and unauthorised migration. Media discourses have been found to influence public perceptions, including those of enforcement officers, of non-belonging and suspiciousness (Weber, 2019). This is followed by two case studies of specific steps and their associated actors within the two chains of social control. The first case study consists of three chapters and focusses on the entry point of the migration control chain, by examining bordering practices carried out by the RNM in the Dutch border areas with Belgium and Germany. The second case study focusses on the end phase of both social control chains. The two chapters of this case study look into the punishment and subsequent deportation of criminally convicted non-citizens (CCNCs). The case studies have been chosen based on the fact that they are situated at opposite ends of the chains of social control, representing the beginning and the end of the chains. Moreover, policing and punishment are key instruments of social control and it is precisely those practices that have been fundamentally altered by recent changes in border control (Pickering et al., 2014). Of course, this also means that other parts of the chains are not covered by this dissertation, in particular the criminal trial phase and immigration detention. An overview of the different case studies, the articles they consist of, and the empirical data collected can be seen in table 1.2. Below the different case studies and chapters are described in more detail.

	Case study	*Data 1*	*Data 2*	*Data 3*
Chapter 2	Media	Newspaper articles		
Chapter 3	Intra-Schengen migration policing	Observations	Focus groups RNM officers	
Chapter 4		Observations	Focus groups RNM officers	
Chapter 5		Observations	Focus groups RNM officers	Survey people who are stopped
Chapter 6	Punishment & deportation	Interviews prison officers	Interviews CCNCs	
Chapter 7		Interviews departure supervisors (DT&V)	Interviews CCNCs	

Table 1.2 Overview case studies

Parts of the data for this dissertation were collected in collaboration with other researchers, with the author being fully involved in all stages of the data collection process. Furthermore, despite various other research outputs stemming from the same underlying data involving which the author of this dissertation was involved as co-author (Di Molfetta and Brouwer, 2019; Van der Woude & Brouwer, 2016; Van der Woude, Brouwer, & Dekkers, 2016; Van der Woude, Dekkers, & Brouwer, 2015), the different chapters of this dissertation are all based on original analysis and writing done independently by the author.

Several chapters of this dissertation have already been published elsewhere or are currently under review. Chapters two, three, four and five have all been published in peer-reviewed journals, with the author of this dissertation as first author. Chapter six and seven are currently under review in peer-reviewed journals as solo-authored articles. Footnotes at the beginning of the individual chapters provide more details about these different publications.

1.4.1 Crimmigration and the media

The first chapter after this introduction deals with crimmigration and the media. It takes the introduction of a bill to criminalise illegal stay as a starting point. Based on the notion that the media play a central role in the discursive construction of migrants, thereby shaping public views and justifying policies, the study examines whether the introduction of this bill was preceded by increasingly negative media coverage of unauthorised migrants. In particular, it seeks to find out whether unauthorised migrant are often discursively framed as criminals. On a broader level, the chapter provides an understanding of the prevalent discourses in the media regarding unauthorised migrants since the turn of the century. As such, it provides a context to better understand the bordering practices discussed in the subsequent case studies.

The study is based on a so-called corpus linguistics approach. This means computer-aided analysis of large bodies of textual data. Such an approach has the advantage that it offers a comprehensive understanding of media coverage of a certain topic over a prolonged period of time, thus also enabling the identification of trends over time. It also reduces the impact of a researcher's bias on the outcomes of the study. In this study, all newspaper articles in Dutch national newspapers on unauthorised migrants between 1 January 1999 and 31 December 2013 were analysed: a total of 28.274 articles. By analysing the frequency of certain words, the strength of a link between two specific words, and a comparison of different data sets, the chapter provides insights in the role of the media on linking unauthorised migrants to crime.

1.4.2 Crimmigration and intra-Schengen migration policing

The first case study focusses on the intra-Schengen borders between the Netherlands and Belgium and Germany. Whereas these borders are no longer supposed to be permanently controlled, Member States have the right to carry out police controls in their border areas, as long as these are not equivalent of border checks. In the Netherlands these type of controls were introduced soon after the implementation of the Schengen agreement in the form of the so-called Mobile Security Monitor (MSM). These controls are carried out by the RNM, the agency taking a central place in this case study. Initially the spot checks were aimed at countering illegal entry and stay only, but over time this came to include tackling identity fraud and migrant smuggling. Moreover, the name of the instrument changed from Mobile Aliens Monitor to Mobile Security Monitor. This expansion raises questions about how the controls are understood and implemented by street-level officers of the RNM, who enjoy high levels of discretionary freedom in deciding who to stop, as well as how they are experienced by individuals who are stopped.

The case study is part of a larger research project into discretionary decision-making in border contexts (Van der Woude, Brouwer, & Dekkers, 2016). As Van der Woude and Van der Leun (2017, p. 28, emphasis in original) argue, "despite the different macro-level explanations that can account for the process of crimmigration, many scholars directly or indirectly refer to the central role of *discretionary decision-making*." Examining the work of frontline officers, their decisions, and the reasoning behind these decisions is thus crucial to understand *how* actual practices of crimmigration control take place on the ground. After all, "immigration officers operating at the border are of vital importance in the decision-making process of who belongs, and subsequently can cross the border, and who does not, thereby continuously differentiating 'insiders' from 'outsiders' (Van der Woude & Van Berlo, 2015, p. 61)." Of course, such practices can only be understood by taking into account the wider legislative and policy context as well as the perceptions of individuals that are targeted by these practices.

The case study draws on different types of qualitative data collected by a small team of three researchers. In particular, it relies on over 800 man-hours of observational study, thirteen focus group discussions with eight to ten different street level officers, and 167 interviews or filled-out surveys by people stopped in the context of the MSM. During observations, many informal conversations with officers also took place in a non-structured way. These different types of data offer the advantage that they combine observed activities of RNM officers in a natural setting with an examination of how these respondents understand and explain these activities. Moreover, findings obtained during observations could be cross-checked for validation during the focus groups discussions, which took place during the latter part of the research project.

A more extensive description of the different research methodologies can be found in the Annex.

The first chapter of this case study deals with the question how RNM officers reconcile the two aims of the MSM, as a tool for both crime control and migration control, and how this affects their decisions. The second chapter also focusses on discretionary decisions, but takes a different approach by seeking to understand how RNM officers decide to stop, and sometimes search, a vehicle. Using research on street-level decision making processes, the article focusses on the use of ethnic, racial, and national categories and how they interact with other factors in these decisions. Finally, the third chapter brings together the perceptions of RNM officers and those of the people who are stopped during the MSM. Drawing on literature on procedural justice and legitimacy, it examines how officers try to ensure they conduct their duties in a fair manner and to what extent different social groups perceive these controls.

1.4.3 Crimmigration, punishment, and deportation

The second case study of this dissertation focusses on the final stages of both social control chains, by taking a closer look at the punishment and deportation of CCNCs. Two agencies are relevant for this case study: DJI (imprisonment) and DT&V (deportation).

Throughout Western Europe the number of foreign national prisoners has surged, creating novel challenges for the criminal justice systems of the countries concerned. One common response has been to increase efforts to return CCNCs to their country of origin. This has resulted in a range of different policy measures to make this process more effective. In the Netherlands, two measures stand out. First, the policy stipulating when a legal resident loses his/her right to stay following a criminal conviction has been repeatedly restricted over the last decade. Second, a special all-foreign prison has been established for CCNCs who do not have a legal right to stay in the Netherlands. The focus in this prison is on deportation instead of resocialisation. To make sure these CCNCs are returned to their country of origin immediately upon completion of their criminal sentence, officers of DT&V are based inside this prison.

The aim of the case study is to understand what this form of 'bordered penality' (Aas, 2014) means for the nature and experience of punishment and to what extent it succeeds in returning CCNCs to their country of origin. To that end, it draws on empirical data collected in the all-foreign prison, consisting of qualitative interviews with 37 CCNCs, 15 departure supervisors, and 8 prison officers. These interviews provide rich insights into how these policies are implemented, experienced, and understood by the different groups involved: CCNCs, prison officers, and departure supervisors. It shows how these developments affect perceptions of fairness and justice and whether they succeed in achieving their aim. The annex discusses in more detail the methodological approach taken.

Chapter six studies the prison experiences of both CCNCs and prison officers in a crimmigration prison. Grounded in literature on the pains of imprisonment, it provides insight into the regime and daily life in the all-foreign prison and examines what this means for prison officers' professional identity and prisoners' experiences. Chapter seven focusses on the aim of returning these CCNCs to their country of origin upon completion of their sentence. It outlines the various policies aimed at motivating CCNCs to cooperate with their own return and discusses whether these policies indeed result in a greater willingness among CCNCs to return.

PART I

Crimmigration and the media

2 Framing migration and the process of crimmigration

A systematic analysis of the media representation of unauthorised immigrants in the Netherlands[1]

2.1 Introduction

Throughout Europe, scholars have found that migration policies are subject to a criminalisation trend. As negative sentiments towards immigrants have come to dominate the political and public discourses, increasingly stricter and more repressive responses to – mostly unauthorised – migratory acts have been adopted, including the resort to criminal law (Berezin, 2009; Bosworth and Guild, 2008; Palidda, 2009; Parkin, 2013). Such developments fit into the broader trend of crimmigration, a term that was first introduced by Juliet Stumpf (2006) to refer to the convergence of criminal law and immigration law and has attracted considerable interest from primarily Anglo-Saxon legal scholars (Chacon, 2009; Hartry, 2012; Legomsky, 2007; Sklansky, 2012; Welch, 2012). European scholars have only more recently started to adopt the crimmigration terminology, thereby identifying the need for a broader definition that encompasses crime control and migration control, in this way allowing for the inclusion of social practices, discourses, perceptions and framing in research (Aas, 2011; Van der Leun and Van der Woude 2012; Van der Woude, et al., 2014). This would also enable more empirical research and make comparative studies possible – something lacking in the primarily legal-oriented scholarship in this field so far.

Within the European context, the Netherlands has been identified as a particularly interesting country in which to study the crimmigration process because of its pioneering role in the adoption of restrictive migrant policies and the strong anti-migration discourse surrounding these policies (Aarts and Semetko, 2003; Lesisnka, 2014; Mutsaers, 2014; Vliegenthart and Boomgaarden, 2007). Over the past two decades a large number of policy measures have been implemented to deter, exclude and remove unauthorised migrants in particular, policies that increasingly focus on detection, detention and deportation (Van der Leun, 2006, 2010; Van der Leun and Ilies, 2010; Van der Leun and Van der Woude, 2012; Van Liempt, 2007). Whereas immigration and integration issues did not receive widespread attention from the Dutch media and public

1 An earlier version of this chapter was published as: Brouwer, J., Van der Woude, M.A.H., & Van der Leun, J. P. (2017). Framing migration and the process of crimmigration: a systematic analysis of the media representation of unauthorised immigrants in the Netherlands. *European Journal of Criminology, 14*(1), 100-119.

in the 1990s, a stark increase has been noticed since especially 2001 (Pakes, 2006; Sniderman and Hagendoorn, 2007). De jure criminalisation has stepped up since 2000, with a strong increase in the number of undesirable migrant resolutions per year and a lower threshold for being criminally liable with the national implementation of the EU returns directive (Leerkes and Broeders, 2010; Van der Woude et al., 2014).

These developments recently came to a symbolic conclusion when the government introduced a bill that would lead to the formal criminalisation of illegal stay, the quintessential step in the crimmigration process and 'the provisional culmination of twenty years of stepping up against illegal residence with criminal legislation' (Van der Woude et al., 2014: 569). Following serious debates, the bill was eventually withdrawn in the spring of 2014. The Liberal Party, the main sponsor of the bill, agreed to this withdrawal in return for a set of tax reforms. Although previous governments also discussed formal criminalisation, it was never so seriously considered, thus raising the question of why this government deemed it necessary and achievable.

Various authors have stated that the media play a central role in the construction of migrants as deviant and criminal, shaping public views and thereby justifying the application of criminal justice responses to unauthorised migration (Gerard and Pickering, 2013; Kim et al., 2011; Mountz, 2010; Spena, 2014). Within the crimmigration literature it has been argued that discursively constructing certain immigrant groups as criminal in the media serves to legitimize the development of crimmigration legislation (Kinney, 2015; Van Berlo, 2015; Van der Woude et al., 2014). Empirical evidence to support this claim is largely lacking though, making the Dutch bill that criminalised illegal stay a valuable case study. In this article we therefore examine whether media representations of unauthorised migrants have been a driving factor behind the proposed criminalisation of illegal stay in the Netherlands. Drawing on theories of agenda-setting, framing and moral panics, we hypothesize that the increasingly repressive policies towards unauthorised migrants in the Netherlands should be preceded by growing attention for this group in the Dutch media, including increasingly negative representations. In particular, we expect newspapers to systematically and increasingly link unauthorised migrants to issues of crime. Because this hypothesis is hard to test through the often used qualitative approaches towards discourse analyses, we have carried out an innovative computer-aided quantitative discourse analysis of *all* articles on unauthorised migrants that appeared in Dutch national newspapers between 1999 and 2013, which does allow for an empirical test of this crucial hypothesis.

2.2 Agenda-setting, framing and moral panics: Why media representations matter

Crimmigration legislation does not arise in a vacuum, but is the result of interrelational discursive processes in which migrants are constructed as social threats. The social construction of the migratory threat essentially rests on reinforcing interactions between political, public and media discourses, with direct causal relationships within this triangle being generally quite difficult to establish (Duffy and Frere-Smith, 2014). The mass media are assigned a central position in these processes, through the selection of topics and issues and through processes of labelling and attributing qualities to groups and individuals, and inferring causes and meaning (Helbling, 2013; Maneri and ter Wal, 2005). The organisation and selection of topics relates to the agenda-setting theory, which suggests that, by paying considerable attention to certain issues, the media have the ability to influence *what* people think about and as such can set the public's agenda (Dunaway et al., 2010; McCombs and Shaw, 1972). Expanding on this notion, and related to processes of labelling and attribution, is the concept of framing (Goffman, 1974): it is not only relevant *what* issues the media write about, it is equally important *how* they write about these topics (Boomgaarden and Vliegenthart, 2009). According to Entman (1993: 52), this means to 'select some aspects of a perceived reality and make them more salient in a communicating context', which can be identified through 'the presence or absence of certain keywords, stock phrases, stereotyped images, sources of information and sentences that provide thematically reinforcing clusters of facts or judgments'.

Caviedes (2015: 900) has argued that 'the more often the press mentions a particular issue and links it to a social ill, the more likely that issue is to be considered a "crisis" meriting political action and resolution'. This resonates closely with Cohen's (1972: 9) concept of moral panics, which entails that a 'condition, episode, person or group of persons emerges to become defined as a threat to societal values and interests'. A defining characteristic of moral panics is that the concern itself and the actions taken are highly disproportionate; they exaggerate concerns when the actual threat itself does not justify criminalisation or the curtailing of rights (Goode and Ben-Yehuda, 2009; Hall et al., 1978). The concept has previously been used to explain the criminalisation of illegal stay in Italy (Maneri, 2011), the criminalisation of immigration in post-9/11 United States (Hauptman, 2013), the criminalisation of asylum seekers in the United Kingdom and the United States (Welch and Schuster, 2005; Welch, 2004) and crimmigration processes in Australia (Welch, 2012).

2.2.1 Terminology

Describing unauthorised immigrants as criminals can happen in direct ways, but more subtle forms are apparent too. In this regard, considerable attention has been drawn to the use of the term 'illegal', which is criticised not only because it 'stresses criminality' and 'defines immigrants as criminals' (Lakoff and Ferguson, 2006: 1), but also for being inaccurate: although a migratory act might be illegal, people themselves cannot be illegal. Moreover, it does not do justice to the complex question of legal and illegal stay, which includes numerous 'in-between' situations described as 'semi-compliance' (Anderson, 2013; Düvell, 2011; Guild, 2004) and the dynamic nature of the phenomenon (Van Meeteren, 2010). As such, it is what Maneri (2011: 80) defines as '"collective categories" that lack any descriptive coherence or precision, but are nevertheless replete with connotations and implicit associations'. Many academics, human rights organisations and EU institutions, but also various international news associations,[2] therefore use terms that are perceived to be more neutral, most notably 'irregular' and 'undocumented', although some academics also explicitly use the term 'illegal migrant' in order to emphasise the role of the state in creating processes that render individuals illegal (Schuster, 2011; Van Eijl, 2008). For the same reason, Bauder (2014) recently argued in favour of the term 'illegalised'. Others also defend use of the term 'illegal' for being clear and accurate, arguing that the alternatives are merely politically correct euphemisms.[3] The debate surrounding terminology has taken on a distinct political character, perhaps most notably in the United States, where liberal and conservative advocates have both sought to get their terminological frames to dominate in the media (Merolla et al., 2013). The preferred word choice then roughly reflects whether someone is in favour of a more restrictive approach or a more rights-based approach. For example, Anderson and Ruhs (2010: 175) argue that '"illegality" is also the term that is often used by those elements of the mass media that promote and reinforce negative public attitudes to immigration, and illegal immigration in particular'.[4]

2 These include the US Associated Press, UK Press Association, European Journalism Observatory, European Journalism Centre, Association of European Journalists and Australian Press Council.

3 'Readers won't benefit if Times bans the term 'illegal 'immigrant', *New York Times, October 2, 2012.*

4 We use the term 'unauthorised migrant' because it is most inclusive of the population we refer too here, and other terms are either too limited in scope (e.g.: not all unauthorised migrants are undocumented) or seem to reflect a particular political stand or viewpoint. See Passel, van Hook & Bean (2004) for some additional discussion.

2.3 METHODOLOGY

In general there is no lack of scholarly attention for the representations of migrants and other minorities in Western media, although Thorbjornsrud (2015) notes that the number of studies that focus specifically on unauthorised immigrants is relatively small. Most of this research has been more or less a critique of the media, focusing on negative depictions of immigrants and minorities that demonstrate an underlying structural bias in the media – or even society at large (Bleich et al., 2015a). Many of these studies have adopted a qualitative approach and often focused on a relatively short time period or a single event, analyzing only a small number of texts (Sciortino and Colombo, 2004). Because a large number of these researchers also take an explicit stand, such studies have sometimes been criticised for lacking representativeness and being subject to 'cherry-picking', where researchers select only those articles that confirm their existing beliefs and initial hypotheses (Hier, 2009; Koller and Mautner, 2004; Orpin, 2005; Stubbs, 1994). Several more recent studies have therefore employed more systematic and comparative methods, resulting in various articles demonstrating the complexity of immigration coverage and challenging the idea that the media are intrinsically biased and consistently engage in negative framing of immigrants and minorities (Bleich et al., 2015b; Caviedes, 2015; Hallin, 2015; Lawlor, 2015; Thorbjornsrud, 2015; Tolley, 2015). Yet, despite these important methodological advances, none of these studies employs what we believe to be one of the most promising approaches towards media analyses: a corpus linguistics approach.

Corpus linguistics (CL) refers to the study of (often very large bodies of) real-life textual data (the corpus) with the aid of computer software (Baker, 2006; Mautner, 2009; McEnery and Wilson, 1996). Corpora are large, representative (or even comprehensive) bodies of naturally occurring language, and, because they are stored electronically, it becomes possible to carry out statistical analyses that can reveal – possibly counter-intuitive – linguistic patterns and frequency information (Baker, 2006). Until now, corpus techniques have only rarely been used for discourse analyses, although the advantages of using CL in media studies have repeatedly been demonstrated (Allen and Blinder, 2013; Baker, 2012; Baker et al., 2008; Gabrielatos and Baker, 2008; Koller and Mautner, 2004; Mautner, 2009). One of these advantages is the fact that a researcher can work with very large amounts of data, which is particularly interesting when studying media content: as Fairclough (1989: 54) has rightly argued, 'a single text on its own is quite insignificant: the effects of media power are cumulative, working through the repetition of particular ways of handling causality and agency'. Computer-assisted analyses of big data sets also greatly reduce a researcher's bias and increase the internal validity of a study, by employing a comprehensive rather than a selective approach (Baker, 2006; Mautner, 2009). Of course, as Tolley (2015: 968) also acknowledges, the distinction between manual and automated analyses is far from clear-cut, with computers amplifying rather than replacing human work (see also Grimmer and Stewart, 2013). But, although much still depends on the individual researcher's choices and his/her interpretation of the findings, 'it becomes less easy to be selective about a single newspaper article when we are looking at hundreds of articles' (Baker, 2006: 12).

For the current study we used the software program 'Wordsmith Tools' to carry out four types of analysis. First, *frequency lists* are one of the most basic applications but a good starting point for the analysis of a corpus (Baker, 2006). They reveal the most frequently occurring words in a corpus, or show how often specific words appear. Through the analysis of *collocates* a more discursive analysis of the way immigrants are described becomes possible on a quantitative level. Collocates are words that appear near another word more often than could be expected by chance only (Blinder and Allen, 2015), and thus they provide 'a way of understanding meanings and associations between words which are otherwise difficult to ascertain from a small-scale analysis of a single text' (Baker, 2006: 96). Wordsmith Tools can identify statistically significant collocates, based on their co-occurrence, the relative frequency of both words in the corpus and the full size of the corpus. Following previous studies, we used a window of 10 words for our analysis, 5 to the left and 5 to the right, using both log likelihood (LL, required minimum score of 6.63) and mutual information (MI, required minimum score of 5.0) to test for statistical significance and strength of the relationship between two words (Allen and Blinder, 2013; Baker et al., 2013; Blinder and Allen, 2015). We focused specifically on the L1 collocate, meaning the word that appears directly before the keyword, because this will often be an adjective directly describing the word of interest (Blinder and Allen, 2015). Following Gabrielatos and Baker (2008), we also use the notion of *consistent collocates* (c-collocates) for words that are collocates in at least two-thirds of the annual sub-corpora. The results of a collocation analysis go further than a mere content analysis, providing 'the most salient and obvious lexical patterns surrounding a subject, from which a number of discourses can be obtained' (Baker, 2006: 114). *Keyness* allows the researcher to compare two data sets and see which words occur significantly more often in one of them, making it a particularly valuable tool for comparisons. Finally, *Concordances* combine quantitative and qualitative methods of content analysis. Baker (2006: 71) describes concordances as 'simply a list of all of the occurrences of a particular search term in a corpus, presented within the context that they occur in'. This context usually means a number of words, to be decided by the researcher, to the left and the right of a search term – for example, 'illegal migrants'. Concordance analyses thus allow for a closer and more in-depth examination and manual reading of a selection of relevant articles, and can act as a bridge towards an informed critical discourse analysis of a smaller number of relevant articles. Here we used it mainly to provide a 'vital validity check' of our quantitative results (Blinder and Allen, 2015: 12).

2.3.1 The corpus

For this study we have created our own specialised corpus, consisting of all newspaper items on unauthorised migrants that appeared in Dutch national newspapers between 1 January 1999 and 31 December 2013.[5] This period was chosen because it also covers a period from before the watershed events at the beginning of the century that have been identified as causing a negative change in Dutch public discourse on immigration (Pakes, 2006); the years 1999-2000 can be used as a period where we would expect more 'neutral' media content.[6] We chose newspapers because their archives are readily available online and, although numbers have been declining, newspaper readership is still relatively high in the Netherlands, with dailies reaching about 70 percent of the population. Of the five main newspapers, *de Volkskrant*, *Trouw* and *NRC Handelsblad* are considered as broadsheets, or 'quality newspapers', with the first two being more left-wing and *NRC Handelsblad* liberal-conservative. *De Telegraaf* has the highest circulation in the Netherlands and, together with *Algemeen Dagblad*, is considered to be a right-wing, 'popular' newspaper. However, unlike in for example the United Kingdom, the distinction between tabloid and broadsheet newspapers holds minor relevance in the Netherlands: the 'popular' newspapers are generally far less populist and sensationalist than, for example, the *Sun* or the *Daily Express* (Bakker and Vasterman, 2007; Broersma and Graham, 2013). The Dutch media landscape further consists of various free dailies mainly distributed on public transport (*Metro*, *Spits*, *De Pers*, and *Dag*, with the latter two existing only briefly) and two conservative Christian newspapers (*Nederlands Dagblad* and *Reformatorisch Dagblad*). To avoid too much repetition we excluded regional newspapers, which, following a number of mergers, often have the same sections on national and foreign news as national newspapers.

Before starting our analyses we manually read a small random sample of newspaper articles. Besides further familiarizing a researcher with its corpus

5 Articles were downloaded from LexisNexis using the Boolean search string "illegalen" or "illegaliteit" or "uitgeproc!" or "ongewenst! vreemdeling!" or "mensen zonder papieren" or "mensen zonder wettig verblijf" or "(irregulier! or illegal! or ongedocumenteerd! or clandestien! or ongeautoriseerd! or niet-geautoriseerd! and migra! or immigrant! or immigratie or vluchteling! or bootvluchteling! or vreemdeling! or asielzoeker! or arbeidsmigra!)". For some considerations regarding the selection of the right query terms, see (Gabrielatos, 2007). We included the term 'rejected asylum seeker' because it is often used interchangeably with unauthorised migrant, at times simply overlaps and in order to see if there were different discourses around different terms.

6 Pakes (2006) identifies three watershed events that contributed to "a sharp and excluding social discourse surrounding issues of crime and law and order. (...) particularly aimed at ethnic minority groups." These are 9/11, the murder of right-wing, anti-immigrant and anti-Islam politician Pim Fortuyn in 2002 by a political environmental activist in 2002 and the murder of film maker and outspoken Islam-critic Theo van Gogh by a radicalised Dutch-Moroccan youngster in 2004.

by already pointing towards interesting language patterns that require attention further in the analysis, this procedure can also help either to find specific terms or synonyms that have been missed in the original search string or to reveal that a high number of irrelevant articles is found with the search string. The final search string we used was the result of various of these trial and error steps and, although one can never be entirely sure to have captured all relevant articles, we believe that in this way we have created a comprehensive 'unauthorised migrants' corpus without a high number of irrelevant articles. Our final corpus contains 28,274 articles from 12 national newspapers and consists of just over 10 million words.[7] All these articles were sorted by publication month and newspaper, allowing us to carry out comparisons between newspapers and over time and identify trends.

2.4 Results

Figure 2.1 shows the number of articles on unauthorised migrants per annum. Because not all newspapers appeared throughout the complete research period – some went out of business, and others started – and results would therefore be skewed towards years with more newspapers, this figure is based on the five main newspapers only,[8] with additional checks confirming that other newspapers showed similar trend lines. Whereas newspaper attention for unauthorised migrants was quite stable until 2006 – fluctuating only slightly each year – there was a sharp decrease in the number of articles per year during the period 2006-9, after which attention steadily increased again. However, the annual number of newspaper articles did not ever reach the same numbers as in the 1999-2006 period. If we look at the distribution of newspaper articles per month in 2010, November and December have by far the most articles. The proposal to criminalize unauthorised stay was introduced in October 2010, practically the lowest point of media attention. Frequency lists and concordance analyses confirmed that the rise in attention for unauthorised migrants during the last three years of our study is primarily due to the political and public controversy over the proposal.

One possible reason for the decline in newspaper articles on unauthorised migrants is the enlargement of the European Union with 10 (mainly East European) countries in 2004, and Bulgaria and Romania in 2007. Overnight this legalised unauthorised immigrants from those countries and itis one of the most important explanations for the decreasing number of estimated unauthorised migrants in the Netherlands (Van der Heijden et al., 2011). At

7 The newspapers were *Algemeen Dagblad, Dag, De Pers, Financieel Dagblad, Het Parool, Metro, Nederlands Dagblad, NRC Handelsblad, NRC Next, Reformatorisch Dagblad, Spits, Telegraaf, Trouw, de Volkskrant.*

8 *Algemeen Dagblad, NRC Handelsblad, Telegraaf, Trouw* and *de Volkskrant.*

the same time there appears to have been a shift in the public debate, where populist resistance against Islam and immigration has been replaced, or at least supplemented, by a fierce resistance against European integration (Wansink, 2007). It therefore seemed plausible that part of the media attention for unauthorised migrants has shifted to migrants from East European countries – and that they are no longer referred to as *unauthorised* migrants. But, whereas a LexisNexis analysis indeed showed a much higher number of

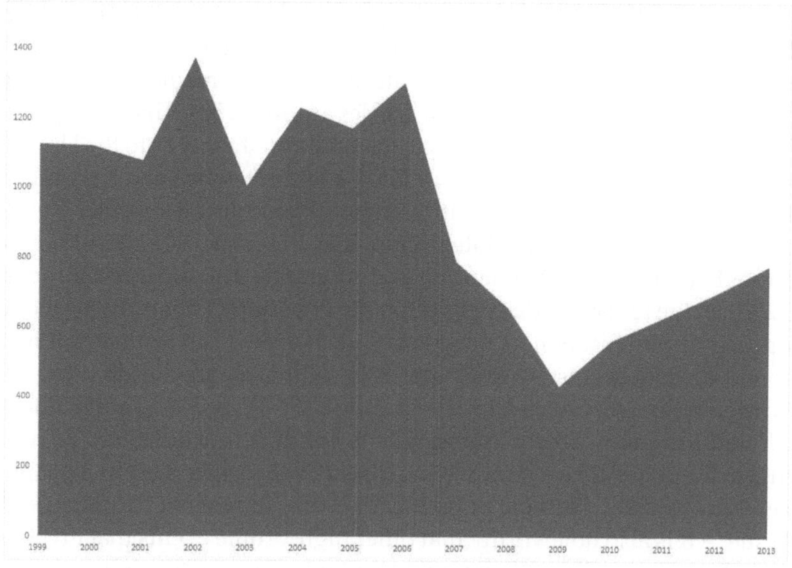

Figure 2.1 Number of articles on unauthorised migrants per year

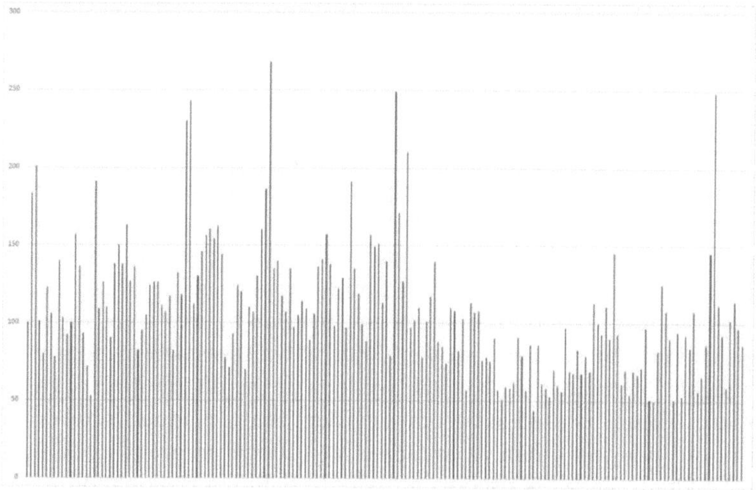

Figure 2.2 Number of articles on unauthorised migrants per month

annual articles about East European migrants since 2004, a content analysis of various nationalities and terms such as 'East European' did not show a declining trend in our corpus – either absolute or relative. This means that, although there has been a general increase in newspaper attention on East European migrants, this cannot explain the decrease in articles on unauthorised migrants. Instead, there does not seem to be one, clear explanation for the decline in newspaper attention for unauthorised migrants.

Looking at the distribution of newspaper articles per month, it becomes immediately clear that there are a few spikes in newspaper attention for unauthorised migrants. Closer examination of these months reveals that these can be explained by specific events that attracted strong media attention for a brief period of time. In June 2000, most articles are about 58 Chinese migrants who died of suffocation in the back of a truck while on their way to the United Kingdom. The high points in February 2004 and September and December 2006 are primarily due to political controversies surrounding the former Dutch Minister for Aliens Affairs and Integration Rita Verdonk, who was known for her tough stance towards unauthorised migrants. The most recent peak in May 2013 is due to serious debates within the governing Labour Party about the proposed criminalisation of illegal stay. It therefore seems that political debates and developments are the main cause of intense media attention on unauthorised migrants. Gabrielatos and Baker (2008: 18) noted a similar effect in the United Kingdom, where immigrants 'were thus functionalised as part of a struggle for political hegemony, being discursively constructed as a people who merely constitute the topic of political debate, somewhat dehumanised as an "issue"'. It is also noteworthy that other high-profile events that involve or could potentially be linked to unauthorised migrants – a fire at the airport immigrant detention centre that killed 11 unauthorised migrants, various (international) terrorist attacks – have not caused the same increase in newspaper articles on unauthorised migrants.

2.4.1 Discourse: Terminology

In Dutch newspapers, 'illegal' is by far the most often used term to refer to unauthorised migrants – over 95 percent of instances. 'Irregular' and 'undocumented' are very rarely used, and sometimes even in different contexts, such as 'irregular rebel groups'. Moreover, this finding applies, without exception, to newspapers across the political spectrum. Similar figures were recently found in the United States, where. in over 95 percent of cases newspapers used the term 'illegal' (Merolla et al., 2013). If we look at the distribution of cases where the term 'illegal' is used, it becomes evident that it is much more often used as a noun ('illegals') than as an adjective ('illegal migrant' or 'illegal immigrant'). When 'illegal' is used as an adjective, the most common noun is 'immigrant', followed by 'migrant' and 'alien'. Instances of 'illegal asylum seeker' and 'illegal refugee' – legally speaking impossible constructions – also appear several dozen times per year. The term 'rejected asylum seekers' ('uitgeprocedeerde asielzoekers'), which does not convey the exact same meaning, is the second most often used term, but the saliency of this term varies widely between years. Use of 'illegal' as a noun does show a steady decline throughout the period, both absolutely and relatively, but this cannot be explained by a replacing term. Rather, it seems to be the result of an increasing focus on the condition of 'illegality' in later years, as a place in which people can 'disappear' or 'end up in'.

2.4.2 A criminal discourse?

Considering the fact that 'illegals' was the most common way to describe unauthorised migrants, and we were interested in how unauthorised migrants as a group were described, we carried out a collocation analysis for this term. Table 2.1 shows an overview of the statistically significant collocates of 'illegals', sorted on the L1 position (the position immediately before 'illegals') for the period 1999-2013, without words such as 'the', 'or', 'and'.

The most important L1 collocate for 'illegals' is 'white', referring to a group of unauthorised migrants who had long resided in the Netherlands but, owing to the enactment of the 1998 Linking Act, suddenly lost most of their rights. The word 'white' is used here with the connotation of a semi-documented position in society and does not refer to physical appearance. The focus on this group is entirely clustered in the initial years, particularly in 1999. Our results also show that numerical terms are often used to describe 'illegals', indicating that an important characteristic is how many there are. Except for absolute numbers ('000', 'million', etc.), these include more vague numerical descriptions ('thousands', 'tens of thousands', even 'millions') and group descriptors ('a lot', 'groups of'). Vollmer (2011: 330) noted that 'number games' play a crucial role in policy discourses on unauthorised migration throughout the EU, where 'higher numbers justify control and enforcement policies, whereas lower numbers ease the political landscape'. 'Stream' is also a strong L1 collocate, which confirms earlier findings that aquatic terms are frequently used in conjunction with migratory movements. Tsoukala (2005) argues that these terms have quickly become standardised in discourses on immigration and create a notion of uncontrollability and threat. What is, however, particularly notable for our main hypothesis is that 'criminal' is one of the most important adjectives used with the term 'illegals', showing that one of the most common ways to describe 'illegals' is as criminals.

N	Word	Total	Total Left	Total Right	L1
3	WHITE	1.936	1.879	57	1.842
7	000	715	648	67	518
11	NUMBER/AMOUNT	646	603	43	477
12	CRIMINAL (Adj.)	541	489	52	450
14	MANY/A LOT	765	629	136	408
17	MILLION	394	375	19	336
18	ALL	451	392	59	264
20	MORE	852	543	309	229
21	AGAINST	696	503	193	219
22	GROUP	388	353	35	195
23	MOST	214	203	11	171
25	THOUSANDS	179	165	14	139
27	CHINESE	159	148	11	138
28	STREAM	181	178	3	133
29	OTHER	377	242	135	124
30	THOUSAND	172	154	18	124
34	HUNDRED	160	147	13	105
36	NONE	738	334	404	104
37	ARRESTED	106	106	0	100
38	ELEVEN	198	189	9	89
40	HOW MANY	89	88	1	82
41	AFRICAN	100	86	14	79
42	TENS	128	117	11	79
46	GROUPS	118	110	8	74
48	TENS OF THOUSANDS	85	75	10	69
49	LESS	170	105	65	68
50	YOUNG	85	73	12	64

Table 2.1 Collocates of 'illegals', 1999-2013

2.4.3 Trends and developments

Although 'criminal' was one of the most important L1 collocates for 'illegals', we were also interested in identifying patterns over time. Therefore we tested whether it was a c-collocate by carrying out collocation analyses for the word 'illegals' in each separate year. This showed that 'criminal' as an adjective[9] scored significant LL scores in all 15 years of our corpus and significant MI

9 In Dutch, the word criminal as an adjective is different than criminal as a noun.

scores in 13 years (in 2000 and 2012 the scores fell just short of the 5.0 requirement). Turning it around, the term 'criminals' is a significant c-collocate of the adjective 'illegal', falling short of the required statistical scores only in 2006 and 2011. The term 'criminals' was also a significant collocate of 'illegals' in all years after 2002, except for 2004 and 2009, thus being a c-collocate for the period 2002-13. This shows that 'illegals' often appear in the same sentence as 'criminal' and 'criminals'.

Both 'criminal illegals' and 'illegal criminals' are thus constructions that can be regularly found, demonstrating that in newspaper articles on unauthorised migrants crime is one of the main topics discussed, and this has been the case throughout the 15 years of our corpus. Similar analyses with the terms 'asylum seekers', 'refugees', 'migrants' and 'immigrants' showed fewer or no references to crime. Although our corpus is not a representative reflection of all newspaper content on these groups – it contains only newspaper articles that also mention unauthorised migrants – this suggests that, in Dutch newspapers, unauthorised migrants in particular are strongly associated with crime.

Yet, although the adjective 'criminal' is a c-collocate of 'illegals', a content analysis of the phrase 'criminal illegals' showed a steady decrease in use of the term between 1999 and 2013. Figure 2.3 shows that, over time, not only did usage of the word 'illegal' show a steady decrease, but Dutch newspapers also described unauthorised migrants less often as criminals. In the last two years of the period studied, only four instances of 'criminal illegals' per year occurred, of which two did not even refer to the Netherlands. Although some other variations appear in the corpus – especially 'criminal aliens', albeit still only one third of the times 'criminal illegals' – there is no contrary trend visible in the use of these terms. Although crime remains an important topic in newspaper articles throughout our corpus, it is far less of an issue in the period around the proposed criminalisation of illegal stay than it was around 2000, and unauthorised migrants are gradually less often directly described as criminal.

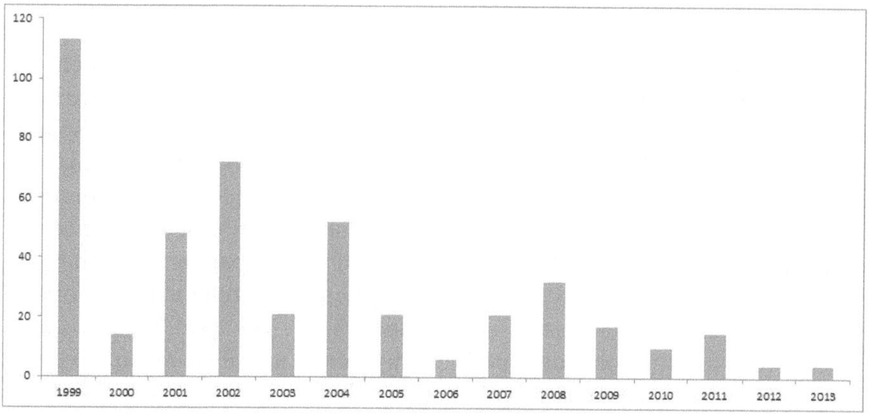

Figure 2.3 Content analysis of the phrase 'criminal illegals'

2.4.4 Differences between newspapers

Whereas there are thus indications of a criminalizing discourse in Dutch newspapers regarding unauthorised migrants, we found considerable differences between newspapers, as illustrated by a keyness comparison between the left-wing 'quality' newspaper *de Volkskrant* and the right-wing 'popular' *De Telegraaf*.

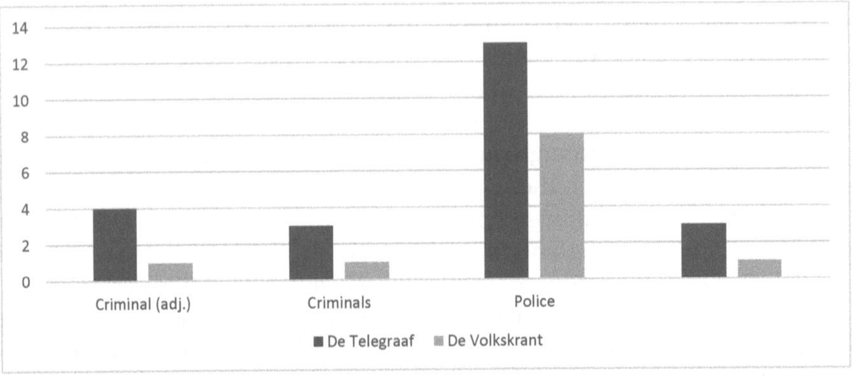

Figure 2.4 Keyness of crime-related terms in De Telegraaf *and* de Volkskrant

Figure 2.4 shows how often various crime-related terms appeared per 10,000 words in both newspapers. The words 'criminal' and 'criminals' appeared three to four times more often in *De Telegraaf* than in *de Volkskrant*. Related terms – 'police' and 'arrested' – were also found significantly more often in *De Telegraaf,* thus lending empirical support to the assertion that right-wing newspapers more often link unauthorised migrants to issues of crime.

2.5 Conclusion and discussion

In this study we have analysed 15 years of Dutch newspaper content on unauthorised migrants. Employing a corpus linguistics methodology, we have been able to identify various patterns in both the frequency of newspaper articles and the discursive elements of how unauthorised migrants are described, thus testing the hypothesis that media content fuels the crimmigration process. Our analysis revealed some familiar ways in which unauthorised migrants are consistently depicted by all Dutch newspapers. The first and foremost is the constant way in which these newspapers refer to unauthorised migrants: 'illegals', or at best 'illegal (im)migrants'. The term 'illegal' is also consistently used in the Dutch political discourse, and it seems to have relevance for arguments regarding actual legislation: in the debate about the formal criminalisation of unauthorised stay at least one politician publicly argued that 'it is of course very strange that something is illegal, but has no punishment to it'.[10] At the EU level there have been attempts to stop use of the term 'illegal' and instead employ the words 'irregular' and 'undocumented'.[11] The Platform for International Cooperation on Undocumented Migrants (PICUM) recently launched a campaign to ban use of the term 'illegal migrant', including a leaflet with preferable equivalents in all major European languages. For the Dutch language the NGO suggests the terms 'mensen zonder papieren' and 'mensen zonder wettig verblijf' (literally: 'people without papers' and 'people without lawful stay'). These descriptions seem rather long for everyday usage and therefore unlikely to become part of popular discourse; although the second option is to some extent an accepted term in Flanders,[12] it does not appear a single time in 15 years of Dutch newspaper articles. Whereas in the United States recent changes in the stylebooks of major media outlets suggest a greater prevalence of alternative terms in the near future (Merolla et al., 2013), in the Netherlands there does not appear to be any meaningful discussion going on about terminology. At the same time, one can wonder if a terminology replacement might not merely lead to what has been dubbed 'the euphemism treadmill' (Pinker, 2007), whereby the replacement terms themselves become offensive over time. Moreover, two recent studies in the United States showed that terminology frames – 'illegal' versus 'unauthorised'/'irregular'/'undocumented' – did not influence public opinion regarding the provision of certain rights for unauthorised migrants, leading the authors to suggest that it might be more useful for migrant rights activists to focus on actual policies and how they are framed, rather than on terminology frames (Knoll et al., 2012; Merolla et al., 2013). In this regard it is interesting to note that the rise in newspaper articles about unauthorised migrants in the last years of our corpus can be solely attributed to the political and public discussion this bill triggered, but newspaper content during this time was not necessarily characterised by the framing of unauthorised migrants as criminal. Some concordance analyses even indicate that various newspapers offered a platform for substantial critique of the proposal, in this way possibly even playing a role in its eventual withdrawal in 2014.

One of the findings that stood out in our analysis was that 'criminal' was one of the most important collocates of 'illegals', providing evidence for a criminal discourse and a merger of references to migration and crime. Dutch newspaper articles about unauthorised migrants deal significantly often with issues of crime; indeed, it is one of the most salient themes. Needless to say, this is the quintessential discourse on which the criminalisation of unauthorised migrants rests. Framing unauthorised migrants as criminals, in combination

10 'Aanpak criminele illegaal is hoofdzaak voor kabinet', *de Volkskrant,* April 1, 2011.

11 European Parliament resolution on the situation of fundamental rights in the European Union 2004-2008, 14 January 2009.

12 We thank one of the anonymous reviewers for pointing that out.

with a strong focus on numbers, serves as a powerful catalyst for what Vollmer (2011: 331) calls 'the demonstration of efficient governance', resulting in repressive and punitive policies with an intense focus on control.
Although these findings are a reason for concern, our main hypothesis proved incorrect: media attention for unauthorised migrants strongly decreased after 2006 and newspaper articles about crime among unauthorised migrants featured mainly in the first years of our corpus. The proposal to criminalize illegal stay came at practically the lowest point of media attention for unauthorised migrants, and seems to have been the result of a change in government rather than of active agenda-setting by the media or another actor. This provides some modest support for Threadgold's (2009: 1) statement that there is 'a small but growing body of evidence that political and policy discourse concerning immigration actually fuel the media discourse, which in turn drives policy'. The present study has clearly demonstrated that the bill to criminalize illegal stay in the Netherlands was not preceded by strong and increasing media attention for criminal illegal migrants. Rather, the framing of migrants as criminals is a more diffuse process in which the media seem to follow rather than fuel politics and policy.

Whereas the initial years of our corpus support the idea of a moral panic episode about 'criminal illegals', this is not something we see in later years. However, we also see that the problem of the 'criminal illegal' keeps lingering on and surfacing every now and then. In this regard it is interesting to see that Cohen (2002) more recently noted that reactions to asylum seekers do not follow the ordinary temporary moral panic model, but are subject to continuous negative, excluding and hostile messages. In their study on UK media reporting around Bulgarian and Romanian EU accession, Mawby and Gisby (2009: 48) argue that this model is 'now a more accurate way to model a cluster of issues, such as immigration in general' and they note that 'this open-ended form of moral panic has seemingly "stepping stoned" its way from asylum seekers to immigrants, to EU enlargement, to general anxieties about crime'. This is relevant, because although our corpus showed that newspaper articles about unauthorised migrants decreased, articles about migrants from new EU countries actually increased, and it is questionable whether the general public is always aware of such distinctions within the broad category of 'foreigners'. If negative attention for unauthorised migrants has merely been replaced by negative attention for foreign EU citizens and other ethnic and racial minority groups, and in the public perception these various categories are assembled into one homogeneous problematic group of outsiders, the decrease in newspaper articles on (criminal) unauthorised migrants will have had hardly any effect on public opinion about this specific group. In light of increasing European integration and the negative backlash this seems to cause in primarily West European countries, it would be worthwhile to examine media content on new European citizens and what this means for the future of the European project.

While this study provided valuable insights into newspaper reporting on unauthorised migrants in the Netherlands, it simultaneously raised various questions that point to interesting areas for future research. Here we have focused only on print media, but analyses of web-based content could be equally interesting. Furthermore, linking the analysis of media content to a more systematic analysis of the political discourse could increase our understanding of who influences whom. Finally, and most importantly, although here we have focused on the Netherlands only, we believe the approach we have introduced is particularly suitable for large-scale comparisons and hope to have laid the foundation for future comparative work between various European countries. This could focus on unauthorised migrants, but it would also be particularly worthwhile to examine how newspapers in different European countries have reported on the recent refugee crisis. The corpus linguistics approach allows for quick replications of analyses with large sets of longitudinal data. Because the statistical tests offer easy to compare outcomes, it is eminently appropriate for a systematic comparison of discourses in various countries.

PART II

Crimmigration and intra-Schengen migration policing

3 At the border of immigration control

Discretionary decision-making within the Mobile Security Monitor[1]

3.1 Introduction

Acting as the 'border (migration) police', the Royal Netherlands Marechaussee (RNM) carries out, among other things, the Mobile Security Monitor (MSM). These are mobile identity checks which have been held in the border areas with Belgium and Germany since the entry into force of the Schengen Agreement in 1995. Since the outbreak of the refugee crisis, these checks have received increasing attention.[2] The MSM is part of the operational control of migrants as regulated in Article 50 of the Aliens Act 2000. Whereas initially this type of immigration checks was merely aimed at counteracting illegal stay, the official objective now also includes combatting human trafficking and identity fraud (Van der Woude, Dekkers, & Brouwer, 2015). This is a proactive form of policing, which means that people can be checked without the need of having a reasonable suspicion of illegal stay or criminal offence (Corstens & Borgers, 2014, p. 297). The RNM officers responsible for implementing the MSM thus have a great deal of discretionary decision power to decide who they will stop for a check and who they want to investigate further.

Traditionally, there has been a great deal of research interest in the discretionary decision-making of police officers (Brown, 1981; Maynard-Moody & Musheno, 2000; Mendias & Kehoe, 2006; Phillips, 2015; for recent Dutch studies, refer to: Çankaya, 2012; Kleijer-kool & Landman, 2016; Landman, 2015). At the same time, it is striking that so far relatively few studies have been published on the performance of actors in the area of immigration control (although see: Aas & Gundhus, 2015; Casella Colombeau, 2017; Pratt & Thompson, 2008; Weber, 2011). This is even more remarkable in the context of the crimmigration process, which refers to the increasing intertwinement of enforcement and control under criminal law and migration law (Staring, 2012; Stumpf, 2006; Van der Leun, 2010; Van der Woude, Van der Leun & Nijland, 2014). This process is visible at the level of the political and public

---

1 An earlier, Dutch, version of this chapter was published as: Brouwer, J., Van der Woude, M.A.H., & van der Leun, J.P. (2017). Op de grens van het vreemdelingentoezicht: discretionaire beslissingen binnen het Mobiel Toezicht Veiligheid. *Tijdschrift Voor Veiligheid, 16*(2), 73-89.

2 The fieldwork for this contribution was carried out before the refugee crisis actually started to dominate the news.

discourse, the level of legislation, but also at the level of implementation and has, among other things, as a consequence that both immigrants and criminals are equally recognised as threats that must be tackled with all available means (Stumpf, 2006; Van der Leun, 2010; Van der Leun & Van der Woude, 2012). Since enforcement under criminal law comes with considerably more procedural safeguards than administrative law, this can have negative consequences for the legal position of the legal persons involved (Chacón, 2012; Stumpf, 2006; Van der Leun, Van der Woude, & De Ridder, 2013).

Various authors consider the decisions of street-level officers (Lipsky, 1980) – and in particular the possibility of stopping persons for a check – as the most important factor in the crimmigration process (Motomura, 2011; Pratt, 2010; Stumpf, 2006). Recently, it has been emphasised repeatedly that there is a strong need for empirical research into the daily practices of officers operating as border or migration police (Cote-Boucher, Infantino, & Salter, 2014; Loftus, 2015). In this regard, Loftus (2015) advises to derive from the rich body of literature regarding regular police officers and to ascertain to what extent the central findings of this could apply to border police officers as well.

In this contribution, we will have a detailed look at the manner in which RNM officers, being involved in the implementation of the MSM, interpret their discretionary decision power. We hereby explicitly focus on the interaction between immigration control and criminal enforcement, and its consequences for procedural safeguards. It is precisely these safeguards that could be jeopardised when law enforcement officials can choose from different types of legislation at their own discretion (Sklansky, 2012; Van der Woude et al., 2015). As illustrated elsewhere, the MSM has a complex legal and policy-based foundation with regard to the precise objective of the instrument, involving the intertwining of immigration control and criminal enforcement (Van der Woude et al., 2015). This raises the question of how this ambiguity about the precise task and associated competences – fitting within the aforementioned process of crimmigration – is interpreted by the street-level officials and which consequences this has for the way in which they perform their tasks. The central question in this contribution therefore reads:

> *How do street-level RNM officers involved in the implementation of the Mobile Security Monitor see their own task, and to what extent and how does this influence the way in which they practically interpret the discretionary decision power they enjoy in this regard?*

This question will be answered based on extensive empirical research, including over 800 man-hours of observation during MSM inspections and focus group discussions with street-level RNM officers involved with the MSM. We will first elaborate on the theoretical foundation for this piece by further explaining the interdependence between the concepts of discretionary decision power and crimmigration. We then provide some background and context by describing the MSM's practice and the discretionary scope the RNM officers have in this aspect. After clarifying the methodology, we will start answering the central question. To this end, we will first show that the RNM officers state that they have to navigate between immigration control and criminal enforcement, thereafter identify two different styles among the RNM officers, and finally discuss how this practically translates into the decisions they make. The article ends with a conclusion and discussion.

3.2 Discretionary decision-making and crimmigration

The RNM officers responsible for the implementation of the MSM resemble regular police officers in many respects. Not only do they represent the government in daily interactions with citizens, they also have a large degree of discretionary power to translate legal frameworks and formal policy into practice. They must apply the often abstract, multi-interpretable and sometimes even conflicting objectives, which are formulated at policy and organisational level, to specific situations (Lipsky, 1980; Van der Woude et al., 2015; Van Gestel & De Poot, 2014). In many cases, they have to interpret specific situations, set priorities and make decisions at their own discretion. Although wide discretionary powers for street-level officials can lead to more just decisions, as individual officials by not or differently applying the law can prevent certain undesirable consequences that the legislator had not foreseen (Schneider, 1992), it can also result in legal inequality and even unlawful decisions (Maynard-Moody & Musheno, 2000). In general, the more unclear the official policy goals are, the more liberty there is for civil servants to make decisions at their own discretion. For example, in a study on Spanish immigration policy, Bastien (2009) found that ambiguous objectives led to more discretion among the officials who had to implement this policy. Vague policy goals can therefore lead to personal convictions or individual professional views influencing the actions of street-level civil servants, and make it more challenging for those street-level officials to be accountable for their decisions.

In recent years there has been ample attention in police literature for the individual and situational factors that can influence the way in which police officers interpret their discretionary decision power during proactive inspections (for an overview, see: Dekkers & Van der Woude, 2014; Johnson & Morgan, 2013). This body of literature shows that discretionary decisions by police officers cannot be viewed separately from what Hawkins (2014) calls the decision field: the entirety of legal frameworks, policy choices and guidelines which form the contours within which professionals make discretionary decisions. So-called 'working rules', the internal culture of the police organisation and informal norms and values of individual agents also influence the decisions whether to stop someone or not (Alpert, Macdonald, & Dunham, 2005; Dunham, 2005; Quinton, 2011; Stroshine, Alpert, & Dunham, 2008). In that respect, the various police styles that police officers have and the influence this has on their actions are also cited (De Maillard, Hunold, Roché, & Oberwittler, 2016; Kleijer-Kool, 2010; Van der Torre, 1999; Wilson, 1978). Terpstra and Schaap (2011) distinguish three different police styles in the Dutch context: order maintainer/service provider, crime fighter, and the professional working style. They also state that for the majority of Dutch police officers, action and tension are important attractive factors of their job, and that agents have a strong incentive to "guard society's norms concerning good and evil and to protect the weak" (p. 188).

Halderen and Lasthuizen (2013) claim that this endeavor to achieve certain organisational goals or social interests regularly leads to a creative use of competences, especially when these competences are limited or legislation is unclear. This fits the claim of Maynard-Moody and Musheno (2000) that decisions by street-level officials are not particularly determined by rules, training and procedures, but mainly by the pursuit for justice. They argue that these officials do not quite use rules and procedures to make decisions, but rather first form a judgment about a citizen or client and then bend the rules and procedures to implement or rationalize their decision. Portillo and Rudes (2014, p. 323) therefore claim that more rules and procedures can paradoxically lead to even more discretion:

> "With more rules in place, street-level bureaucrats have greater discretion to determine which rule(s) to apply in a given situation. More, and contradictory, rules leave more options available for application and less the ability to monitor their application."

Although this depends on the way in which those rules are implemented, this is nevertheless an interesting observation with regard to the aforementioned process of crimmigration. According to David Sklansky (2012), crimmigration cannot be viewed separately from a broader trend of what he calls 'ad hoc instrumentalisation'. With this he means a way of thinking about the law and legal authorities in which formal distinction between legal domains is of secondary importance and government officials can simply choose the most effective instrument for solving a problem in each individual case. According to him, this way of thinking is strongly influenced by skepticism with regard to the necessity and possibility of limiting the discretionary decision power of street-level officials. In the last decades, the development towards a managerialist and instrumentalist criminal justice system is clearly perceptible in the Netherlands as well (Van der Leun et al., 2013; Van der Woude et al., 2014).

According to Sklansky, this instrumental approach to law is intrinsically linked to crimmigration. Due to the increasing intertwinement of criminal enforcement and immigration control, street-level officials have a broader spectrum of possibilities to stop or investigate a person, which increases their discretionary decision power. Sklansky mentions a toolbox of legal instruments that enforcers can use to deal with unwanted individuals, whether they are criminals or migrants. Given the instrumental considerations and the emphasis on effectiveness, enforcement not only takes on a strong ad hoc character, but the procedural safeguards retire to the background as well. Furthermore, the many options available to enforcers can quickly lead to a lack of transparency, because "this way little or no insight is provided into the grounds on which individual civil servants base their choices and decisions" and these civil servants often face little accountability for their actions as long as no formal complaints are filed (Van der Leun et al., 2013, p. 227).

3.3 Discretionary power within the Mobile Security Monitor

The MSM was established in 1992 in response to growing concerns about illegal migration and cross-border crime following the disappearance of internal borders in the Schengen area. Nevertheless, the instrument was originally solely aimed at immigration checks, as is also apparent from the initial name: Mobile *Aliens* Monitor. As it quickly became clear that the RNM was regularly confronted with criminal offences during the execution of the MSM, it was decided in 2006 to expand the official objective to include combatting migration-related forms of human trafficking and identity fraud. Although the MSM remained primarily a form of immigration control, a name change took place in the years following this adjustment: instead of Mobile Aliens Monitor, Mobile Security Monitor has since been used, initially only in the policy discourse but meanwhile also in the law. This seems to at least symbolically shift the focus from immigration control to criminal enforcement (Van der Woude et al., 2015).

Although MSM checks are also carried out on international trains, at airports and on the water, this contribution focuses on the MSM as it is performed on the road. As described in Article 4.17a of the Aliens Decree, these inspections take place in an area of twenty kilometers within the national borders with Belgium and Germany. To prevent them from having the effect of border controls, checks may take place during a maximum of six hours a day and ninety hours a month per road.[3] During a regular, 'static' MSM check, one or more motorcyclists observe the passing traffic right behind the border and select potentially interesting vehicles. The motorcyclist then accompanies these vehicles to the so-called 'inspection location' a little further inland, where other RNM officers carry out the actual check. In a few cases however, during so-called 'dynamic' checks, both selection and check are done by RNM officers who drive around in the border area by car.

3 According to Article 4.17b of the Aliens Decree 2000, this limit can be deviated from under exceptional circumstances. This also includes an increased influx of foreign nationals. The deployment of the MSM has therefore been intensified since November 2016.

The MSM possesses two important discretionary decision moments. The first moment is the decision to select a vehicle for a check, or the selection decision. A reasonable suspicion of illegal stay or criminal offence is not a prerequisite for selecting a vehicle. The Aliens Act solely states that the checks are carried out "based on information or experience-based evidence regarding illegal stay."[4] Apart from international and national non-discrimination principles, the circular does not provide any specific restrictions regarding the selection of a vehicle (Van der Woude, Brouwer, & Dekkers, 2016). RNM officers therefore have a lot of freedom to assess which persons and vehicles may be 'interesting' and should be checked. As construed elsewhere, they at least partly based themselves on external characteristics that could suggest that a passenger was an (unauthorised) migrant, making skin color an important factor (Brouwer, Van der Woude, & Van der Leun, 2017). Although the RNM officers were generally aware of the sensitivity of this profiling method, they felt that this was inevitable in view of their duties as enforcers under the alien law. Eastern European vehicles were also stopped a lot, as it was thought that they were often involved in certain forms of cross-border crime. However, these selection criteria are potentially problematic in view of the prohibition of discrimination and the right of EU citizens to free movement in the Schengen area.

The second moment of decision happens after a vehicle has been selected for a check and regards to the decision to further investigate a selected vehicle or person. During the check, the passengers are verified for identity, nationality, and legal residence in the Netherlands.[5] If they can confirm these three elements through valid documents, the check is complete and they may continue. However, if one or more passengers do not have valid documents, the RNM officers may further investigate the car and any person in the vehicle, aiming to determine the nationality and identity of that person in some way (for example by finding documents).[6] In addition, the RNM officers acting as general investigating officials are permitted, through the so-called 'continued application of powers' (Corstens & Borgers, 2014), to switch from immigration control to criminal investigation if they spontaneously encounter a specific suspicion of a criminal offence during the performance of a MSM check. In such situations, the relevant RNM officer changes his 'migration law cap' to a 'criminal law cap' (Van der Woude et al., 2015).

In many respects, the MSM therefore clearly fits in with the previously described trend of crimmigration. It is performed by RNM officers who have a great deal of discretion and generally do not have to account for the decisions made. In addition, the instrument has a complex legal foundation, which

4 Article 4.17a, para. 2 Aliens Decree 2000.
5 Article 50, para. 1 Aliens Act.
6 Article 50, para. 1 Aliens Act *juncto* Article 50, para. 5 Aliens Act *juncto* Article A2/3 Aliens Circular 2013.

reveals a slightly ambiguous objective aimed at both immigration control and (limited) criminal enforcement. Then, there is also the name change in official policy documents. All these elements seem to increase the discretionary scope of the street-level RNM officers and give them the freedom to develop their own professional views and act accordingly. Before we address the question to what extent this actually is the case, we will first provide a description of the research methodology.

3.4 Methodology

This contribution utilizes data collected through various research methods between October 2013 and November 2015 in the context of the larger research project 'Decision-making in Border Areas' (Van der Woude et al., 2016).[7] During this period, researchers participated in 57 MSM controls, resulting in more than 800 man-hours of observation. Observational research was chosen because it is a method ideally suited to study the behaviour of police officers and other street-level officials in a 'natural' setting, and thereby gain insight into their actions and decisions and the way in which they must be interpreted (Ley, 1988; Reiss, 1971). The disadvantage of this research method is that it influences the obtained results (Spano, 2005). For example, it cannot be ruled out that the presence of the researchers facilitated that the RNM officers were more likely to act according to the rules. An attempt was made to eliminate this by joining at least six shifts with each brigade,[8] which means many RNM officers were very regularly seen and spoken and a certain degree of trust emerged. Moreover, this reduced the chance they would consistently display 'unnatural' behaviour for a long time. Nevertheless, a certain amount of observer effect cannot be excluded.

The research team always consisted of two people who attended the entire shift. The number of RNM officers per shift varied greatly, ranging from shifts with only four RNM officers to large shifts with more than ten RNM officers and on one occasion several other law enforcement agencies. A shift normally lasted six to eight hours and always started with a briefing. The researchers made use of this moment to introduce themselves, to briefly explain the research and to offer the possibility to ask questions. During the shift, an observation form was used, which systematically recorded the characteristics

---

7 The data collected for this project consists of 800 man-hours of observation, thirteen focus group discussions with RNM officers involved in the operational implementation of the MSM, 167 surveys conducted among persons who were checked within the framework of the MSM and eighteen in-depth interviews with staff members, policy staff and government officials working at the Royal Netherlands Marechaussee, the Ministry of Defense and the Ministry of Security and Justice. Only the observation data and the focus group discussions were used for this contribution.

8 Five brigades of varying sizes are involved in the MSM on the road.

of the selected vehicle, the events taking place during the check, the interaction between the RNM officers and the people being checked, and the outcome of the check. On this form, the researchers also noted the reasons RNM officers gave for the various decisions they made.

Observations took place in different ways. In most cases the researchers were at the inspection location, where they had a good view of the selected vehicles brought in and the course of the inspection. During dynamic checks, the researchers were usually in the back of the car. Due to practical reasons, in those cases less use was made of the observation form. During observations, a lot of conversations took place with the RNM officers present. Thus, insight has been gained into RNM officers' actual decisions as well as their interpretations. Considering there were often several officials present at the control location, many different RNM officers were interviewed. These conversations happened in a fairly informal nature, without a prearranged topic list. Moreover, as this type of conversations took place in an environment familiar to the RNM officers, the chance of socially desirable answers was reduced. The researchers kept field notes in the form of short notes and catchwords, which were further elaborated into fieldnote reports after each shift.

In addition to the observations, thirteen focus group discussions were held with eight to ten RNM officers of various ages and years of service who were involved in the operational implementation of the MSM. Focus groups can provide insight in complex or unclear phenomena – such as the manner in which RNM officers interpret their discretionary decision power – as well as the influence of and dynamics within the researched group (Finch, Lewis, & Turley, 2013; Krueger & Casey, 2014). This research method is not suitable for finding out individual opinions about the discussion topics and the group process can influence the mutual discussion. The goal of the focus groups, however, was to obtain data that offers a good insight into the collective views of the RNM officers. At most brigades we held two focus group discussions, at one brigade we held one and at one larger brigade we held four. These discussions took place after the majority of the observations had already been carried out, hence the subjects and preliminary findings that emerged during the observations could be submitted to the participants for reflection. This ensured enrichment and amplification of the data. In this sense, during these discussions, the perceptions of the RNM officers were extensively discussed with regard to their own tasks and the corresponding authorities.

The focus group discussions were recorded and transcribed verbatim. All field notes and transcripts were then coded and analysed using Atlas-Ti. A list of codes was prepared in advance by the researchers, which was supplemented and – in mutual consultation – adjusted during the coding itself.

3.5 Between immigration control and criminal enforcement

During the fieldwork, it became clear that street-level RNM officers had different visions on what their own tasks consisted of. Almost all RNM officers indicated that the MSM is primarily an instrument for immigration control and cited the fight against illegal migration as an important or the most important objective. At the same time, according to Article 141 of the Code of Criminal Procedure, RNM officers are also general investigating officials; hence they are authorised to criminal enforcement if during a check they, in accordance with the aforementioned doctrine of continued application, *spontaneously* encounter a punishable fact other than human smuggling or identity fraud. Many respondents explicitly saw themselves as more than solely enforcers in the context of the Aliens Act and considered other forms of crime important, in addition to human trafficking and identity fraud: drug crime, money laundering, and possession of weapons were often mentioned. Some of these respondents felt supported in this view by the name change of the MSM. Despite the fact that this change was not accompanied by actual changes in the aim of the MSM or the tasks of the RNM officers, some of the respondents nevertheless felt that it was more than just a semantic change.

> "Within that 20 km zone you are no longer specifically concerned with foreigners, you are also concerned with safety. There is a different name to that (...) You also have things like money laundering you pay attention to."

Respondents indicated that they saw an important role for themselves in protecting the Dutch state against all kinds of danger. For example, one of the RNM officers stated that they attempted not to select too many drug runners, but that was sometimes difficult because all RNM officers had "blue blood" in them. In addition, it was regularly articulated at the start of a shift that today they would try to "catch criminals" again. In that sense, there seems to be little difference between RNM officers and regular police officers, who consider "catching criminals" as their most important task (Kleijer-kool & Landman, 2016; Landman, 2015). A logical consequence of positioning oneself so explicitly as a crime-fighter was that the tasks were interpreted broadly. As one of the RNM officers indicated during a focus group discussion:

> "The police are meant for the security on the street and the RNM for the security of the state. This also includes catching people who have been reported as being armed and dangerous, flight hazards or connected with drug crimes."

This broader interpretation of the aim of the MSM seemed to stem partly from the idea that if one only focused on the offences prescribed by law, this would result in an unnecessary restriction on the presence of the RNM officers in the border areas. Many RNM officers opined that it would be a waste of capacity to use the MSM only for the control of migrants.

> "We are general investigating officials and we are stationed there anyway [in the border areas, JB]. We are there and I think, let's get the most out of the six hours that we are allowed to stand there instead of shutting our eyes."

In accordance with the expectations based on the theoretical literature, there were substantial differences between the RNM officers in the way they saw precise scope of the MSM's aim and the way in which they interpreted their task. Similar to the different police styles that have been identified with regular police (Terpstra & Schaap, 2011), a distinction was sometimes made in this context between 'immigration officers' and 'police officers'. This refers to the fact that some RNM officers were mainly focused on cases related to immigration law, while others were more interested in fighting crime. Simultaneously, there were also many RNM officers who made little distinction and indicated that they saw both as an important part of their task. As a result, criminals and foreigners were sometimes mentioned in one breath and a clear distinction was not always made.

> "You have people, I am one of them myself, I grab everything that comes to my attention. I don't care if it's a foreigner, or Article 8 [Road Traffic Act, JB] or a weapon, or an uninsured car, I don't care. Look, I just want to catch a crook and whether that is a foreigner or something else, I don't care."

The younger RNM officers in particular seemed to find 'catching criminals' more exciting than checking out potentially unauthorised migrants. It was regularly indicated that the highest satisfaction was achieved by encountering criminal cases. After one of the RNM officers had checked a car thinking the occupants were Albanians, he said he believed that Albanians are often involved in crime and that he would rather deal with such types than an "illegal African". The fact that many RNM officers were particularly keen to go for the criminal cases was repeatedly demonstrated during the observed controls. It often happened that a vehicle was selected that, according to the RNM officers, was not particularly interesting in terms of aliens law, but whose passengers might still have outstanding fines or simply had "the face of a crook". For many RNM officers, catching a criminal was the part that made the work worthwhile and stories about an arrested criminal were told frequently. This is in line with the findings of research into regular police officers, which shows that catching 'crooks' is a crucial factor in their job satisfaction (Kleijer-kool & Landman, 2016). In addition, the RNM officers were often visibly enthusiastic if a car was checked whose occupants had criminal antecedents or were signalled for crimes.

A specific case can illustrate this. During one of the checks, a taxi was checked with two young boys of about twelve years old sitting on the back seat. They had no identity documents with them, but said they were German and Croatian. They claimed to be on their way to their grandmother to pay a hospital bill and that they received money for it from their mother. The RNM officers present indicated that they had little faith in the story and decided to search the trunk. When a transparent bag of golden jewellery was found in a large loaf, there clearly was a slight euphoria among the RNM officers about this, which expressed itself through mutual congratulations and 'fist bumps'. In the weeks that followed, the matter was regularly brought up again at this brigade.

3.6 DECISION-MAKING IN AN AMBIGUOUS CONTEXT

As stopped a vehicle within the MSM framework, unlike in the case of domestic immigration control, is not required to be based on a reasonable suspicion of illegal stay, individual RNM officers have substantial freedom to decide who they will select for a check. During the fieldwork it became clear that RNM officers not only have a great deal of discretion in their decisions to stop vehicles, but also to decide whether a stopped vehicle or person will be further investigated. If someone does not have the correct papers, it must be decided whether or not to investigate this person and whether or not the car will be searched. Sometimes this decision is based on an estimate of the chance that someone will be staying in the country illegally. This was the case, for example, when two German boys with a North African appearance were checked and did not carry a passport. The supervising RNM officers decided fairly quickly to let them continue because they did not speak "immigrant German" and one of them did have the German passport of his brother. Often the decision was based on the possibility of finding any incriminating facts. When a car with four Eastern European young men was searched because one of them did not have a passport with him, one of the RNM officers present indicated that this would not happen if it concerned an older couple or a decent family, because in that case after all, the chance of finding something punishable would be considerably smaller. Another time, a vehicle with a Dutch license plate and three Dutch-speaking men was fully searched after the driver could only present a Dutch driver's licence (which is not a valid cross-border document), because the men lived in a nearby caravan camp and were known to the RNM officers for past criminal facts.

An important factor that influences the way in which RNM officers fill in their discretionary decision power is the way in which they see their own tasks. As explained above, despite the name change, the MSM is still essentially an instrument that is primarily aimed at immigration control, which is reflected in the competences of the RNM officers. According to Article 50 of the Aliens Act, they have no authority to search a vehicle if all passengers can present valid identity documents. This limitation with regard to searching a vehicle regularly caused frustration when RNM officers felt that something was wrong but according to their competences were not allowed to open the trunk for example.

> "That is the only disadvantage, that we are based on the Aliens Act. If we have the documents, our task is done and you should not look in the car anymore. Or he happens to be reported with regard to drugs or possession of weapons and then you can turn the whole car inside out, other than that you have no real reason to actually open the trunk."

Despite this kind of frustration, some RNM officers indicated that they had no choice but to simply accept this. However, this was viewed differently by respondents who felt they had a broader competence, or at least should have. RNM officers regularly indicated that they could not agree with the limitations of the aliens law, because the competences were inadequate to effectively monitor security.

> "I don't understand why they are so difficult about those trunks, why don't they just adjust it. Let us just have a look in it, because after all it's just about safety."

To overcome this limitation, several respondents indicated that they had to be 'creative' with their competences. It is crucial to mention that RNM officers expressed they did not necessarily violate the rules or abuse their powers; instead, they stated that they were merely making the best use of the possibilities offered by the various forms of legislation. This can be well illustrated with a specific case. Towards the end of a dynamic check, a station wagon was stopped in a residential area with a fairly young boy behind the wheel, without a clear specific cause (which was confirmed by the RNM officers at a later inquiry). During the check it appeared that he still had a number of outstanding fines and he was taken to the brigade for a further check. On the way, the boy asked one of the RNM officers why they had stopped him, to which he replied that he had been stopped because he had not turned on his traffic indicator. Later at the brigade, the RNM officer explained that he was always looking for a loophole, no matter how small, and that in this case they would base the check on traffic law.

The RNM is of course not unique in this creative use of competences and diverse legislation, as this also surfaces in research with the police (Halderen & Lasthuizen, 2013). Nevertheless, the combination of immigration law and criminal law competences offers the RNM officers extra possibilities. Frequently, the RNM officers explicitly referred to the possibility of using different forms of legislation.

> "Well, when I check a car I first have a look at the documents, but automatically you are also looking directly into the vehicle. If you smell something, you open that whole car in the context of drugs. When you look in the door frame, maybe you see a weapon and if they don't have any documents, then you turn the whole

car inside out. So you have to play a little bit with the legislation and that is how you also come across the fun parts."

As indicated in the theoretical part, more rules and laws can paradoxically lead to more discretion. Many RNM officers indeed appeared to see opportunities in combining the benefits of immigration control and criminal enforcement. The question of whether the legislation was always used in a just manner did not seem to be of central importance. In accordance with the concept of ad hoc instrumentalism, they made use of the legislation that was most effective in a given situation. However, enforcement through criminal law is covered with considerably more legal safeguards than enforcement through administrative law. The Aliens Act makes it possible to stop a vehicle within the framework of the MSM and to check all passengers without a reasonable doubt of illegal stay or a criminal offence. Then, based on either the lack of the correct documents or the suspicion of a criminal offence, it can be decided to investigate a person or vehicle in more detail. As one of the respondents explained:

> "We are civil servants in charge of border control and that is regulated in the administrative law and then we merely exercise oversight. The great thing about immigration law is of course that you can check everyone, because otherwise it is only the driver. (...) And if someone does not have papers with him, you can also search the vehicle as stipulated in article 50 [Aliens Act, JB] and then of course you will bump into something, for example marijuana, and then you put on your police cap. Continue applying your powers and then you suddenly change from being a supervisor to an investigating officer."

At the same time, there were clear differences in this area between brigades and even between individual RNM officers per brigade. These differences were sometimes prompted by a lack of clarity about the aim of the MSM and the extent of their own competences. During one of the observed services, for example, the team leader opened a trunk due to the presence of long rolling paper (a piece of paper with a sticky edge that is often used for joints) in the car. One of the RNM officers present then asked a more experienced colleague whether the presence of long rolling paper was indeed sufficient reason to search the trunk, on which he made clear that this was not the case. Especially if there was no weed smell or the driver had no red eyes, this was not sufficient, because long rolling paper itself is not prohibited. The younger RNM officer indicated that this was his opinion as well, but that he had his doubts after he saw the team leader do this.

3.7 Conclusion and discussion

In this contribution we looked at the way in which street-level RNM officers carrying out the MSM give substance to their discretionary decision power. These RNM officers have a lot of discretion to convert the official policy goals into action. At the same time, these policy goals are somewhat ambiguous: the MSM has a complex legal framework in which immigration control overlaps with criminal enforcement, which is reinforced by the name change from Mobile Aliens Monitor to Mobile Security Monitor. Within the context of the crimmigration process and ad hoc instrumentalism, this increases the discretionary decision power of the street-level RNM officers and allows their own professional views and beliefs to play a role in decisions.

The results show that in practice, RNM officers do indeed navigate between immigration control and criminal enforcement. They try to find their own way in this, with each having their own accents. As with regular police officers, there are therefore different styles among the RNM officers who carry out the MSM: some mainly focuses on immigration control, while others seem more focused on combatting crime and are strongly driven by the desire to increase the security of the Dutch state. RNM officers in the latter group find 'catching criminals' more exciting and get more satisfaction from it than from monitoring potential unauthorised migrants, which seems to fit the concept of striving for justice.

One's own professional opinion has specific consequences for the way in which the discretionary decision power and the corresponding competences are handled. As explained in the theoretical part, more rules and laws can lead to more discretion, considering street-level officials simply have more options to choose from. In the context of the MSM, even the *assumption* of more rules, combined with an ambiguous objective, already resulted in more discretionary space. Since the MSM is still primarily an instrument for immigration control, the RNM officers identified as 'police officers' in particular opined that the existing competences sometimes offer insufficient possibilities. To nonetheless achieve these goals, they regularly made creative use of their powers, 'playing' with the various areas of the law.[9] This fits with the ideas of crimmigration and ad hoc instrumentalism: both unwanted migrants and criminals are tackled by the most effective means available, regardless of the legal area.

9 On November 1, 2016, the Supreme Court ruled on the creative handling of competences by the National Police. In the context of dynamic traffic controls, there was no misuse of powers – a malicious creative use of powers – according to the Supreme Court, since it could not be established that the supervisory powers were used solely for investigation purposes (Supreme Court 1 November 2016, ECLI:NL:HR:2016:2454). This ruling by the Supreme Court requires nuance about the – legal – objectionability with regard to the perceived creative use of powers by the Royal Netherlands Marechaussee in the context of the MSM.

Thus, the actions of the RNM officers contribute to the further fading of the boundaries between immigration control and criminal enforcement.

Both the emphasis on 'catching criminals' and the creative use of competences are also apparent from research that took place at the police (Halderen & Lasthuizen, 2013; Kleijer-kool & Landman, 2016). What distinguishes the RNM officers from the regular police, however, is the combination of immigration control and criminal enforcement within the context of the MSM. As a result of the intertwining of immigration control and criminal enforcement, they have a more extensive toolbox with various instruments which can be used during a check, with competences arising from both administrative law and criminal law. RNM officers thus have a multitude of tools for stopping and searching a vehicle. In line with Sklansky's (2012) ad hoc instrumentalism and the claims of Maynard-Moody and Musheno (2000), they can first form an opinion about a vehicle or person and then use one of the options in the extensive toolbox they have at their disposal to justify their decisions. This means that it is not always transparent on which grounds a certain decision is made, especially for the persons being checked. Moreover, enforcement through criminal law is covered with considerably more procedural safeguards than supervision on the basis of administrative law.

Although the present article was mainly aimed at an empirical study of implementation decisions, the normative question arises as to whether this combination of different competences – so typical of the crimmigration process – is desirable in view of equal treatment of the persons checked and the protection of legal certainty and if so, to what extent sufficient safeguards have been built in. Where discretionary decision power may be required for street-level actors to translate abstract rules into specific situations, such fundamental considerations should not be left to the level of implementation.

4 (Cr)immigrant framing in border areas
Decision-making processes of Dutch border police officers[1]

4.1 Introduction

In recent years a growing body of scholarly literature has documented how crime control and migration control have become increasingly intertwined, creating an ever expanding group of out- siders (Stumpf 2006). This process of 'crimmigration' has been visible on the discursive, legislative and enforcement level (Brouwer et al. 2017, Van der Woude et al. 2014). On the enforcement level an important role is played by street-level bureaucrats (Lipsky 1980) with often high levels of discretion. Motomura (2011), for example, argues that immigration officers' ability to stop and arrest persons is a major driver behind the crimmigration process, as it enables ethno-racial profiling and can mark the entry point for immigrants into the criminal justice system. In this context particular attention has been drawn to the border as a site where 'bona fide global citizens' need to be distinguished from 'crimmigrant others' (Aas 2011), with various authors arguing that high levels of discretion for border policing officers result in processes of what Lyon (2007) calls social sorting (Fan 2013, Pickett 2016).

Despite the fact that immigration officers in border areas seem to play a crucial role in deciding who belongs, there have been very few empirical examinations of the decision-making processes of border policing officers (see for notable exceptions: Gilboy 1991, Pratt and Thompson 2008, Weber 2011, Pickering and Ham 2013, Casella Colombeau 2017). Meanwhile a wealth of studies has addressed decision-making processes of regular police officers, and the issue of ethno-racial profiling in stop-and-search contexts in particular (Holmberg 2000, Waddington et al. 2004, Wilson et al. 2004, Alpert et al. 2005, Dunham 2005, Schafer et al. 2006, Stroshine et al. 2008, Parmar 2011, Quinton 2011, Fallik and Novak 2012, Tillyer 2012, Mutsaers 2014). Whereas this body of research has provided valuable insights in the way regular police officers exercise their discretion in crime control, border policing officers have a fundamentally different task – as their main focus is migration control – and they are often equipped with powers in both crime control and migration control (Sklansky 2012). This raises questions about what kind of people and

1 An earlier version of this chapter was published as: Brouwer, J., Van der Woude, M.A.H., & Van der Leun, J.P. (2018). (Cr)immigrant framing in border areas: decision making processes of Dutch border police officers. *Policing and Society, 28*(4), 448-463.

situations arouse their suspicion and how they employ their discretion. Various authors have therefore recently stressed the need for empirical studies of street-level bureaucrats involved in border policing (Cote-Boucher et al. 2014; Loftus 2015).

In this article we examine the decision-making processes of border policing officers in internal border areas of the Netherlands. Europe's internal borders are no longer supposed to be enforced after the implementation of the Schengen agreement in the 1990s, meaning that EU Member States have experienced a loss of sovereignty and their ability to monitor who enters their country through the internal borders. Since the summer of 2015 the arrival of large numbers of primarily Syrian and African refugees has made states wanting to take more firmly control of their national borders again, a process further accelerated by the terrorist attacks in Belgium and France and the discursive and political connection between these two crises. Whereas some states have temporarily reinstalled permanent internal border checks, others have increased immigration and security checks in their border areas (Van der Woude and Van Berlo 2015). Such checks are allowed under article 23 of the Schengen Border Code (SBC), as long as these do not have an effect equivalent to border control. In the Netherlands – and a few other European countries – these security checks already came in place soon after the implementation of the Schengen agreement, due to concerns about an influx of irregular migrants and an increase in cross-border crime (Groenendijk 2003, Atget 2008, Casella Colombeau 2010, Schwell 2010). The Dutch interpretation of article 23 SBC resulted in the instalment of the Mobile Security Monitor (MSM), a form of border policing[2] in the country's border areas with Belgium and Germany with the aim to combat illegal entry and stay, identity fraud and human smuggling. These controls are carried out by the Royal Netherlands Marechaussee (RNM), a military police force that performs both civic and military duties. RNM officers have a high level of discretion in their selection of vehicles and persons, as a reasonable suspicion of any criminal activity or illegal entry or stay is not required. This raises the question how these officers decide whom to stop.

Drawing on extensive observational study and focus group interviews with street-level officers, this article aims to provide insight into the reasoning behind, and outcomes of, discretionary decisions of officers carrying out the MSM. We focus specifically on the question how ethnic, racial and nationality categories shape the decision whom to stop and the underlying ideas that seem to drive these decisions, while also placing these individual decisions within

2 Although there is officially no longer a border, we nonetheless employ the term border policing to refer to these controls. This is done because the term border control would imply that there is still a visible border that is permanently enforced, while the term migration policing encompasses a wide range of immigration enforcement activities that go beyond these controls (Weber and Bowling 2004).

the wider organisational and political context. After discussing relevant literature on discretion and street-level decision- making processes, we show how officers' individual street-level decisions are fundamentally shaped by a combination of legal and organisational ambiguities regarding the official aim of the MSM, combined with the emergence of a political and public discourse in which certain ethnic and immigrant groups are increasingly framed as 'dangerous others'. Our analysis offers insights into selection decisions that go beyond the more common discrimination-oriented analyses. In the final section of this paper we look at the way in which such perceptions are formed and transmitted among officers, before concluding with a discussion of our results in light of on-going societal and academic debates about selectivity more in general.

4.2 Decision-making processes in context

One of the defining features of street-level bureaucrats is that they need to translate often vague or conflicting laws and policy goals into concrete action. To that end they enjoy considerable discretionary freedom, which led Lipsky (1980) to argue that street-level bureaucrats should in fact be seen as the real policy makers. According to Hawkins (2014, p. 187), criminal justice decision-making involves 'interpretative and classificatory processes from individual decision-makers'. Especially during proactive controls that do not require a reasonable suspicion or concrete evidence of any criminal behaviour, officers have little choice but to rely upon categorisations and typologies (Holmberg 2000, Wilson et al. 2004, Bowling and Phillips 2007). Faced with limited time and information, street- level decision makers may then highlight certain features while ignoring others, thus developing a 'perceptual shorthand to identify certain kinds of people as symbolic assailants' (Skolnick 1966, p. 45; See also Tillyer and Hartley 2010). When this shorthand is influenced by stereotypes there is the possibility that extra-legal factors such as age, ethnicity, gender, race and social class come to inform the decisions, potentially resulting in over-policing of specific groups.

Despite this focus on the individual decision-maker, Hawkins (2014) emphasises that discretion is critically shaped by both the wider 'social surround'- the broader societal setting that is shaped by economic and political forces – and a 'decision field' of organisational rules and objectives. Literature on the discretion of regular police officers established early on that collective occupational norms, as well as law and formal policy, shape the way in which individual officers use their discretion (Skolnick 1966). In more recent years a wealth of research has demonstrated how police decisions are complex processes involving a host of factors (Johnson and Morgan 2013). These includes organisational and legal rules (Engel and Johnson 2006, Miller 2009) but also internal norms and values, including both conscious and unconscious stereotypes (Graham and Lowery 2004, Wilson et al. 2004). Police culture and occupational ideologies have been found to play an abiding role in informing officers how they do their work, both through formal training and informal socialisation processes (Loftus 2010). As to the latter, various scholars have pointed out the role of storytelling and the canteen culture, as playing an important role in making sense and giving meaning to events (Van Hulst 2013).

Loftus (2015, p. 188) has accordingly noted that in order to fully understand border policing it is crucial to pay attention to both 'the broader social, political and legal context' and 'the culture and practices of those involved in the daily upkeep of border priorities'. Before turning to the actual decision-making of officers carrying out the MSM, we therefore first outline the decision field and social surround in which these officers make their decisions.

4.3 Monitoring security in an expanding European Union

The MSM has since its instalment in 1994 developed from an instrument aimed at migration control to an instrument aimed at both migration control and crime control (Dekkers et al. 2016, Groenendijk 2003). The original aim of the MSM was to combat and prevent illegal stay, as was reflected by the name Mobile Aliens Monitor. In 2006 the aim was formally expanded to also include the migration- related crime forms of human smuggling and identity fraud. Although still primarily a form of migration control, starting in 2010 official policy documents began to refer to the MSM as Mobile Security Monitor – the abbreviation remaining the same as the Dutch words for alien and security have the same first letter (Dekkers et al. 2016). This name change was purely cosmetic, as no extra investigative legal powers were given to officers in the field. It nonetheless signals a broader understanding of the aim of the MSM and, consequently, the reasons officers might base their selection decisions on. RNM officers furthermore hold regular police powers and therefore can shift towards criminal law-based powers when suspicion of a criminal fact arises during a control, while there is no accountability mechanism in place to ensure that officers base their stops on immigration-related rationales only (Van der Woude and Van der Leun 2017, Van der Woude and Brouwer 2017).

Tillyer and Hartley (2010) claim that general negative sentiments in society towards migrant groups can affect the views held by street-level bureaucrats and therefore lead to prejudices informing the decisions they make. In the Netherlands a discourse has developed in which various ethnic minority groups are linked to crime and other social issues (Eijkman 2010, Svensson and Saharso 2014). Especially youngsters with a Moroccan background are seen as disproportionally involved in various forms of street crime and often negatively portrayed in the media (Boomgaarden and Vliegenthart 2007). Both Svensson and Saharso (2014) and (Van der Leun and Van der Woude 2011) argue that this discourse, combined with the emergence of a Dutch version of the culture of control (Garland 2001, van Swaaningen 2005, Pakes 2006), has increased the risk of ethno- racial profiling by the police and other controlling organisations. Recent debates around ethno- racial profiling by the police are also to a large extent centred around the question whether young men with a Moroccan background are disproportionally targeted (Amnesty International 2013). At the same time, the expansion of the European Union has in recent years led to concerns about mass immigration from Central and Eastern European countries (CEE countries) and heavy media attention for crimes by Eastern Europeans in the Netherlands (Pijpers 2006, Rosmalen and van Es 2014). This has led some to argue that the traditional hype about problematic Moroccans has been supplemented with a moral panic regarding CEE migrants (Pijpers 2006, Rosmalen and Van Es 2014). A recent study found that although Dutch police officers do stereotype Polish persons, they are still heavily concerned with youngsters with a Moroccan background (Bonnet and Caillault 2014).

4.4 Methodology

This paper draws on qualitative data collected in the context of a larger research project on discretionary decision-making in border contexts (Van der Woude et al. 2016). Data for this project consist of observational data, transcripts of focus group interviews with officers and in-depth interviews with senior policy officials. For this paper we used the observational and focus group data, collected between November 2013 and March 2015, before the Syrian refugee crisis really started to dominate newspaper headlines. Researchers – always in duos – joined a total of 57 MSM shifts, leading to over 800 man hours of structured observation. Observations were combined with brief conversations and on-site informal 'interviews' and discussions with officers: non-structured talks that naturally occurred during observations. Such participant observation in a 'natural' setting combined with interviews and discussions has proven to be a valuable research method to capture both the actions of people and the underlying reasons for the decisions that are made (Quinton 2011, Loftus 2015, De Maillard et al. 2016, Buvik 2016).

In order to build up trust and acceptance and get a comprehensive understanding, all six brigades that carry out the MSM were visited at least six times. A regular shift lasted around eight hours, started with a briefing and included plenty of time drinking coffee in the canteen; both function as important sites for storytelling, briefings in a more factual manner and the canteen as a place of informal conversation (Van Hulst 2013). Researchers usually spent most of the day on the control location, where they could observe the selected vehicles and the actual control, ask about the reasons behind a specific stop and chat with officers during the sometimes long periods waiting for a new vehicle. Individual field notes were drawn up at the end of each shift by both researchers, thus giving the opportunity to cross-check certain observations.

Besides participant observation, thirteen focus group discussions were organised with street-level officers to cross-check findings from the observations and further discuss a number of issues. Questions were structured around several topics that had either been part of the research from the start or had emerged as particularly interesting during the observations. Two sessions were organised at each brigade, except for one larger brigade where we held four sessions, and one smaller brigade where we only had one session. Each focus group was conducted by three researchers, with one taking the lead in asking the questions. The number of respondents varied between eight and ten, with differences in experience, rank and age. Participants were encouraged to react and disagree with each other, in order to create dynamic discussions and obtain rich data. The discussions lasted any- where between 1,5 and 3,5 hours and were recorded and subsequently transcribed. Both field notes and transcripts were afterwards systematically analysed with AtlasTi, a software package for qualitative data analysis, coding them according to the various themes associated with the sub-questions of the larger research project.

Our data consists of what van Maanen (1979) calls 'operational data' and 'presentational data'. Whereas operational data refers to observed activities and spontaneous conversations, presentational data consists of appearances as put forth by the research participants. Presentational data is often ideological, normative or abstract. Rather than the actual actions of participants, presentational data is often an idealised view constructed by the people that are studied. Below we will draw on both forms of data: we use operational data to draw up observed activities and decisions, but as we are primarily interested in the rationales and ideas that lie behind such decisions, we strongly rely on presentational data. All quotes below have been necessarily translated into English by the authors.

4.5 Targeting immigration

The decision to select persons and vehicles for a check was usually made by a motor driver who selected 'interesting' vehicles just after the border. He or she then directed the vehicle to a control location further inland, where other officers carried out the actual control by checking the identity papers of the persons stopped. Other times officers would drive around in vehicles and carry out both the stop and the control themselves. Because traffic normally passed at high speed, officers frequently indicated there was very little opportunity for a thorough examination of the passing vehicles and its passengers. They had to decide within a split second whether to select a vehicle or not, sometimes without clear view of the passengers due to darkness or bad weather. Officers were therefore usually only able to see very basic features of the passengers, such as a beard, skin colour or certain clothing. They furthermore had little to no prior information on the vehicles that were passing. Although most shifts started with a briefing in which attention was paid to wanted persons, this information was often provided by the police and usually not so much related to illegal migration or migration-related offences.

As the MSM is first and foremost a form of migration control, officers regularly indicated that the primary aim of the instrument was to prevent illegal entry and stay. However, they received very little information on how to recognise unauthorised immigrants. For example, neither the general education all RNM officers receive nor the specific training to become a motor driver contains elements on the selection of vehicles or persons. Officers repeatedly stated that they believed this would not be very useful anyway, as the realities on the street cannot be captured in formal training or written instructions. As one officer said, 'you really only learn it when you are at the workplace'. In general, officers relied on their own judgements about how to filter out potential unauthorised immigrants. Besides the nationality of the license plate, the number of passengers and the state of the vehicle, they strongly relied on skin colour as a visible marker of 'foreignness' to detect potential unauthorised immigrants. Almost all RNM officers we met were white males and perceived non- whiteness as an important indicator of foreignness. In practice this meant that during our observations primarily black or Arab-looking people were stopped. This became particularly apparent during one of the controls that took place partly in daylight and partly after dark. During the day we observed mainly black and Arabic-looking persons being stopped. However, this became increasingly varied after dark as it was much harder to see the persons inside a vehicle. Officers indicated several times that a vehicle with only white passengers would not have been stopped during daylight.

Over the course of our fieldwork numerous stops were justified by officers on the basis that the vehicle looked rather old, was a particular type or had a foreign license plate, in combination with the 'foreign appearance' of the driver and passengers. An interaction between one of the researchers and an officer that occurred during the observations can illustrate this. When the researcher asked the motor driver why he had selected a particular vehicle, he responded by asking whether the researcher had seen the license plate. After the researcher saw that it was a Belgian license plate, the officer asked him in a rhetoric tone whether he thought the two passengers – who had Arabic features – looked Belgian to him. The officer then continued by saying that of course it was possible they were, but that he was nonetheless curious to check, also because they came into the Nether- lands from Germany in a vehicle with a Belgium license plate.

At the same time, this focus on 'non-Western looking' persons did not result in many stops of people with an Asian appearance. One officer told us that Chinese persons were not often stopped during these controls because, unlike African and Middle Eastern people, they tend to stay in one place and not drive around so much. Yet when a vehicle with one Asian man and two Asian women was stopped during one of the controls we observed, an officer stated this was not very interesting and they were not their core targets. Whereas black or Arabic persons were frequently referred to as the main target of stops – something that translated into actual targeting practices – there was much less reference to Asians.

Whereas skin colour was thus an important factor behind immigration-related stops, sometimes other factors were employed to infer 'foreignness'. During one control, researchers were in a car with two officers after dark, when the officers decided to follow a vehicle with Dutch license plates. As they had not been able to see inside the vehicle they checked the license plate in the systems. When they heard that the vehicle was registered by someone with an African sounding name, the driver said 'that is a name we can work with' and decided to stop the vehicle for a check.

4.6 Border policing and ethnic profiling

Although most RNM officers were aware of the sensitivity of using racial or ethnic categories as a factor in their decisions and societal concerns about discrimination, they nonetheless often freely admitted that these categorisations played a role in their selection. As one of them said:

> "When people ask if we select on the basis of skin colour, then we have to readily admit that. Somebody's skin colour is for us the first sign of possible illegality. But, because we select on the basis of skin colour does not automatically mean that we discriminate."

Such openness was always coupled with a resolute denial that this selection criterion was driven by any racist intentions or motives. Instead, officers argued that their specific task of preventing illegal immigration leaves them little choice but to base their stops at least partially on skin colour as proxy of being a migrant. Indeed, they saw it as inherent to their work in the context of immigration law. Respondents emphasised their intentions rather than the outcomes. And as one officer explained:

> "It is also the fact that many of those countries have a visa requirement. Look, we did not invent the visa requirement for Africa. That by chance it is black people that come from there is not our fault, that is what we have to control, if there had been living only white people that had visa requirements we would have been checking white people."

Such statements are in line with Satzewich and Shaffir's (2009, p. 231) argument that 'the occupational culture enables the police to draw upon a vocabulary of explanations [that] permits them to deny responsibility when faced with the allegations that their profiling is racially motivated'. According to them these kind of rationalisations help officers deal with possible feelings of guilt or shame, and generally offer a better explanation for police behaviour than intentional racism.

At the political level, concerns with respect to potential discrimination during the MSM have continuously been countered with reference to professionalism. Officers are supposed to act on the basis of more objective criteria rather than solely rely on appearance (Dekkers et al. 2016). RNM officers indeed regularly pointed out that stops were based on a combination of factors and not appearance alone. The origin of the license plate, the number of passengers, their clothing, other appearance- related factors and sometimes their behaviour were all factors that could play a role in the decision to stop a vehicle. In the debate on ethno-racial profiling there is disagreement about whether markers for ethnic categories are never allowed to play a role in decisions to stop, or whether it is acceptable when these markers are combined with other factors informing a decision (Smith 2004). Such considerations were also found among RNM officers:

> "Naturally we are here to find illegal immigrants, so somebody's appearance and skin colour are important factors. Of course these are not allowed to be the only factors, I also know that and I agree with that."

More elaborate combinations of factors were also presented. For example, one officer gave a more detailed description of how a combination of factors could be invoked to stop a vehicle with North-African looking persons, drawing on knowledge and ideas about illegal immigration patterns.

> "You notice that we get a lot of cars from France, Spain, Italy, those are interesting for us. There are of course a lot of people from North-Africa, Algerians and Moroccans who don't have their documents straight. It is simply known that they often come here with family members illegally so if you see something like that coming it is just interesting. When it is somebody driving alone it is less interesting, but if it is several people with North-African appearance you make sure to stop it."

At the same time, it was somewhat contradictory that although license plates were the main other indicator of 'foreignness', a relatively large number of vehicles that we observed being stopped had Dutch license plates. During our observations it regularly seemed that a 'foreign appearance' was the primary or only reason for a stop, especially when vehicles had a Dutch license plate. For example, one time an officer indicated he had stopped a vehicle because he had the feeling 'it was not right'. When asked if he could explain that feeling, he responded that 'those three guys [the passengers, JB]' had aroused his interest. After talking a bit more, it became clear that he found it striking that three men with, according to the officer, 'clearly non-Dutch facial features' were driving a vehicle with a Dutch license plate.

This touches upon a complicated discussion about whether ethno-racial profiling is about intentions or outcomes. Obviously these practices result in ethnic disparities among those who are stopped during the MSM and may send a message of non-belonging to the relatively large number of legal residents or citizens that are stopped on account of their 'foreign appearance'. At the same time this does not directly mean that RNM officers are driven by beliefs about the inferiority of certain groups of people. Alpert et al. (2005, p. 410) note that certain organisational or legal factors 'can lead to discriminatory policing without individual-level discrimination'. This seems particularly true for proactive forms of border policing aimed at preventing illegal immigration; it is the instrument that leaves individual officers little choice but to use their powers in a discriminatory way, with skin colour playing an important role.

4.7 Targeting crime

Although the MSM is primarily aimed at preventing illegal entry and stay, there is a lack of clarity about what exactly falls within the official aims. This ambiguity was rarely considered an issue by officers, who generally seemed more interested in fighting crime than controlling illegal immigration. However, it had a large impact on the factors influencing officers' decisions. The controls under study are carried out by a military police organisation and officers often talked about 'catching bad guys'. They frequently invoked crime-related justifications for a stop that were derived from perceptions about certain groups or nationalities being disproportionally involved in specific types of crime.

> "I also just think that there is evidence and there are facts that certain target groups or nationalities all have their own business [meaning specific crimes, JB]."

> "Yes, yes, it is just from experience. I mean we take, get certain groups that just indeed have a certain business they are in. We see that every time again."

The focus on crime resulted in different groups being targeted. Various RNM officers expressed the idea that 'Moroccan', or more generally 'North-African', young men were disproportionally involved in – especially drugs-related – crime. This resonates with the study of Bonnet and Caillault (2014), who found that Dutch regular police officers were heavily concerned with 'Moroccans' being involved in criminal behaviour. RNM officers pointed to arrest and prison statistics as concrete evidence of this overrepresentation. Thus while North-African looking people were regularly stopped because of potential illegal entry or stay, especially when their car had a foreign license plate, officers also indicated a few times that a stop involving young Moroccan-looking men was primarily based on crime- related reasons. A North-African background could thus be a factor in stops both related to migration control and crime control. However, in the Netherlands there is a large population with a Moroccan background that can no longer be seen as foreigners or immigrants. Instead, they are typically born in the country and hold Dutch citizenship; Moroccan is usually seen as an ethnic, rather than national, category. As such, the ambiguity about the exact aim of the MSM on a political and policy level translates into the targeting of groups that are not necessarily interesting in the context of what is sup- posed to be primarily an instrument of migration control.

Although North-African young men were regularly linked to various forms of crime, most commonly and openly associated with criminal behaviour were people from CEE countries – primarily Bulgarians and Romanians, to a lesser extent also Hungarians and Polish. Such perceptions were usually said to constitute 'known facts' and being based on 'evidence'.

> "I think that there is just evidence that if you say "human trafficking", those are Bulgarians, it is just like that."

> "No but if a Romanian is driving a vehicle with an Italian license plate then you already know something is not alright. They drive through all of Europe to commit criminal offenses and that is also proven."

During our observations, a relatively large number of vehicles with Eastern European license plates were stopped, and officers regularly indicated that a Bulgarian or Romanian license plate was already sufficient reason for them to make a check. Although other Eastern European countries were sometimes also mentioned – in particular Albania – the relatively high number of vehicles from Poland, Bulgaria and Romania that drive to the Netherlands meant that they were most often stopped.

The targeting of these groups was primarily based on the origin of the license plate, as this was an easy visible marker and the nationality of individuals form Eastern European member states are generally harder to recognise on the basis of physical characteristics. Nonetheless, officers said it was a particular challenge to also be able to select Eastern European people when they were driving a vehicle with another license plate, something that regularly happened. For example, during one of the controls researchers were sitting in the back of the vehicle when a car with a German license plate was stopped. According to the officer he had stopped the car because he believed the driver and passengers to be Albanian, and Albanians were often involved in crime in the Netherlands. Justifications for such stops were based on the merging of a variety of crime risks that range from mobility-related offences such as human trafficking and false identification papers to more mundane crimes as pickpocketing and theft.

> "That has to do with crime there. We have come across a lot of false documents from Romanians and Bulgarians, many false ID-cards and that is one of our priorities."

> "And the Bulgarians and the Romanians and especially the Bulgarians are known for false papers and Romanians too, but Romanians are also well known for pickpocketing etcetera, human trafficking."

Overall, there was a common understanding among RNM officers that 'there is almost always some- thing wrong' with members of these groups in the border areas concerned. This led to extreme statements proclaiming that nine out of ten times Eastern European drivers have burglary tools in their trunk, or that Romanian looking people in a vehicle with a British or Spanish license plate were nine out of ten times thieves.

These 'profiles' were based on shared ideas rather than on information provided by the organisation. At the same time, it was interesting to note that such common-sense profiles were far from static. Nationalities that used to be targeted quite frequently could become less interesting over time, as during our research was the case with people from Poland. While Polish vehicles were considered interesting for various crime-related reasons in earlier years, respondents regularly stated that this was now much less the case. Although they were sometimes mentioned in the same breath with Bulgarians and Romanians, other times clear distinctions were made and it was argued that Polish people nowadays mostly came here to work and had their papers in order. As one officer noted:

> "In the beginning we checked them quite a lot. Those vans and stuff. But it turns out that most of it is work-related."

That did not necessarily translate into practice though, as we still quite regularly observed Polish vehicles being checked during the controls. However, officers were now much less positive about the likelihood of actually encountering something wrong than they were in the past.

This normalcy of nationality as a proxy for a high risk background reflects the findings of Pratt and Thompson (2008, p. 682), who argued in their study on Canadian border officials that 'while race is an unacceptable basis of discretionary risk assessment at the border, nationality is continually reproduced as a legitimate consideration'. Dutch border police officers equally seemed to find that assumed nationality (often based on license plates) was far less controversial as a (partial) selection criteria than ethnic or racial features, especially for crime-related stops. One officer even saw it as a clear advantage that they stopped a lot of Bulgarians and Romanians, because this meant there was less opportunity for complaints about racism than when they primarily would stop black or Arabic- looking persons. Only once an officer raised questions after he said that Romanian license plates were almost automatically stopped:

> "I am actually not allowed to say that, am I? That Romanians are always stopped? Is that discrimination?"

This heavy reliance on nationality as a risk category is not without problems in light of the envisaged ideals of a 'cosmopolitan European Union of transnational citizens' (Van der Woude and Van Berlo 2015). The abolition of internal border controls in the Schengen area and the subsequent freedom of movement is one of the core components of the European Union as an area of freedom, security and justice (Carrera 2005). As Maas (2014, p. 802) has rightfully argued, 'free movement is arguably the foundation for all further European rights', and for a large number of Europeans it is the very essence of what the EU means (Gehring 2013, Parker and Catalan 2014). The introduction of European Union citizenship furthermore means that all citizens of EU Member States have the right to move and reside freely within the EU and that discrimination by Member States on the basis of nationality is prohibited – all EU citizens must be treated equally (Carrera 2005, Nanz 2009). Whereas Bulgaria and Romania are not yet part of the Schengen area, these countries are part of the European Union and their citizens therefore should enjoy the fundamental right to freedom of movement without being subjected to discrimination (Jorgensen and Sorensen 2012). Although it has previously been noted that the freedom of movement rights do not equally apply to third-country nationals that have legally entered the Schengen area (Atget 2008, Loftus 2015), realities on the ground demonstrate that citizens of some EU Member States face restrictions on their mobility as well – most notably the Eastern European countries that recently joined. Based on their alleged involvement in various forms of (cross-border) crime, these citizens are one of the primary targets of the MSM, which as such functions as a form of selective border control for those EU citizens that are deemed less worthy of free travel, and to a certain extent creates a hierarchy within EU citizenship (see Gehring (2013) and Parker and Catalan (2014) for a similar account with regard to Roma EU citizens). Being designated bona fide travellers by the European Union but identified as dangerous others by border policing officers, these people therefore do not profit to the fullest from the purported area of justice, freedom and security. As we will elaborate on below, this also seems to be related to considerations of class.

4.8 EU EXPANSION AND THE ROLE OF CLASS

The MSM is a direct result of the lifting of borders following the implementation of the Schengen agreement, and policies at the European level – combined with ideas about high levels of crime among Eastern European immigrants – shaped the decisions made at the border. Officers would regularly draw upon such policy developments as one of the main reasons they now 'had so much to do with Eastern Europeans'. They expressed frustration about the fact that citizens of these new EU Member States now had free access and similar rights as other EU-citizens, as this limited the possibility to tackle various issues.

> "You do see a trend now that you see a lot of organised crime, especially groups, often Eastern European groups that now cause a burglary wave. Pickpockets that cause trouble in Amsterdam, are often Romanians, Bulgarians. They cross the border somewhere and it is not the external border. Of course we see the urgency, but your hands are tied to European policy."

Here, mobility sits at the core of the perceived problem. Where the easing of visa restrictions has rendered CEE nationals more mobile, RNM officers see this primarily as an increased risk of importing crime. Political concerns about a post-Schengen increase in cross-border crime that led to the instalment of the MSM are thus translated into the targeting of citizens of new EU Member States. This link between EU expansion and a subsequent perceived rise in crime numbers also became apparent through the following story one of the researchers overheard an officer telling a younger colleague who was new to the team.

> "Bulgarians often have something to do with human trafficking, while Romanians are very often involved in theft, robbery and scams. Now they are even talking about making Moldova visa-free. Somebody there earns an average of 2.500 euros per year, while in Bulgaria at least they still earn 11.000 per year. You can thus more or less guess what will happen."

Besides disseminating common-sense knowledge to a relatively new member of the team, this officer also immediately presents a cause for this 'fact', by pointing out the easing of visa requirements in combination with low average incomes in Eastern European countries. This was common among officers, who regularly cited the vast differences in average income between Eastern and Western European countries as an explanation for crime among CEE migrants.

> "You have to imagine, these people come from a part of Europe where the average income is quite low. Between 200 and 400 euros for a weekend in the Netherlands is for these people very expensive. Are they hiring a hotel room for the weekend, what are these people doing here? It's not bad, they can just go on holiday but of course that raises suspicion so you need to come up with a story."

One officer who linked Bulgarians and Hungarians to the theft of copper from the railroads noted that it involved not only lower educated people, but also people holding university degrees. They were unable to find jobs in their country and could earn up to 4.000 euros per month this way. Similarly, Eastern Europeans truck drivers were considered to form a higher risk for people smuggling, as their generally very low income means they are easily recruited for the smuggling of persons. In line with what Loftus (2007) observes, this seems to point to the important role of class in shaping categorisations and influencing practices. Yet whereas class issues were an important explanation for officers' perception that crime risk was high among Eastern Europeans, this was different for the specific sub- category of Roma (Gypsies). Various officers expressed the belief that crime was an integral part of their culture, thus reflecting a tradition of long-standing discrimination and stereotyping of Roma people throughout the European continent (Guild and Zwaan 2014).

Class-related factors were not only invoked to arouse suspicion, but could also indicate that some- body should not be stopped. A common example of the latter was the 'business man': described as somebody wearing a suit and driving an expensive car, officers indicated that this was not very interesting for them, no matter what the person further looked like. Our observations further seem to suggest that considerations of class also played a role after the selection of a vehicle. When a minivan with a Romanian license plate and six men inside was stopped, one officer immediately said that this would not be very interesting. He argued that these people looked too well-groomed and were very polite; therefore, he considered them to be part of the Romanian middle class. Their vehicle was also too clean, while the 'bad ones' usually look very sloppy and drive a smelly vehicle. Another time an officer deemed a stopped vehicle less interesting because it had new tires. According to him 'it might sound a bit silly, but worn-out tires say something about how you live your life'.

4.9 Generating and disseminating knowledge on whom to select

By presenting certain links between ethnicity or nationality and criminal behaviour as hard facts ('evidence', 'facts', 'it is just like that', 'that is shown'), and through their continuous repeating, officers created a common-sense knowledge about these perceptions. This common-sense knowledge about these associations was not only generated through officers' own (and their colleagues') experience, but also seen confirmed through external sources. For example, during one shift various officers discussed a 'documentary' they had seen about Bulgarians and Romanians who came to the Netherlands to receive various benefits only to go back home to live a luxurious life. Another officer said that one just needed to follow the media a bit to come to the same conclusion:

> "It is generally known, doesn't matter where you are from, if you follow the media a bit, that skimming is done by Romanians and that burglaries during the dark days are by Bulgarians, Romanians and Polish. That is just known."

At one brigade officers were particularly outraged by a newspaper item that claimed that the government had pressured a television show on criminal investigations to show less suspects with a Moroccan background and instead paint a more representative picture of society.[3] Officers stated that if this was the reality you should just show it, and you should not 'bury your head in the sand' for political reasons. It was telling that this news was brought up by different officers at one specific brigade, whereas at other brigades it was never mentioned. This suggests that officers share such information with each other and, accordingly, influence each other through their stories. It simultaneously shows that it is hard to speak of 'one' border police culture: every brigade seems to differ, also in its canteen culture.

The resulting targeting practices further reproduced and sustained such perceptions, because new officers learn profiling 'on the job' from more experienced colleagues (see also Pratt and Thompson (2008) with regard to Canadian border control officers). Dutch RNM officers generally indicated that the organisation provided very few instructions or information on whom to stop during the MSM, and profiling does not form part of the official training prior to becoming a border policing officer. Instead, new recruits were often coupled to a more experienced officer and learned about risk profiles from these more experienced colleagues and through their own experiences. In this way prevailing beliefs are transmitted to new officers and existing targeting practices are kept in place. As one officer explained:

> "You learn it automatically yes, you start working and see every time that motor drivers [who makes the selection, JB] bring in the same cars, then you think at some point, you get a bit of a feeling for it of course."

Most officers we spoke to agreed that experience is crucial for good profiling, because it involves combining so many factors. The main way to get such experiences is by simply practicing a lot and looking carefully at and learning from more experienced colleagues. As several officers explained, such experience was mainly the result of stops that led to an actual arrest.

> "I think that you just figure out for yourself where you find the most cases. If you very often find [false identity papers, JB] in an old vehicle with, for example, a Romanian license plate, then eventually that automatically becomes something of which you say like "hey, there I have the biggest chance of catching something".

---

3 A Dutch police officer in the study of Bonnet and Caillault (2014) mentioned the same television show as a source of evidence fort he criminal overrepresentation of persons with a Moroccan background.

For yourself, that is your experience and you will expand that more and more when you work here longer."

Such experience was not necessarily always based on actual outcomes of a stop though, as some- times even a mere gut feeling that something was wrong with a selected vehicle was seen as a reason to select similar types of vehicles or persons in the future. This also had to do with some officers' strong confidence in the accuracy of their own judgements, which left little room for alternative explanations that could help to make sense of a situation. For example, during one briefing officers were asked to pay attention to a vehicle that had been stopped the week before with a Romanian woman and several Albanian and Romanian men. The woman had said that she worked voluntarily as a prostitute, but officers had not trusted the situation and therefore made a note in the systems. The team leader later told the researchers that in one hundred percent of the cases where officers had the gut feeling that a woman was working involuntarily as a prostitute, they were right. In this way officers thus have their views confirmed without objective facts backing them up and without reflecting upon the potential side effects of these selection practices, leading to a vicious circle in which stereotypes can be reproduced time and again. More generally, there was regular talk about the high 'success rate' of especially more experienced officers. Whenever we observed a control with little concrete results, this led to visible frustration and disappointment among officers, who would offer various reasons – ranging from the date and time of the control to the lack of suit- able vehicles on the road – why this was the case.

Although some individual officers did reflect upon the inherent risk of developing generalisations about crime among certain categories of foreigners, they never referred to this type of reflection as being part of the training and professionalisation on the job. Moreover, a more objective attempt to measure the success of existing practice-based profiling strategies – for instance by every now and then making a comparison with the outcomes of a random sample – is lacking. This high trust in and dependency on experience and sharing of experiences carries a risk of institutionalised tunnel vision. The latter is not only a matter of potential discrimination; it may also lead to overlooking new developments.

4.10 Conclusion and discussion

In this paper we have explored how ethno-racial and national categories play a role in Dutch border policing officers' decisions whom to stop while policing the country's internal border areas. As the underlying research has shown, these decisions seem to be shaped by a lack of clarity about the exact aim and scope of the MSM, the emergence of a specific Dutch culture of control and policy developments at the European level. Such selection processes appeared to be largely based on informal and experience-based stories and officers' own experiences. Receiving very little concrete information on what to look for during a control, but often having to decide within a split second whether to stop a vehicle or not, officers use a combination of factors to select vehicles and persons that they think have the highest chance of resulting in the detection of something wrong. Ethnic, national and racial categories are important factors in these decisions to stop a vehicle. However, the role of these categories differs depending on whether someone is stopped for potential illegal stay or for possible criminal conduct. Our study indicates that 'foreign appearance' was used as a central indicator for the possibility of illegal entry or stay and skin colour was therefore an important factor in migration- related controls. The legal framework and official aim of the MSM played an important role here, as officers were very aware of possible accusations of racism and thus explicitly referred to their task of preventing illegal stay to justify their use of skin colour as a selection criterion.

However, the ambiguity regarding the exact aim of the instrument – in combination with high levels of discretion and officers' ambitions to fight crime – meant that people were frequently stopped for crime-related reasons as well. In such cases other factors played a role, including assumptions about the high criminal propensity of certain ethnic or national groups, in particular Northern African ethnic minorities and Eastern European nationals. Officers frequently expressed frustration about EU expansion and open border policies, as this meant that Eastern European immigrants increasingly came to the Netherlands.

A number of factors on various levels thus ultimately shaped officers' decisions to select a vehicle. On the organisational level, the dual aim of the MSM means that officers face limited restrictions on whether they decide to target illegal immigration or crime, and most officers seemed more interested in fighting crime. The personal factors that influenced the decision to stop someone – especially ethno-racial and national categories – were strongly connected to the aim of the stop. In particular, whereas skin colour was used as an acceptable factor in immigration-related stops, for stops based on crime control rationales officers usually invoked ethnic and national categories. These categories were based on ideas about the overrepresentation of certain groups in crime that strongly reflect the prevailing political and public discourse in the Netherlands. In practice, however, the dual powers of RNM officers render it often difficult to make a clear-cut distinction between these two aims.

Selection processes are inherent to the MSM and, in a broader sense, to proactive policing in general. Dutch border policing officers have little choice but to rely upon selection criteria, but the ambiguity about the exact aim and scope of the instrument means that migration-related factors freely interact with broader security considerations as rationales for stops. Moreover, there are no concrete organisational guidelines for officers which make clear how they should conduct immigration checks without taking into account that people 'look' like immigrants, among other reasons. As a result, ethnic, racial, and national categories intersect in various and shifting ways with age, class, gender and other factors to create a variety of risk profiles that sit at the juncture of crime, security, and migration.

Although Dutch RNM officers share many similarities with regular police officers, their specific task and powers mean there are important differences too. Our results demonstrate the need to move beyond individualised analyses of discretion and point to the importance of taking into account local and organisational contexts. Existing research on ethnic profiling has tended to focus on North America and the United Kingdom (Miller et al. 2008) and concentrated on the question whether black persons are disproportionally stopped during proactive police controls compared to white people. In the context of internal border policing in the Netherlands this is only one part of the story, and moreover a direct result of the specific task of the officers carrying this out. Other ethnic and national groups are also frequently stopped during the MSM for reasons that range from potential illegal entry and stay to the risk of theft, thus indicating the plurality of targeting practices and the need to move beyond the mere use of skin colour as primary or only form of categorisation (Bonnet and Caillault 2014). Our findings show that the development of stereotypes are closely related to a country's migration history and ethnic composition, and that the 'symbolic assailant' strongly depends on specific national, local and organisational contexts.

5 Border policing, procedural justice and belonging

The legitimacy of (cr)immigration controls in border areas[1]

5.1 Introduction

Borders have always been important markers of inclusion and exclusion, defining both national sovereignty and the boundaries of belonging (Villegas, 2015). However, in recent decades the nature and meaning of the border has undergone significant changes, so that the traditional notion of a border guard standing at a demarcated line to check every traveller is no longer the only accurate depiction. Instead, the monitoring of movement no longer exclusively occurs at national borders, but equally at various sites inside sovereign territories (Pallitto & Heyman, 2008).The contemporary border is delocalised and can be better understood through the notion of 'bordering' (Muller, 2010). Driven by techniques of identification and surveillance, states increasingly rely on practices of internal border control (Lyon, 2007). In this way the relationship between borders and territory has disappeared, or diminished at least, although in recent years there has been a renewed focus on actual physical borders and a proliferation of high fences, walls and barbed wire.

This is particularly true in Europe. As the continent has seen its internal borders disappearing following the implementation of the Schengen agreement coupled with the freedom of movement for everybody holding European citizenship, states have started to seek other ways to control unwanted mobility (Van der Woude and Van Berlo, 2015). While passport controls are no longer employed at the intra-Schengen State borders, identity and security checks carried out by law enforcement agencies in 20 km zones around these former physical borders mean that the border is in other ways still very much present (Atget, 2008; Brouwer, Van der Woude, & Van der Leun, 2018; Casella Colombeau, 2017). Although many of these bordering practices were first and foremost administrative, Aas (2011) notes that they are often carried out by police forces or incorporate various crime-fighting objectives.

What is crucial about these new 'borders', is that they are not encountered in the same way by everyone. The border only materialises for people whose citizenship is questioned or who are otherwise deemed a risk, making questions of identity particularly salient (Blackwood, Hopkins, & Reicher, 2015;

1 An earlier version of this chapter was published as: Brouwer, J., Van der Woude, M.A.H., & Van der Leun, J.P. (2018). Border policing, procedural justice and belonging. The legitimacy of (cr)immigration controls in border areas. *British Journal of Criminology, 58*(3), 624-642.

Shamir, 2005). Various studies have highlighted how contemporary bordering practices result in 'social sorting' processes (Lyon, 2007) that are frequently shaped by the merging of crime control and migration control – also referred to as crimmigration control (Aas, 2011; Stumpf, 2006). According to Aas (2011), the distinction between what she refers to as 'bona fide travellers' and 'crimmigrant others' is not only based on citizenship, but also on alleged criminal status. This makes the border encounter an important moment for questioning someone's membership or ascribing one disreputable, dangerous or criminal identities (Muller, 2010; Villegas, 2015). This can be experienced as a form of 'identity misrecognition' and seriously challenge people's ability to exercise their 'everyday citizenship' (Blackwood et al., 2015).

Despite ample attention for these social sorting practices of current border regimes (Lyon, 2007; Pickering & Ham, 2013), the perceptions of individuals that are subjected to them have so far received little empirical attention. This omission is remarkable, given the importance of such perceptions for the legitimacy of bordering practices. According to procedural justice theory, legitimacy in criminal justice contexts is primarily the result of the perceived fairness of procedures (Tyler, 2003). A central component in this body of literature is the notion of shared group membership and the importance of social identity for legitimacy judgments (Bradford, 2014). Whereas a wealth of research on procedural justice has focussed on experiences with the police, there are good reasons to assume that it holds equal relevance for border policing actors (Hasisi & Weisburd, 2011). But whereas the police has important self-interests for treating citizens in a fair and respectful manner – as good relationships with the community are essential for their cooperation and thus an effective policing model (Bradford, Hohl, Jackson, & MacQueen, 2015; Sunshine & Tyler, 2003) – this seems to be less the case for border policing organisations. After all, these generally do not work in and with communities – except the communities that live in the border area where these controls take place. In general, the relationship between citizens and border police officers is primarily based on the former wanting something from the latter – in practice entrance into territory –, thus creating a power imbalance. Litmanovitz and Montgomery (2015) therefore argue that it is important to take into account officers' perceptions of procedural justice and legitimacy.

This article examines both officers' perceptions and the experiences of people that are stopped in the context of the Dutch 'Mobile Security Monitor' (MSM), a form of border policing in the border areas of the Netherlands with neighbouring Belgium and Germany. Although the internal borders in the Schengen area are no longer supposed to be enforced, article 23 of the SBC does allow Member States to carry out security checks in border areas, if these do not have an effect equivalent to border control. In the Netherlands, these selective security checks are carried out by the Royal Netherlands Marechaussee (RNM), a military police force that performs both civic and military duties. Although the original aim of the MSM was the prevention of illegal entry and stay, over time this expanded to include human smuggling and identity fraud (Van der Woude & Brouwer, 2017). People can therefore be stopped for suspected illegal stay as well as involvement in criminal activities. The MSM is a highly discretionary proactive instrument, as a stop does not require a reasonable suspicion of illegal stay or criminal activity. This raises the question how officers' themselves understand procedural fairness and legitimacy and how these controls are perceived by the different groups of people that are subjected to them.

5.2 Legitimacy, procedural justice and belonging

Policing studies generally maintain that legitimacy is formed through two separate but interrelated components: The perceived effectiveness of the police and its operations and the way police officers treat the people they encounter while performing their duties (Sunshine & Tyler, 2003; Tyler, 2003; Tyler & Wakslak, 2004). According to procedural justice theory, experiencing fair treatment by the police is the strongest predictor of police legitimacy. Procedural justice is usually seen to incorporate the fairness of the decisions made by officers and the quality of treatment during an interaction (Sunshine & Tyler, 2003). When the police is seen as neutral, polite and respectful they will be considered legitimate in the public's view (Bradford, Murphy, & Jackson, 2014; Tyler, 2003; Tyler & Wakslak, 2004). Research suggests that procedural fairness is especially important for people in the case of police-initiated contact (Hunold, Oberwittler, & Lukas, 2016).

The *Group Value Model* (GVM) of procedural justice theory is based on the idea that police officers are representatives of the social majority group and their actions reflect broader community outlooks (Jackson & Bradford, 2009). As such, they play a key role in communicating messages of belonging and non-belonging, with serious membership implications for those who are deemed disrespectable and branded as outsiders (Waddington, 1999). Although most studies have focussed on the regular police, it seems likely that this might be equally relevant for border policing officers. After all, borders are key spaces for issues of citizenship and identity, with passport controls as a crucial tool for detecting those who do not belong (Lyon, 2007).

According to the GVM, people care so much about the way they are treated by the police because it says something about how the police views them (Bradford, 2014). Experiencing fair processes and being treated with respect signals inclusion and strengthens the attachment to the group (Antrobus, Bradford, Murphy, & Sargeant, 2015; Blader & Tyler, 2009). Unfair policing, on the other hand, communicates exclusion and may signal that one is not considered a bona fide group member (Sunshine & Tyler, 2003). People react strongly to police actions they perceive as unfair because it challenges their feelings of belonging to the social group the police is seen to represent

(Bradford et al., 2015). This means that people's level of social identification with the authorities will influence the extent to which procedural justice has an effect on legitimacy. Especially people with strong feelings of belonging to a social group will value their status within this group and therefore care more about being treated in a fair manner by authorities (Antrobus et al., 2015). In contrast, in interactions with authorities that represent a group someone does not care about, these relational considerations will be less relevant in predicting attitudes towards authorities and instrumental concerns will be more important (Murphy, Sargeant, & Cherney, 2015). Accordingly, what factors are most crucial in determining the perceived legitimacy of the police might differ greatly according to the ethnic or social group one belongs too (Bradford et al., 2015).

Two recent studies show that judgments about whether certain police conduct is considered to be 'fair' indeed depends to a great extent on social, contextual and background factors (Radburn, Stott, Bradford, & Robinson, 2016; Waddington, Williams, Wright, & Newburn, 2015). Research suggests that ethnic minority group members are generally more likely to perceive they are being treated in an unfair manner and that the feeling of being profiled plays a crucial role in their legitimacy judgments (Tyler, 2005; Weitzer & Tuch, 2002). Especially being subjected to stop-and-search controls in the context of pro-active policing activities elicit complaints (Hunold et al., 2016). In their study on profiling and police legitimacy, Tyler and Wakslak (2004) showed that whereas white people often believed profiling to be a legitimate form of neutrally fighting crime and to be justified by general policing goals, minorities more frequently believed this to be the result of prejudice on behalf of police officers. Such findings have not been limited to policing studies: In their study of security screening processes in an Israeli airport, Hasisi and Weisburd (2011) found that Arab passengers perceived these processes as less legitimate than Jews and this was mainly due to the perception of being profiled and other treatment-related elements.

Most research on procedural justice and police legitimacy has focused on the experiences and perceptions of citizens, somewhat neglecting the perceptions of police officers (Mastrofski, Jonathan-Zamir, Moyal, & Willis, 2016). This is unfortunate, because the way officers see and understand procedurally fair treatment is equally important (Litmanovitz & Montgomery, 2015). Officers clearly do not treat every citizen in the exact same way and there are thus differences in the extent to which police-citizen encounters are characterised by procedural justice. Research suggests that disrespectful behaviour of citizens results in less procedural justice, because officers perceive these people as less deserving of procedurally fair treatment (Mastrofski et al., 2016; Pickett & Ryon, 2017). Particularly relevant for this study, Litmanovitz and Montgomery (2015) found that Israeli border guards experienced a high level of social distance between themselves and Arab citizens they policed, meaning they saw them as less worthy of procedural justice. This suggests that police officers are less likely to treat people in a procedurally just way when they do not consider them to be part of their own group.

5.3 Methodology

For this paper we have adopted a qualitative approach, using fieldwork observations of MSM controls and semi-structured interviews or surveys with people who have been stopped. Data was collected between November 2013 and March 2015 in the context of a larger research project on discretionary decision-making and legitimacy in Dutch border areas. The overarching aim of this research project was to examine the culture, decisions and practices of border policing officers and to assess the legitimacy of both the MSM and the RNM (Van der Woude, Brouwer, & Dekkers, 2016).

Whereas qualitative methods have been regularly used to study legitimacy in prison settings (Crewe, 2011; Liebling, 2004), it has only been scarcely employed for studies on police legitimacy (for important recent exceptions see Davies, Meliala, & Buttle, 2016; Harkin, 2015a). There are nonetheless several advantages to such an approach. As Harkin (2015a) claims, it can offer insights and complexities that are left largely untouched by more quantitative survey-based approaches, including rationales behind judgments about police legitimacy. Furthermore, Jonathan-Zamir, Mastrofski & Moyal (2013, p. 846) argue that researchers should examine procedural justice through direct observations in natural settings in order to incorporate "other useful viewpoints such as those of the police or a third party." Because we draw on interviews with both officers of the RNM and people who have been stopped, in combination with observational study, we have been able to incorporate various perspectives and gather relatively 'thick' data.

5.3.1 Observational and focus group data

Three trained observers – one senior researcher and two PhD-students – spent a combined total of 800 hours observing MSM controls, always in pairs. Usually RNM motor drivers stood just after the border, selected 'interesting' vehicles and then directed these to a control location further inland, where other officers carried out the actual control by checking the identity papers of the stopped persons. We systematically collected data on 330 stopped vehicles, by filling in standardised forms detailing the process and interaction. Observations were combined with brief conversations and on-site informal 'interviews' and discussions with officers: non-structured talks that naturally occurred during observations and were particularly suitable to capture border policing culture. Individual field notes were drawn up at the end of each shift by both researchers, giving the opportunity to cross-check certain observations. Besides participant observation, thirteen focus group discussions were organised with street-level officers to cross-check our findings from the observations and further discuss a number of issues. Both field notes and transcripts were afterwards systematically analysed with AtlasTi, coding them according to the various themes associated with the sub-questions of the larger research project.

5.3.2 Survey data

During the actual controls one researcher would focus on the characteristics of the vehicle and persons and reasons for the stop, while the other asked people if they were willing to participate in an academic study. Vehicles were approached while RNM officers were checking the papers, as at this time there was usually no interaction between the officers and the stopped persons. RNM officers also agreed to give the researcher space to conduct the interview. The researcher was clearly distinguishable from RNM officers and always stressed before an interview that he or she did not work for the RNM but was part of an independent academic research team. He or she also emphasised that all information would be treated anonymously and confidentially. Depending on the origin of the vehicles' license plate and the language proficiency of the researcher, people were approached in Dutch, English, French or German. When feasible the interview was conducted orally, sometimes resulting in lively conversations. To also include people that did speak any of these languages, a survey was designed and translated into eleven different languages.[2] When a language barrier stood in the way of an oral interview, this survey was handed to the respondent in his or her preferred language. This greatly enhanced the number of respondents, including groups otherwise completely missed, but it inevitably led to more basic information.

The survey contained a set of open questions about people's perceptions regarding the fact that they had been stopped, why they thought they had been stopped, whether they trusted the RNM officers had done the right thing and if the reason for the stop had been explained to them. We also asked people's country of birth, the country of birth of both their parents and, in order to capture their own sense of social identity, to what ethnic or national group they felt they belonged most. To measure legitimacy, we included two sets of five-point Likert-type scale ranging from 1 (strongly disagree) to 5

2 The survey was translated into Albanian, Bulgarian, German, French, Hungarian, Italian, Polish, Romanian, Russian, Spanish and Czech. We want to thank Rogier Vijverberg for his assistance with designing the survey and thank the following persons for the translations: Andrea Varga, Benjamin Kiebeler, Magdalena Szmidt, Ekaterina Kopylova, Francesco Cacciola, Sarah Castéran, Theodora Petrova, Bogdan Popescu, Silvia Rodriguez Rivero, Marie Skálová, Burbuqe Thaci and Luca Valente.

(strongly agree). The first set of five statements focussed on the perceived effectiveness and acceptability of the instrument, while the second set of four questions focussed on treatment by the officers.[3] For the analysis of these statements we only used the surveys that responded to all statements in the concerned set.

5.3.3 Respondents

A total of 167 respondents were interviewed or filled out a survey. Not all surveys were filled out completely and respondents often provided relatively short answers. Table 5.1 shows the breakdown of the surveys and interviews per language. The language of the survey or interview does not necessarily equate the nationality of the respondent. However, the most common languages roughly correspond with data we collected about the nationality of people who were stopped, with the exception of Belgium, which is divided here between French and Dutch-speaking respondents.

As we are primarily interested in seeing if there were any differences depending on people's ethnic and national background, we categorised the survey results in three groups: 'non-Dutch citizens', 'Dutch majority citizens' and 'Dutch ethnic minority citizens'. Non-Dutch citizens (N=127) are neither born in the Netherlands nor have any of their parents born in the Netherlands. Except for seven Belgian and two Suriname respondents, none of these respondents spoke Dutch. Dutch citizens (N=40), on the other hand, are either born in the Netherlands themselves, have at least one parent born in the Netherlands or were born abroad to non-Dutch parents but identified themselves nonetheless primarily as Dutch (often because they have been living in the Netherlands since a very long time and might even hold Dutch citizenship). All these respondents spoke Dutch. In order to make a distinction between majority group members and ethnic minority group members, we looked at the country of birth of the parents. When a respondent was born in the Netherlands to two Dutch-born parents, we classified him or her as majority group member (N=13). When at least one of the parents was born abroad, we classified the person as an ethnic minority (N=21).[4] There were six Dutch-speaking respondents we did not collect any of this data on; these are left out of the analysis.

3 This set also consisted of five statements, but one of these was about the duration of the control. Because this has little to do with treatment by officers, we have left it out in our analyses for this article.

4 This classification is not entirely unproblematic, as this can include non-visible ethnic minorities (for example someone born to a German mother and Dutch father). However, all these respondents had a non-western background.

Language	Number
Dutch	50
German	32
French	23
Polish	16
Romanian	12
English	8
Russian	6
Bulgarian	5
Hungarian	4
Czech	4
Spanish	3
Albanian	2
Italian	2
Total	167

Table 5.1 Number of surveys filled out per language

5.4 Decision-making, treatment and officer perceptions of procedural justice

The MSM is an ambiguous instrument, combining migration control with elements of crime control. Originally designed as an instrument to combat illegal entry and stay, since 2006 the official aim includes human smuggling and identity fraud. Around the same time an unofficial name change took place from Mobile Alien Monitor to Mobile Security Monitor, with the abbreviation staying the same in Dutch. As RNM officers hold regular police powers, in practice the controls are based on both suspicion of illegal stay and criminal activity (Brouwer et al, 2018; Van der Woude & Brouwer, 2017). This reflects Shamir's (2005, p. 214) claim that the policing of mobility is based on "'paradigm of suspicion' that constructs individuals and often whole groups as having suspect identities related to the risks of immigration, crime and terrorism, (…) each on its own account and often coupled with one another."

As noted above, fair decision-making is a core element of procedural justice. In the context of stop-and-search activities, the feeling of having been unfairly profiled is particularly crucial. One of the most important decisions during the MSM is the decision to stop someone for a control and RNM officers have a considerable amount of discretionary freedom in doing this. Although there is a smart camera system in place that can read license plates of vehicles, in practice this is barely used (Dekkers, Van der Woude, & Van der Leun, 2016). Instead, officers largely rely on their own judgments in selecting interesting vehicles.

Elsewhere we have shown in more detail how officers use their discretion and make decisions regarding who to stop (Brouwer et al, 2018). They often rely on various indicators to determine whether a vehicle is of interest, but ethnic, national and racial categories play a particular dominant role. These differ, however, depending on whether a stop is based on possible illegal stay or criminal activity. Because the primary aim of the MSM, as laid down in article 50 of the Aliens Act and article 4.17a of the Aliens Decree, is migration control, officers had to detect potential unauthorised migrants. To that end, they tried to see whether passengers had a 'foreign appearance'. Skin colour was an important part of this, as officers regularly implied that being Dutch primarily meant being white. According to one officer:

> "Look, we are here in the context of the Aliens Act. Dutch people are by nature white – of course there are also non-white Dutch people – but you do take that into account. Belgians as well. So if a car with a Belgian license plate passes the border here, and it has a couple of non-white people in it, it means that is an indicator."

Officers did not see this as discrimination, but rather as a logical consequence of their specific task of preventing illegal migration. At the same time, they also frequently stopped vehicles for crime-related reasons. In these cases they strongly relied on the license plates of vehicles – as an indicator for nationality – to check primarily Eastern European vehicles. Although these people are EU citizens and should therefore enjoy freedom of movement within the Schengen area, they were thus frequently stopped on the basis of potential criminal activity. Besides Eastern European nationals, RNM officers also focused on Northern African ethnic minorities in relation to criminal activities. Officers generally did not perceive such decisions to be unfair, as they, according to them, were based on "experience and intelligence."

Besides fair decisions, quality of interpersonal treatment is another core element of procedural justice. Almost all RNM officers stressed the importance of treating the persons they encounter during controls in a respectful and friendly manner. As one officer explained, "if you treat people with respect, you will also get respect in return." They often described this with the official term 'hostmanship', which means making people feel welcome through a friendly and understanding approach. Many RNM officers work at Schiphol International Airport, where they are the first point of contact for people coming to the Netherlands. During their formation they are therefore trained in friendly and respectful interactions. Although the MSM is a significantly different setting than border policing work at the airport, many officers nonetheless invoked the principle of hostmanship when talking about the way they approached people. As a more senior officer explained:

> "We try to treat people as humans, not as criminals. They are after all only stopped for a control and are not considered criminals until something is actually found.

The fact that 90% of the people have done nothing wrong is a good reason to treat everybody in a good way."

Some officers suggested that especially more experienced officers are capable of approaching people in such a manner. For example, one officer stated during a focus group that mainly younger colleagues tended to act in a somewhat authoritarian manner. He furthermore argued that with a few senior officers on the control location, the whole atmosphere during a control was more calm, something confirmed by our own observations. More generally, the vast majority of interactions we observed went in a relatively calm and friendly manner.

5.5 Perceptions of those policed and differences between social groups

As noted above, we categorised the survey results in three different groups. Our results show that whereas non-Dutch citizens and Dutch majority citizens were generally very positive about both the RNM and the MSM, ethnic minority citizens were much more critical.

5.5.1 Perceptions of non-Dutch citizens

The majority of the respondents were non-Dutch citizens, with no apparent link to the Netherlands (N=127). Most of these people indicated their national-

N=72 (Average 3.77)	*1*	*2*	*3*	*4*	*5*	*Average*
I have confidence that these stops will prevent illegal migration	6 (8.3)	11 (15.3)	10 (13.9)	22 (30.6)	23 (31.9)	3,63
I have confidence that these stops will prevent crime	6 (8.3)	11 (15.3)	10 (13.9)	23 (31.9)	22 (30.6)	3,61
This is an acceptable measure to prevent illegal migration	3 (4.2)	7 (9.7)	10 (13.9)	28 (38.9)	24 (33.3)	3,88
This is an acceptable measure to prevent crime	4 (5.6)	8 (11.1)	8 (11.1)	27 (37.5)	25 (34.7)	3,85
In general, I am positive about this measure	4 (5.6)	9 (12.5)	14 (19.4)	20 (27.8)	25 (34.7)	3,74

Table 5.2 Non-Dutch citizens on instrument – N (%)[5]

5 For all tables, the scores are 1 = strong disagree; 2 = disagree; 3 = neutral; 4 = agree; 5 = strongly agree.

ity as the main social group they belonged to, although three respondents primarily adhered to a common European identity. The survey results show that the vast majority of this group perceive the MSM controls as not at all problematic, or even positive (see table 5.2). This is not surprising: since these people essentially identify themselves as foreigners, the fact that they have been stopped merely confirms their own identity.

Most people were rather indifferent about the fact that they had been stopped, giving statements as "it is normal when one is entering another country" and "it is necessary to perform identity checks on the foreigners entering the Netherlands." Even other EU citizens, who enjoy the fundamental right to freedom of movement within the Schengen zone, did not seem to find it problematic that their trip was temporarily halted. Cherney and Murphy (2011) argue that procedural justice can only be successful if the laws the police are seen to enforce are perceived as legitimate. The fact that European citizens were positive about the MSM and the RNM therefore suggests they did not perceive this form of border policing in the supposedly borderless Schengen area as problematic.

As can be seen in table 5.3, most non-Dutch respondents were also very positive about the treatment they received, indicating that they found the RNM officers friendly and professional. This might have been influenced by their experiences with border policing officers in their own and other countries. Griffiths (2018) argues that Polish migrants in the UK hold favourable attitudes about the local police, because they compare them with the perceived corrupt police in Poland.

N=82 (Average 4.03)	*1*	*2*	*3*	*4*	*5*	*Average*
During this stop the officer(s) treated me with respect	1 (1.2)	2 (2.4)	6 (7.3)	21 (25.6)	52 (63.4)	4,47
The officer(s) listened to me during this stop	1 (1.2)	2 (2.4)	14 (17.1)	23 (28.1)	42 (51.2)	4,25
During this stop the officer(s) talked to me in a way I could understand	1 (1.2)	4 (4.9)	6 (7.3)	21 (25.6)	50 (61)	4,40
I felt intimidated during this stop[6]	3 (3.7)	8 (9.8)	16 (19.5)	18 (22)	37 (45.1)	3,98

Table 5.3 Non-Dutch citizens on treatment – N (%)

6 Because this statement is negatively formulated the scores have been reversed for consistency.

When asked why they thought they had been stopped, a lot of people answered with responses such as "routine check" or "control". This suggests they did not really care about why they had been stopped. Although most respondents in this group thought they had been stopped because of their foreign license plate or their foreign appearance, they did not necessarily see this as problematic (N=47). Only four people explicitly said they believed they had been stopped because of their skin colour: two Dutch-speaking Belgian respondents and two Dutch-speaking Surinamese respondents. These respondents were also the most critical in this group.

41 persons indicated that they did not know why they had been stopped. These respondents also sometimes mentioned that they had not committed any offense – such as speeding – and that there had thus not been a good reason to stop them. While some respondents were aware that the MSM is primarily a form of immigration control, others thought it was a traffic control or had to do with crime control; various respondents also referred to RNM as police officers. This suggests that at least some of the respondents were confused about the exact nature and primary aim of the MSM.

5.5.2 Perceptions of Dutch majority citizens

Thirteen Dutch respondents were part of the majority group. As can be seen in table 5.4, Dutch majority citizens were generally very positive about the MSM as an instrument. Among the five respondents who were slightly less positive about the effectivity of the MSM (but still gave an average score between three and four), three of them motivated this by saying that criminals would not be caught this way and that more controls are needed for it to really have an effect. Largely positive interactions with the RNM officers meant that all respondents in this group were also very positive about their treatment by the RNM officers, as can be seen in table 5.5. Only one person gave an average score below 4.25, which seemed primarily motivated by the lack of explanation about the reason of the control.

Some of these respondents indicated they found it annoying they had been stopped, but most said they understood these controls took place, or even stated that it was very good. Several respondents believed they had been stopped because they were driving a car with a foreign license plate, while one person thought the reason had been that his passenger was a foreigner (Egyptian) and had a dark skin. However, in none of these cases did this have consequences for respondents' legitimacy judgments. Instead, the only mild form of criticism among this group of respondents was a lack of clarity about the reason for the stop: some of the respondents did not fully understand the purpose of the controls and felt they had been wrongly stopped.

N=12 (Average 3.85)	*1*	*2*	*3*	*4*	*5*	*Average*
I have confidence that these stops will prevent illegal migration	1 (8.3)	1 (8.3)	4 (33.3)	5 (41.7)	1 (8.3)	3,33
I have confidence that these stops will prevent crime	0 (0)	3 (25)	1 (8.3)	4 (33.3)	4 (33.3)	3,75
This is an acceptable measure to prevent illegal migration	0 (0)	1 (8.3)	2 (16.7)	4 (33.3)	5 (41.7)	4,08
This is an acceptable measure to prevent crime	0 (0)	1 (8.3)	1 (8.3)	6 (50)	4 (33.3)	4,08
In general, I am positive about this measure	1 (8.3)	0 (0)	2 (16.7)	4 (33.3)	5 (41.7)	4

Table 5.4 Dutch majority citizens on instrument – N (%)

N=13 (Average 4.58)	*1*	*2*	*3*	*4*	*5*	*Average*
During this stop the officer(s) treated me with respect	0 (0)	0 (0)	1 (7.7)	3 (23.1)	9 (69.2)	4.62
The officer(s) listened to me during this stop	0 (0)	0 (0)	1 (7.7)	5 (38.5)	7 (53.8)	4.46
During this stop the officer(s) talked to me in a way I could understand	0 (0)	0 (0)	0 (0)	7 (53.8)	6 (46.2)	4.46
I felt intimidated during this stop[7]	0 (0)	0 (0)	1 (7.7)	1 (7.7)	11 (84.6)	4.77

Table 5.5 Dutch majority citizens on treatment – N (%)

5.5.3 Perceptions of ethnic minority Dutch citizens

Twenty-one respondents were Dutch citizens who were either born abroad themselves or had at least one parent born outside the Netherlands.[8] Most

7 Because this statement is negatively formulated the scores have been reversed for consistency.

8 The most common foreign backgrounds were Morocco (6), Turkey (4), Iraq (3) and Suriname (2)Three of these have relatively large populations in the Netherlands. Turkish and Moroccan populations formed when people from these countries migrated to the Netherlands

of these respondents (16) identified themselves primarily as Dutch. Two respondents indicated they felt they belonged to two ethnic or national groups (including Dutch), one respondent felt primarily Turkish, one respondent primarily Arabic and one person did not answer this question.

Out of these twenty-one respondents, thirteen believed they had been stopped because of their skin colour or 'foreign appearance'. For example, one woman said that when she saw the RNM officer on his motor coming in front of her car, the first thing she thought was: 'of course we are getting stopped, I am in the car with a Moroccan and a Turk'. Another respondent said in response to the question why he thought he had been stopped: "Because I am a foreigner, like all persons that I have seen being stopped." As can be seen in table 5.6, this group was on average more critical about the instrument than the other two groups.

N=18 (Average 2.98)	*1*	*2*	*3*	*4*	*5*	*Average*
I have confidence that these stops will prevent illegal migration	3 (16.7)	2 (11.1)	6 (33.3)	3 (16.7)	4 (22.2)	3,17
I have confidence that these stops will prevent crime	6 (33.3)	2 (11.1)	5 (27.8)	2 (11.1)	3 (16.7)	2,67
This is an acceptable measure to prevent illegal migration	4 (22.2)	2 (11.1)	5 (27.8)	2 (11.1)	5 (27.8)	3,11
This is an acceptable measure to prevent crime	5 (27.8)	2 (11.1)	5 (27.8)	3 (16.7)	3 (16.7)	2,83
In general, I am positive about this measure	5 (27.8)	2 (11.1)	2 (11.1)	4 (22.2)	5 (27.8)	3,11

Table 5.6 Dutch ethnic minority citizens on instrument – N (%)

Eight respondents were particularly critical about the MSM, with an average score below 3. Five of them indicated they thought they had been stopped because of their skin colour or because they were 'foreigners', while the other three said they had no idea. A few respondents were also critical about the treatment they received by RNM officers, although not as much as about the instrument (see table 5.7).

N=21 (Average 3.74)	*1*	*2*	*3*	*4*	*5*	*Average*
During this stop the officer(s) treated me with respect	1 (4.8)	1 (4.8)	2 (9.5)	7 (33.3)	11 (47.6)	4,14
The officer(s) listened to me during this stop	2 (9.5)	1 (4.8)	4 (19)	8 (38.1)	6 (28.6)	3,71
During this stop the officer(s) talked to me in a way I could understand	3 (14.3)	2 (9.5)	1 (4.8)	8 (38.1)	7 (33.3)	3,67
I felt intimidated during this stop[9]	4 (19)	3 (14.3)	4 (19)	2 (9.5)	8 (38.1)	3,33

Table 5.7 Dutch ethnic minority citizens on treatment – N (%)

Only three respondents were overall very negative about their treatment by the officers. Here too the feeling of having been stopped because of a 'foreign appearance' was often brought up in explanations. As a Kenyan-born respondent said:

> "I would like to know why they are selective on skin colour. I am slightly intimidated, noticed that the car of a friend before me was not being stopped and then saw a motor driver carefully scrutinising my car. That was an unpleasant moment, I knew then that I would be stopped: five black men in a car, come on!"

Besides the feeling of having been stopped because of a 'foreign appearance', another important factor behind negative perceptions seemed to be the lack of clarity about what these controls were for and what the reason for the stop was. The most critical respondents all stated that the purpose of the control was not explained to them and that they felt they had been stopped because of their appearance. As one Dutch respondent with a Moroccan background elaborated:

> "This motor driver comes up next to you and you immediately think, 'what have I done wrong?' Then more generally, they are not polite, curtly and do not explain anything. Look, now I am with a friend who understands I have done nothing, but imagine I am with my girlfriend or family. They immediately ask all kinds of annoying questions."

---

as 'guest workers' in the 1960s and 1970s, while Suriname is a former Dutch colony. The other backgrounds were Algeria, Angola, Egypt, Kenya, Sri Lanka and Syria.

9 Because this statement is negatively formulated the scores have been reversed for consistency.

His passenger then added:

> "Look around you, madam. There are only foreigners here, black people. They let the Dutch ones just pass."

This last statement is particularly telling. Despite the fact that both men were born in the Netherlands and Dutch citizens, they referred to the 'Dutch ones' as other people who were not being stopped. Conversely, the people who were stopped were all 'foreigners, black people'. Other Dutch ethnic minority citizens equally referred to themselves as 'foreigners'. This seems to suggest that these respondents interpret these stops as confirming that only white people can pass as being Dutch. Although they self-identify as being Dutch, the controls signal to them that they are not necessarily seen as such by the RNM.

Following the procedural justice framework, it is these kinds of experiences that seem most damaging for the legitimacy of the MSM and the RNM. When people felt they had been stopped because of their supposed foreign appearance and received no satisfying explanation about the aim of the control or the reason for the stop, they were generally most critical about the MSM and – to a lesser extent – their treatment by the RNM. These experiences occur mainly among Dutch ethnic minority group members who identify themselves as Dutch. As can be seen in figure 5.1, this results in substantial differences regarding overall satisfaction between the three groups.

There was thus considerable ambivalence among the people who were stopped during the MSM, with different perceptions of fairness seeming to stem for an important part from people's social identity. Although people identifying as non-Dutch regularly believed they were stopped because they were foreign, they did not perceive this as unfair. Dutch majority citizens frequently believed that officers had made a mistake in stopping them and therefore did not perceive this as unfair or challenging their identity. Both these groups were also positive about the treatment they received from the RNM, resulting in overall high legitimacy scores. This was different for Dutch citizens who belonged to an ethnic minority. Many of these respondents believed they had been stopped because of their 'foreign appearance' and thus their skin colour, even though they identified as Dutch. Although this group was not outspokenly negative about the way they were treated during the stop, this form of identity misrecognition meant these respondents saw the RNM and the MSM as less legitimate than the other two groups.

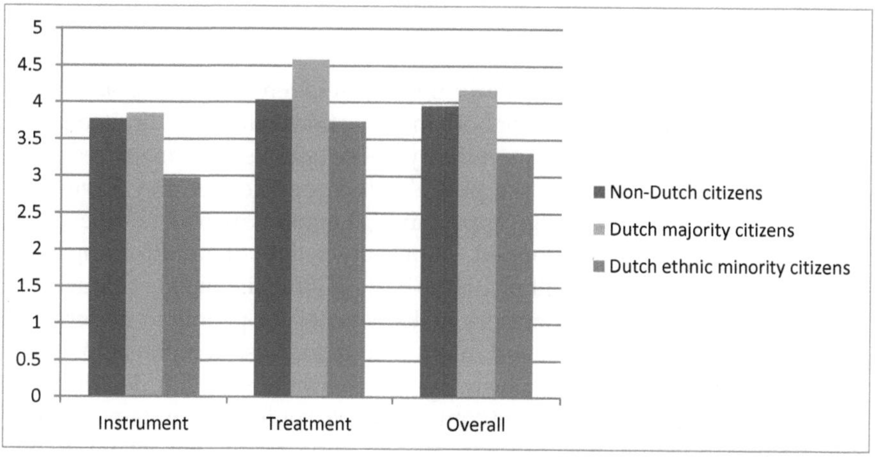

Figure 5.1 Average scores per group

5.6 Conflicting perceptions of procedural fairness

Our results suggest that the feeling of having been stopped on the basis of one's skin colour, in combination with a lack of explanations about the aim of the MSM and the reason somebody has been stopped, are crucial factors in negative judgments regarding the legitimacy of the MSM and the RNM. RNM officers were mostly aware that explaining the aim of the MSM and the reasons behind a stop could help reducing negative responses from citizens. According to one of them:

> "Look, what I think we do well is that, immediately when a car arrives, we say who we are and what we do. This way people know what it is and this often creates much more understanding."

We indeed noticed during the observations that officers usually shortly stated that it was an ID-control at the onset of a check. Out of 224 stops that we recorded this type of observational data on, officers stated 183 times that this was an identification-control conducted by the RNM. Yet, as one officer indicated, a lot of people did not hear this. Furthermore, we noticed that these short statements were often quite unclear or not in a language people could be expected to understand. Indeed, more than half of our respondents said it had not been explained to them why they had been stopped; many people thought it was a 'general control'. While it could be expected that language barriers are an important explanation for this, our results show that Dutch people say slightly more often that the reason of the control was not explained to them. Moreover, the brief statement that it was an id-control was not always satisfactory to respondents:

> "They didn't say anything at all. They only said 'control, ID'. Not explained why, very bad."

Such explanations seem particularly important given the ambiguous nature of the MSM. It is an instrument for both immigration control and limited forms of crime control, carried out by a military police organisation; many respondents referred to the RNM as 'the police'. When people feel they have been stopped because of their 'foreign appearance', it requires more detailed explaining why people have been stopped – especially in light of non-discrimination provisions that prohibit profiling on the basis of ethnicity or skin colour only. Such explanations can furthermore make it easier for people to understand why they have been stopped and might help to increase acceptance. Various officers stated that when they were honest about the selection decision and carefully explained the aim of the control, people could even understand they had been stopped because of their 'foreign appearance'. For example, one Dutch respondent with a Moroccan background said he believed he had been stopped because he "looked foreign, Moroccan". He furthermore stated that officers had explained to him that it was an immigration control and that he therefore understood that only 'foreigners' were stopped. Although he was critical about the effectiveness of the MSM in preventing crime, he did think it could help in preventing illegal migration. He was generally positive about the MSM and said that he did not mind that he had been stopped because it gave him a safe feeling.

At the same time, it is important to acknowledge that such explanations can also increase the dissatisfaction of people who have been stopped. As one respondent answered to the question what he thought about the fact that he had been stopped:

> "Racist. I understand that it is an immigration control, but I have a Dutch license plate."

For officers, the fact that they were conducting migration controls meant that it was logical to take a person's skin colour into consideration in their selection decisions. Although most officers stressed the importance of explaining the task of the RNM and the aim of the MSM, some also expressed frustration about how in their experience primarily black people were very quick to accuse them of racism. This sometimes caused annoyance among officers, who were less willing to explain their actions when they immediately faced accusations of racism or discrimination. As one of them explained:

> "On the one hand I think to myself, 'what are you complaining about?' I am here for a specific piece of legislation and you may not like that, that is all fine, I will try to explain that. (...) But I do think to myself, you could also do some research yourself. I mean, the police do their controls, we do controls, tax inspectors do

their controls (…) we are all busy with things, and just because I am wearing a blue uniform I would have to explain each time why I decided to stop you."

Various officers indicated that especially Dutch persons were outspokenly critical when they were stopped. They explained this through Dutch culture, which they perceived as very assertive, and the fact that Schengen has become normalised for Dutch people. One officer did not understand complaints from Dutch citizens who believed they had been stopped because an officer perceived them as foreigner.

"You often hear that they go completely out of their mind, get completely furious, give a Dutch identity card and say: 'you stop me because I am foreigner!' Why? You have a Dutch identity card, don't make such a fuss."

This comment is particularly illustrating for the different viewpoints of officers and some Dutch ethnic minorities who are stopped during the MSM. This is perhaps not entirely unsurprising, as past research has shown that powerholders and majority group members can downplay negative experiences of minority group members (Blackwood, 2015). Most officers perceived the impact of a control limited; they commonly reasoned that when everything is in order a person can leave quickly and that the interference and inconvenience is therefore very minimal. What they failed to acknowledge in this way, is that the very fact that somebody has been selected for a control can be perceived as communicating that he or she is not regarded as full citizen. Being selected for a pro-active immigration control in what someone perceives to be 'his' or 'her' country can constitute an important form of identity misrecognition, no matter how brief the actual interaction is. Our results suggest that explaining the aim of the controls and reason behind a stop can at least diminish these feelings.

5.7 Conclusion and discussion

In this article we have looked at the experiences and perceptions of people who have been stopped in the context of the Mobile Security Monitor, a form of internal border policing in the border areas of the Netherlands. Furthermore, we have explored officers' perceptions of the necessity and 'deservedness' of procedural justice and legitimacy. Our findings suggest that non-Dutch persons who have been stopped in the context of the MSM mostly do not perceive this as problematic. These people generally felt they had been treated in a fair manner and did not find they had been unjustifiably selected for an immigration control: after all, they *are* foreigners who want to visit the Netherlands. Even though within the Schengen area borders are no longer supposed to be enforced, very few people contested the authority of the RNM to carry out border policing activities, and this included European citizens. Whereas under

EU-law all European citizens ought to be treated equally and without discrimination, most of these people might not think of themselves as equally entitled to free entry into the Netherlands as Dutch citizens.

Among Dutch citizens who were stopped there was a clear distinction between majority group members and ethnic minority group members. Majority group members were generally very positive about both the instrument and the RNM officers, while minority group members were considerably more critical about both the MSM and the RNM officers. One explanation for this might be that marginalised people feel less sure about their place in society and therefore care a great deal about the status that is being communicated by fair treatment at the hand of authorities (Antrobus et al., 2015). For example, Blackwood (2015) claims that especially minority group members care about what other groups think about them, and that they look in particular to authorities as representatives of the wider social group. Most ethnic minority respondents identified themselves as primarily being Dutch and felt they had been stopped because of their skin colour or because of their 'foreign appearance'. Several of them also stated it had not been explained to them what the aim of these controls was or why they were stopped.

Although most respondents did not explicitly address it as such, these judgements seem to be linked to people's social identification, as primarily people who felt they belonged to the same social group as RNM officers seemed to care about the identity-related information that is communicated through the decisions of these officers. Whereas sentiments about being stopped on the bases of 'foreignness' and a lack of clarity about the aim of the controls and the reason for a stop were also present among non-Dutch citizens and Dutch majority group members, this did not translate in equally negative judgments about the legitimacy of the MSM or the RNM.

While officers generally stressed the importance of a procedurally fair treatment – and most interactions were indeed rather friendly and calm – they also sometimes expressed frustration about being easily accused of discrimination and the need to explain the reasons for selecting a vehicle. This seemed to be the result of a perception that the impact of a stop is very limited. Moreover, officers did not perceive their selection decisions as unfair. Although they acknowledged to rely on skin colour as an important indicator of foreignness, they believed this was a logical consequence of their focus on migration control. Furthermore, reliance on certain ethnic and national categories was primarily based on experience and intelligence. In other words: In their eyes this was a form of justified profiling. This points to fundamental differences between citizens and officers regarding the fairness of decisions and highlights the importance of taking into account the perceptions of both sides to better understand issues of procedural justice and legitimacy. It also lays bare the problematic nature of these pro-active and selective forms of border policing, especially when they intersect with crime control. Decisions to stop can be based on both the expectation of illegal entry or suspicion of criminal activity and for the people who have been stopped the exact reason is often unclear. This increases the chance that bona fide Dutch citizens with a migrant background are being stopped, while for them it is unclear why exactly they have been selected.

The question is what these findings mean for the legitimacy of the MSM and the RNM. Harkin (2015a) points out that procedural justice theory fails to account for the broad support for the police that often exists among large parts of the population in spite of scandals or unfair treatment. In line with Waddington (1999) he argues that as long as unfairness is directed at people belonging to excluded groups – such as migrants or ethnic minorities – this might not necessarily result in diminished legitimacy among the majority population (see also Radburn et al., 2016). Although a few people felt they had been treated unfairly during the MSM, most people did not see these controls as problematic. This is likely to be the same among the majority Dutch population that is never stopped in the context of the MSM. Moreover, unlike the regular police, border policing agencies generally rely much less on the explicit cooperation of citizens. As such, there seem to be little incentives for the RNM to appreciate the negative experiences of certain ethnic minorities (Cf. Blackwood, 2015). Why, then, is it nonetheless important to address these concerns, besides the notion that everyone should have the right to be treated fairly and with respect (Murphy et al., 2015)?

Another model of procedural justice theory can help to formulate an answer. The *Group Engagement Model (GEM)* shares several similarities with the GVM, but differs in some other aspects. The core idea of this model is that people are more likely to cooperate with authorities they identify with (Madon, Murphy, & Cherney, 2017). Strongly relying on social interactionist and labelling theories, the model furthermore stresses that authorities can actually *shape* social identities (Blader & Tyler, 2009; Bradford et al., 2015, 2014). Especially in Europe's contemporary multicultural societies, where ethnic minorities' sense of belonging is increasingly being questioned, identity-related information from authorities might be important.

In a recent study, Bradford, Murphy and Jackson (2014) showed that procedurally just policing can increase a sense of national identity and stimulate feelings of societal inclusion. Conversely, perceptions of unfairness can lead to diminishing levels of group identification. Referring specifically to racial profiling as an important example, Tyler and Blader (2003, p. 358) argue that "experiencing stereotyping and prejudice within the groups that people belong to is damaging to their sense of self, which may in turn lead them to maintain a psychological distance between their identity and group membership." In this regard Harkin (2015b, p. 48) draws attention to "intimidating or embarrassing activity such as stop-and-search" that "communicate and promote exclusion, alienation and disenfranchisement of individuals or groups from mainstream society" and "may stigmatize, deprive or at least erode groups of their social reputation." In such cases not only people's respectability and their position as law-abiding citizen is at stake, but their very status of full citizen (Bradford et al., 2014).

Experiencing unfair treatment might thus lead to a diminishing sense of belonging and feelings of disengagement from the subordinate group. This might not only have serious psychological consequences for the individual involved and lead to a reluctance to engage with members of the group the authorities represent, but can also decrease legitimacy and ultimately make it less likely for people to cooperate with authorities in the future (Madon et al., 2017). Especially when unfair treatment is experienced on numerous occasions and by different actors, this might lead to diminishing levels of trust and further marginalisation (Blackwood, 2015). This suggests that in order to evaluate the activities of contemporary border policing actors it is necessary to move beyond broad majority support and place more emphasis on the viewpoints of minorities that are actually subjected to these powers.

Part III

Crimmigration, punishment, and deportation

6 Bordered penality in the Netherlands
The experiences of foreign national prisoners and prison officers in a crimmigration prison[1]

6.1 Introduction

In many European countries the growing merger between criminal justice and migration control – also referred to as crimmigration – has had drastic implications for the nature of the prison population and the characteristics of punishment (Aas, 2014; Stumpf, 2006). First, as migration acts have increasingly been criminalised and many states have lowered the threshold for terminating migrants' legal right to stay following a criminal conviction, the number of foreign national prisoners (FNPs)[2] in many – primarily western – European countries has considerably increased (Ugelvik, 2014). Second, states increasingly see deportation as a legitimate instrument of crime control and a way to protect public safety (Turnbull & Hasselberg, 2017). As a result, the punishment of FNPs has undergone drastic changes, being aimed primarily at deportation instead of deterrence and rehabilitation. This has serious consequences for how punishment is experienced (Bosworth, Hasselberg, & Turnbull, 2016).

It has been observed that penal interventions directed at non-citizens are no longer limited to defining society's moral boundaries, but also about establishing the boundaries of belonging and membership (Bosworth, Aas, & Pickering, 2017). As various scholars have pointed out, the result of such developments is the emergence of a parallel criminal justice system for non-citizens that takes on aims that are traditionally within the realm of migration control (Fekete & Webber, 2010; Kaufman, 2015). Aas (2014, pp. 525-526) refers to this parallel penal system as 'bordered penality', observing that "when deprived of their freedom, non-citizens are increasingly placed in separate institutions, or institutional arrangements, and afforded different procedural treatment and standard of rights than citizens." When the criminal justice system is directed at FNPs, it becomes more openly exclusionary: the aim is no longer rehabilitation and preparing prisoners for their return into society, but to permanently exclude them from the territory (Bosworth, 2011a). Citizen-

1 Under review (revise and resubmit) for publication in Punishment and Society, as: J. Brouwer. Bordered penality in the Netherlands. The experiences of foreign national prisoners and prison officers in a crimmigration prison.

2 Unless indicated otherwise, in this paper the term FNP refers to prisoners without a legal right to stay in the country where they are imprisoned.

ship, or rather membership, has come to constitute a "legitimate sorting device" between inclusive and exclusive sanctions (Turnbull & Hasselberg, 2017, p. 136).

The most direct expression of bordered penality is the creation of separate prisons specifically for FNPs. In several European countries such 'crimmigration prisons' have emerged that exclusively hold FNPs and "where immigration control purposes either are added to, or replace, such traditional aims of prisons as punishment, deterrence and rehabilitation" (Ugelvik & Damsa, 2018, p. 1026). For example, under the hubs-and-spokes policy in England & Wales, several prisons have been designated all-foreign prisons, with immigration staff embedded and prison officers working as quasi-immigration agents (Kaufman, 2015). Quite similarly, Kongsvinger prison in Norway has since several years been exclusively reserved for FNPs who are less than two years from their likely deportation (Ugelvik & Damsa, 2018). Although the practical implementation differs, these prisons have in common that FNPs are expected to be deported upon completion of their sentence, thus rendering rehabilitation activities aimed at return into society irrelevant (Pakes & Holt, 2017). The prison has thus become an instrument of border control, playing a role in shaping national identity and the borders of citizenship (Kaufman, 2014).

In their comparative study of crimmigration prisons in England & Wales and Norway, Pakes and Holt (2017) claim these are the only countries in Europe with separate prisons for FNPs. However, since 2014 the Netherlands also has a specific prison for FNPs, located in the small town of Ter Apel. So-called departure supervisors of the Repatriation and Departure Service (DT&V), a specialised organisation responsible for returning unauthorised migrants to their country of origin, are working inside this prison to ensure FNPs are deported at the end of their sentence. Despite these significant developments, empirical research into the punishment of FNPs in the Netherlands is virtually non-existent (Bolhuis, Battjes, & van Wijk, 2017; Boone & Kox, 2012). This article therefore analyses more in-depth these recent changes in the punishment of FNPs in the Netherlands and examines how this is understood and experienced by FNPs, but also by prison officers. The latter group has been somewhat neglected in the handful of empirical studies on crimmigration prisons.

As various scholars have argued, there is a need for combining macro-level, broad analyses of penal policies with more in-depth, empirical examinations of prisoner experiences (Bosworth et al., 2017; Crewe, 2015; Ugelvik & Damsa, 2018). On the one hand, analyses of macro-level penal policies can be significantly enriched by empirical assessment of prisoner experiences. On the other hand, understanding how imprisonment is experienced requires taking into account the wider context of macro-level penal policies. In other words, a comprehensive understanding of the why and how of prisons requires studying penal policies, prison characteristics, and prisoner experiences in conjunction. To that end, the article first provides an examination of the Dutch penal policy framework vis-à-vis FNPs and the characteristics and regime of the all-foreign national prison in Ter Apel. This is followed by an exploration of the experiences of those working and being imprisoned in Ter Apel prison, drawing on in-depth interviews with FNPs and prison officers. In doing so, the study contributes to a small but growing body of scholarship concerned with providing a more empirical understanding of how bordered penality policies are implemented and experienced 'on the ground' (cf. Turnbull & Hasselberg, 2017).

6.2 Foreign national prisoners in the Netherlands

Table 6.1 shows the number of foreigners imprisoned in the Netherlands on September 1 of each year, based on data from the annual SPACE reports of the Council of Europe. Slightly more than twenty percent of the prisoners are foreigners, roughly the same as the European average. Because of the growing use of alternative sanctions, in recent years the total number of prisoners, including foreigners, has considerably decreased.

It is important to realise that not all foreigners lack residence rights. The figures in the last column come from DT&V and show the number of deportable prisoners released from prison throughout each year – they have either been deported or released as unauthorised migrant. These numbers are therefore not directly comparable to the number of foreigners, which counts the number of foreign prisoners on September 1 instead of throughout the year. However, there is a clear trend discernible: whereas the number of foreigners has gradually decreased since 2010, the number of deportable FNPs has increased. Besides the fact that non-citizens are generally excluded from non-custodial sentence, two other factors are likely to have played a role in this: 1) the rules on revoking someone's residence permit following a criminal conviction have become much stricter, resulting in more migrants losing their right to stay; and 2) the systems of crime control and migration control have become much more integrated in recent years, resulting in earlier detection of non-citizens in the criminal justice system.

During the same period, punishment of FNPs has drastically changed. Although resocialisation[3] is traditionally considered a crucial element of punishment in the Netherlands, in recent decades the development of a distinctive Dutch culture of control has meant that the principle seems to have lost some of its importance (Downes & Van Swaaningen, 2007; Pakes, 2004). Various authors have noted how a strong law and order discourse has emerged that combines a strong focus on the protection of the public with growing concerns about immigration and (crime committed by) foreigners and ethnic minorities (Pakes, 2004; Van Swaaningen, 2005). Driven by discourses that fit within Feeley and Simon's (1992) new penology, crime control policies

3 Resocialisation, rather than rehabilitation, is the term commonly used in the Netherlands.

increasingly focus on identifying and targeting specific offender groups that are considered particularly dangerous (Downes & Van Swaaningen, 2007). Moreover, the main aim of penal interventions has shifted to temporary or permanent exclusion of unwanted individuals, through practices described as "banishment modern style" (Van Swaaningen, 2005, p. 296).

Year	*Total prisoners*	*Foreigners*	*Percentage*	*Deportable*
2018	9.315	1.710	18.4%	1.140
2017				1.150
2016	8.726	1.832	21%	1.090
2015	9.002	1.994	22.2%	1.200
2014	9.857	2.081	21.1%	1.220
2013	10.547	2.321	22%	1.120
2012	11.324	2.380	21%	910
2011	11.579	2.636	22.8%	800
2010	11.737	2.830	24.1%	780

Table 6.1 Foreign National Prisoners in the Netherlands

Nonetheless, resocialisation is still considered an important aim of punishment for most prisoners in the Netherlands. It has therefore been argued that the Dutch criminal justice system can best be characterised as a system of bifurcation, with inclusive sanctions for some groups of offenders and exclusive sanctions for others (Boone, 2012a; Cavadino & Dignan, 2006). Given the concerns about criminal immigrants, it is not surprising that the absence of citizenship serves as an important factor in drawing the line between inclusive and exclusive punishment (Boone, 2012a). Indeed, Boone (2012b, p. 1) states "that irregular migrants are almost totally excluded from the regular rehabilitation opportunities in the Netherlands." As such, the bifurcation of the Dutch criminal justice system is strongly reminiscent of Aas' (2014) bordered penality. This is also illustrated by a 2009 letter from the Minister of Justice to the parliament about the policy regarding criminal foreigners:

> "Within the return policy, high priority is given to the return of criminal migrants and migrants demonstrating anti-social behaviour. This is why from the viewpoint of 'deport or detain', all efforts are focused on deporting criminal illegals. If this

> is not (yet) possible, efforts will be made to detain the criminal illegal as long as possible, with the aim of eradicating nuisance for society."[4]

Dutch bordered penality policies culminated in 2014 in the creation of the dedicated foreign national prison in Ter Apel. The prison previously operated as a regular prison, but because there were often not enough prisoners in this part of the Netherlands, it was repeatedly nominated to be closed. As an important source of jobs in an area with relatively little economic activity, the designation as an all-foreign prison meant the prison could stay open. The prison has a capacity of 434 places, holds only male prisoners, and, unlike many other prisons in the Netherlands, usually has few empty cells.

The reasons for placing FNPs together were twofold. First, in the proposal for the creation of a separate prison regime for FNPs, the former Minister of Security and Justice explicitly stated that

> "this group [CCNCs, JB] differentiates itself from other detainees in that resocialisation aimed at return in the Dutch society is not at stake and principles such as prison leave, regionalisation [placing offenders in a prison near their family members, JB] and detention phasing [placing detainees in more open regimes to prepare them for release, JB] are not applicable."

The prison regime in Ter Apel is considerably more austere than in regular prisons, as most of the activities aimed at preparing prisoners for reintegration are not available here (Boone, 2012a). FNPs are also not eligible for regular early release from prison but can only have their sentence shortened if they agree to be deported. This is related to the second reason for placing FNPs together: it offers better possibilities to work on their deportation during imprisonment. Departure supervisors of the DT&V have their offices located on the prison grounds and regularly meet with FNPs in order to organise their departure from the Netherlands. As such, migration control has become a firmly integrated part of the punishment of FNPs in the Netherlands.

6.3 THE PAINS OF CRIMMIGRATION PRISONS

Building on Sykes' (1958) famous pains of imprisonment, Crewe (2011a, 2015) argues that different prisons lead to different experiences and that even within a prison people might have very different experiences. In order to better understand these differences, he proposes a conceptual framework that comprises four elements that make up the pains of imprisonment. The first element is depth and refers to the feeling of being far away from society, of "being buried way beneath the surface of freedom" (Crewe, 2015, p. 54). The second

4 Parliamentary Documents II 2008/2009, 19637, no. 1263.

element – weight – refers to how imprisonment can be a psychological burden for prisoners, bearing down upon prisoners' shoulders. This is often strongly related to the behaviour of, and relationships with frontline staff. As Ugelvik and Damsa (2018, p. 1029) write, "'weight' is not about prison conditions as such, but the way particular conditions can be seen to communicate something about prisoners' moral status." Next, tightness is related to the increased 'softness' of penal power (Crewe, 2011b), which results in growing emphasis on the responsibility of prisoners to change for the better. Finally, breadth deals with the imposition of continuous disciplinary control after a custodial sentence.

When it comes to penal experiences, FNPs were long considered a forgotten group, but in recent years this has started to change. Several studies have shown how FNPs tend to feel particularly isolated in prison, as they face cultural and language barriers, struggle to stay in touch with family members, and have difficulties obtaining information about prison life and their immigration status (Bhui, 2007; Kaufman, 2015; Ugelvik & Damsa, 2018). Warr (2016) described three distinctive pains experienced by FNPS: the deprivation of certitude, legitimacy, and hope. In a Dutch study conducted before the establishment of the all-foreign prison in Ter Apel, Kox et al (2014) found that FNPs in the Netherlands experienced similar pains as other prisoners. However, there were three additional pains that were explicitly related to their status as unauthorised migrants. First, FNPs struggled considerably more to stay in touch with the outside world. Second, a lack of possibilities to prepare for their release, uncertainty regarding their release date, and the threat of possible deportation created considerable emotional distress. Third, language barriers prevented effective communication with staff members and other prisoners. All these factors considerably aggravated the risk of social isolation for FNPs.

Both Kaufman (2014, 2015) and Ugelvik and Damsa (2018) have explored more directly the role of bordered penality policies and crimmigration prisons for the experiences of FNPs. Writing about England & Wales, Kaufman (2014) shows how under the hubs and spokes policy questions of belonging became part of everyday prison life. As a result, a stigma of being 'foreign' and concerns about deportation played a crucial role in FNPs' daily experiences. She accordingly argues that "policies like hubs and spokes *shape* the 'pains of imprisonment' (p. 139, emphasis added)." Similarly, Ugelvik and Damsa (2018, p. 1040) write about FNPs' experiences in Kongsvinger prison that "the crimmigration prison produces its own specific pains and frustrations." They find three pains specifically related to the crimmigration prison: the pain of discrimination, the pain of long-distance relationships, and the pain of deportability.

Whereas there is the beginning of a body of scholarship on the experiences of FNPs in crimmigration prisons, to date research with prison officers in these institutions is still very limited. The conduct of prison officers is considered to be central to the legitimacy of a prison, and therewith the existence of a safe and humane environment. Liebling (2011) argues that two factors are central to the work of prison officers. First, the importance of relationships between prisoners and prison officers. Second, the challenge of maintaining a balance between "welfare and discipline, or care and power" (p. 485). Research with prison officers in the Netherlands found that besides maintaining order and safety, resocialisation was seen as an important aim of their work. Especially the feeling that they could contribute in a positive way to the future of prisoners was an important part of the satisfaction of the job (Molleman & Van Ginneken, 2013). Indeed, there is some research on prison officers in bordered prisons that found that they often felt uncomfortable with the differential treatment of FNPs and struggled with the lack of traditional justifications of punishment (Bosworth, 2011b).

6.4 Methodology

A total of 37 FNPs were interviewed in Ter Apel prison. Respondents were sampled with the aim of capturing as much diversity as possible, both in terms of national background, age, prison sentence, time spent in the Netherlands before being arrested, and remaining prison time left. The interviews were conducted by different researchers, mostly to enable sampling of respondents who did not have a language in common with the lead researcher. Whereas this greatly increased the number of potential respondents and the diversity of the final sample, factors such as age, gender, nationality, and personality of the interviewers are likely to have influenced the interview and therefore the nature of the data. At the same time, recent research on FNPs in Norway by two completely different researchers suggests such differences do not necessarily lead to different findings (Damsa & Ugelvik, 2017). Moreover, findings that came back in interviews conducted by different researchers can be said to be particularly strong.

Interviews lasted anywhere between twenty minutes and more than an hour. They took place in the offices of the Repatriation and Departure Service, as this was one of the few places inside the prison where one can establish an acceptable level of privacy. Although this sometimes generated some issues of distrust, this could quickly be addressed when researchers explained who they were and what the interview was for. Every respondent signed an informed consent form before the interview started and was given the opportunity to ask questions about the interview, the research project or the researcher. Where possible, respondents were interviewed in their native language or another preferred language; translators were never used. All interviews were recorded and subsequently transcribed, except for two respondents who preferred not to be recorded. Transcripts of interviews in another language than English have been translated by the interviewer.

Interviewing prisoners generally provided rich and thick narrative data on the subjective experiences of FNPs, perceptions of imprisonment in Ter Apel, and the impact this had on their life and future. At the same time, it is important to stress the limitations of primarily relying on verbal exchange, and for example not include participatory observation or other more ethnographic research methods. Respondents certainly had their own agendas during the interviews and might have exaggerated or even made up certain claims. Whereas this is perhaps less relevant when studying prisoners' experiences, particularly critical accounts of prison life in Ter Apel were always corroborated with other FNPs, prison officers, and other staff members for accuracy.

Following the interviews with FNPs, eight semi-structured interviewed were conducted with prison officers working in Ter Apel. All these interviews were conducted in Dutch by the author of this article. Prison officers differed strongly in their age and years of experience. These interviews lasted between forty minutes and almost two hours and all of them have been recorded and subsequently transcribed. All interview transcripts have been analysed and coded according to relevant research themes using the qualitative software program NVivo. Throughout this paper pseudonyms are used to ensure the anonymity of respondents.

6.5 Experiencing the crimmigration prison

One of the defining characteristics of Ter Apel prison is that it acts as a precursor for deportation, with migration control being implemented during imprisonment and little emphasis being placed on educational opportunities and meaningful activities. Many of the opportunities that are available in regular prisons are simply not available in Ter Apel prison. FNPs normally spend the morning at work, while the afternoon is reserved for 'recreation', or vice versa. In order to compensate for the lack of organised activities, and according to some officers reduce the risk of aggressive or disorderly behaviour, FNPs have a comparatively large amount of time labelled as recreation, when they can move around the prison relatively freely. Although officers sometimes organised some activities to improve the quality of life in prison, such as a billiard tournament or sport activities, these were all ad-hoc projects organised by dedicated individuals and not part of any structural framework.

Diversity is high in Ter Apel prison. At the time of research, there were over sixty different nationalities, although there is a clear disproportionate representation of certain countries and regions. This includes former Dutch colony Suriname, Algeria, Morocco, Turkey, Eastern Europe – especially Albania, Poland and Romania – and Colombia. Some of them have lived in the Netherlands for more than twenty years, with a wife and children; others had been arrested upon arrival at the airport and had not spent a minute in the Netherlands as a free person. Some FNPs wanted to leave the Netherlands as soon as possible; others wanted to stay at all costs. As will be further illustrated below, such differences have a direct influence on FNPs' penal experiences.

6.5.1 Prison officers in a crimmigration prison

Most of the interviewed prison officers already worked in Ter Apel prison before it became an all-foreign national prison and therefore had to adapt to these new circumstances. Officers normally largely rely on verbal communication to establish order and maintain safety in the prison, but the cultural and linguistic diversity of the FNP population frequently made it challenging to establish a relationship with the prisoners. Moreover, the aim of their work was no longer the same, as resocialisation is not a part of the prison regime in Ter Apel. Despite these considerable changes, officers had not received any special training or other form of preparation to work with FNPs.

Prison officers all indicated that the specific regime for FNPs meant they sometimes struggled to find meaning and satisfaction in their work. Besides maintaining order and safety in the prison, prison officers normally guide prisoners and prepare them for return into society. For many of them, helping prisoners get their life 'back on track' is an important part of the satisfaction of the job (Molleman & Van Ginneken, 2013). In Ter Apel prison they have very limited possibilities to do so, as formal education and training possibilities are notably absent. As one officer stated, imprisonment was now primarily about "getting them through the days as good as possible until they are deported." Another officer, who had been working in Ter Apel prison since 2008, explained:

> "When we got the FNPs here, for a long time I was looking what my motivation was. Because these men, after serving two-third of their sentence, simply go back to their country of origin and there is no resocialisation programme or anything. So for a very long time I was trying to see: 'what is my own motivation here?' And I still struggle with that. I still find it difficult that these men are simply placed back without any perspective. That I think: what is the motivation here? Because I have no possibilities to do anything for these boys, nothing, nothing."

With all FNPs facing deportation at the end of their sentence, most officers believed their role included preparing prisoners for their return to their country of origin. This mainly consisted of getting FNPs to understand and accept the inevitability of their deportation and trying to make them feel better about returning to their country of origin. Officers lacked the tools and knowledge to do much more. Asked what he tried to do to prepare FNPs for their return to their country of origin, one officer replied:

> "Very little. I wouldn't even know what is going on in such a country. We have over sixty nationalities here, so yeah... Someone goes to Nigeria, how am I supposed to prepare him for that? I wouldn't know."

None of the officers challenged the bifurcated system in itself or the legality of taking away someone's residence permit following a criminal conviction. However, almost all spoke of individual cases that made them struggle with the exclusionary logic of the migration control system. They especially problematised the lack of resocialisation activities for FNPs serving long-term sentences or FNPs they perceived as Dutch. Such cases seemed to collide with their belief in the ideals of second chances and reintegration. As one officer argued:

> "Well look, society wants them out of the country. And, at least partly, I agree with that. But, I do think in a number of cases, I have my doubts. (...) Those are boys who went to school here, they did everything here. They are Dutch, they are really Dutch. They speak the language, often better than most people here in the north. And those are being deported. And then I think: you're taking the wrong one. If you put some energy in them, they'll get to work, and will even be useful to society."

Another officer indicated that because long-term residents had been raised in the Netherlands, Dutch society also has a responsibility towards these people. Such sentiments illustrate the fundamental difference between criminal justice and migration control. Whereas the previous is generally based on temporal exclusion followed by reintegration into society, the latter results in permanent exclusion. Prison officers' occupational belief in resocialisation, derived from the criminal justice system they are part of, therefore sometimes conflicted with the more openly exclusionary outcomes of the migration control system.

6.5.2 Isolation and uncertainty in the crimmigration prison

As described above, studies on FNPs have commonly found that they struggle with feelings of isolation and uncertainty about their migration status and release. Notwithstanding more fundamental criticism of the bifurcated logic of a crimmigration prison, the unique characteristics of the all-foreign prison in Ter Apel actually helped to mitigate these issues to a certain extent. By placing all FNPs in the same prison, it is more likely that prisoners encounter someone from the same country or who speaks the same language. Although the prison administration is careful not to place too many people of the same nationality in the same prison wing, ensuring at least a minimum number of prisoners who speak the same language seemed to prevent feelings of isolation. Most FNPs primarily spent their time with fellow prisoners that come from the same country or region or speak the same language. For example, Zhang (China) explained that he mainly socialised with the few other Chinese prisoners in Ter Apel prison, who had been deliberately placed in the same prison wing by the prison administration:

> "We have a little Chinese community here. We are five of us and we stay together mostly. I do not really speak with people from other cultural background anymore, because you know the scenario is different. There are so many people from different countries and with different backgrounds here, that I really feel that I need to stay with my own people because I feel more comfortable in this way."

For many FNPs, being in the company of prisoners from the same background helped to prevent isolation *within* the prison walls, something I refer to here as *internal* isolation. For example, Mario (Italy) only spoke Italian, a language that is likely to be little spoken in a regular prison in the Netherlands. Although even in Ter Apel prison he was the only Italian, he had found a group of fellow prisoners he could speak with in his own language:

> "I spend most of my time with a group of guys from Albania because they speak Italian, so it is nice, I feel comfortable with them. I am the only Italian in this prison."

Such language-based communities also provided important support to FNPs who did not speak any Dutch or English, as prisoners could act as unofficial translators in conversations with officers or in other situations. Another important aspect of preventing isolation in Ter Apel prison is the opportunity to buy food in the prison grocery store and make use of a communal kitchen facility. Many FNPs were particularly pleased with the opportunity to cook and eat together with fellow prisoners with whom they shared the same cultural background, reflecting the importance of food in performing identity work in crimmigration prisons (Ugelvik, 2011). However, only FNPs with sufficient financial means could profit from this possibility – others had to eat the standard microwaved prison meals.

Whereas concentrating FNPs in one prison thus helped to reduce feelings of internal isolation, many FNPs reported strong feelings of *external* isolation: they were far away from the people who were most important to them. The location of the prison plays an important role in this. Whereas prisoners are normally incarcerated in facilities close to their homes, this does not apply to FNPs. As there is only one designated foreign national prison in the Netherlands, any prisoner without the right to stay in the country is automatically send there. Although the Netherlands is a relatively small country, Ter Apel prison is located in a rather remote area, far away from the major cities and the main international airports. This creates an extra obstacle for relatives living abroad who want to visit. As Nick (Suriname) said: "We've been taken away the visits from family, it's very hard." Although visiting rules are interpreted more flexible in Ter Apel prison than in regular prisons, FNPs still receive considerable less visitors than other prisoners. Attempts were made to address this issue, for example by allowing FNPs time on Skype, but this was still rather limited due to the few computers available.

There might appear to be a certain logic to the exclusion of FNPs from the right to be incarcerated close to their home. After all, they are foreigners who are perceived to be not living in the Netherlands. However, many FNPs have been living in the Netherlands for a considerable amount of time, often with family members. In most cases, these people live in one of the major cities in the western part of the country, far away from Ter Apel. This makes it complicated for their loved ones to regularly visit them. For example, Bajram's (Kosovo) wife and child lived in the southwest of the Netherlands. He had previously been imprisoned near the town where they lived, but with the creation of a specific prison for FNPs, he had been relocated to Ter Apel prison. Since then, the number of times they visited him had considerably declined.

> "You see, my family lives in [city], which is about 280 kilometres from here. And the little one goes to school and in the weekend there are never visits here. So they came once, one time in eight weeks, and that is it."

As Ugelvik and Damsa (2018) note, the 'depth' of imprisonment always relates to a 'surface', which is not simply the world directly outside the prison walls, but rather where their family and other loved ones are. The isolated location of Ter Apel therefore significantly contributes to the experience of 'deep' imprisonment.

Besides isolation, another commonly reported pain of FNPs in existing studies is the uncertainty about how and when their detention will end (Turnbull & Hasselberg, 2017; Warr, 2016). FNPs are often not sure whether they will be deported, released or get transferred to migration detention. Prison officers are generally not equipped or knowledgeable enough to deal with these issues. In Ter Apel prison these issues are at least to a certain extent addressed by the presence of departure supervisors of the DT&V. While the constant presence of DT&V provides FNPs with a stark reminder of the ultimate aim of their imprisonment, departure supervisors are often able to provide FNPs with valuable information about their migration case. Especially for FNPs who actually want to return to their country of origin, collaboration with DT&V means they often know in an early stage the final date of their prison sentence and return to their country of origin. For example, Diego (Ecuador) had a Spanish residence permit and wanted to return to Spain as soon as possible. By cooperating with DT&V, his departure supervisor had been able to quickly organise his return and inform him about his release date:

> "I have everything prepared. I was sentenced to four years, and I have to stay here for 22 months. They asked me where I wanted to go after my sentence was done, and I said to Spain, and now everything is ready."

With migration control already implemented during the execution of the penal phase, there is also less chance that FNPs are transferred to immigration detention after their prison sentence. Crimmigration – understood as the intertwinement of processes of crime control and migration control – can thus have favourable outcomes compared to when these two procedures would be executed consecutively. However, this mainly applies to FNPs who are willing to leave the Netherlands. For respondents who wanted to stay in the Netherlands, the threat of deportation was the most important pain they experienced (for a more in-depth discussion of these specific pains of deportation, see: Di Molfetta and Brouwer (2019)).

6.5.3 Identity and belonging in the crimmigration prison

A key function of any carceral institution is stripping away prisoners' identity and imposing on them a new 'prisoner' identity (Goffman, 1961). Crimmigration prisons, however, impose a specific kind of identity upon their prisoners. With only non-citizens transferred to these institutions, and the absence of resocialisation activities, they play a role in shaping and enforcing the boundaries of membership: what is at stake is who belongs and who does not (Aas, 2014). Incarceration in Ter Apel accordingly no longer only communicates moral condemnation, but also that one does not belong (Kaufman, 2014). This exclusionary logic was clearly felt by FNPs. In the words of Bajram (Kosovo):

> "I have been in prison before, but here you are treated differently, they look at you differently. You are seen here as an alien."

As Ugelvik and Damsa (2018, p. 1039) argue,

> "the experience of being singled out and consigned to a special prison for foreign nationals adds 'weight' because it contributes to a perception of being unwanted and of being the victim of discrimination."

Similar to their study, in Ter Apel prison references to discrimination and racism were common – this encompassed the wider penal policy and the Dutch criminal justice system. Opinions regarding prison officers in Ter Apel were rather mixed, ranging from accusations of discrimination and racism to positive assessments of their friendliness and professionalism. David (Serbia) explained:

> "In a Dutch prison, whatever problem you have they suddenly fix it; you just have to talk with the prison staff. While here, nothing happens, they just make you lose time. But not all of them. There are some people in the prison staff that are very helpful and nice, but some of them are a bit racist I think. Or perhaps it is just the mentality here in the north, in this part of the Netherlands."

Further weight is added to the prison experience in Ter Apel, because FNPs enjoy fewer rights and privileges than other prisoners in the Netherlands. Many respondents believed they were deliberately being punished extra harshly because of their status as foreigners. They regularly emphasised how other prisons in the Netherlands, but also in other European countries, were considerably better than Ter Apel prison. Respondents particularly criticised the lack of meaningful resocialisation activities, which made it extra hard for them to accept their imprisonment.

> "If I'm sitting in a Dutch normal prison, I will put my attention to 'onderwijs' [education, JB], to school, to learn something. But here you have nothing, even the work is not serious work." (Hamdi, Albania)

> "When you commit a mistake, you have to pay for it, you have to deal with it. But they should help us to do so, but it is not the case: when you come out, you will do so with more rage and anger than before. That's my summary: this prison is not doing what it should for helping us reintegrating into society after paying our debt." (Jose, Colombia)

FNPs responded to this in different ways. In particular, there were considerable differences between FNPs who saw themselves as foreigners and those who believed they had the right to stay in the Netherlands. The first group perceived the bifurcation policy as fundamentally unfair, as they believed that all prisoners should enjoy the same rights, regardless of their citizenship status. These FNPs frequently invoked experiences or stories they had heard about other European countries, where non-citizens supposedly enjoy equal rights and no formal distinction was made on the basis of nationality or citizenship. For example, Carlos (Colombia) was born in Colombia, but had a Spanish resident permit. He claimed that whereas in Spain FNPs are treated the same as all other prisoners, in the Netherlands this was not the case.

> "In Spain, foreigners are given the chance to go home and come back to the prison. In Spain they want to rehabilitate you; that you study, that you work. It would seem that they only want more delinquents here. I have been working my entire life, and when I came here, I said to myself: 'Ok, I will fulfil my duty.' I am a prisoner here, but being so I would like to learn a job or study, but they won't give me that option, that's just for Dutch people. The only thing they do here is creating more criminals."

These FNPs saw their differential treatment compared to Dutch prisoners as illegitimate, but did not necessarily contest their presence in an all foreign prison in itself. This was different for prisoners who self-identified as Dutch, often because they had been living in the Netherlands since a very young age or because their family was living there. Many had spent time in other Dutch prisons, either during previous sentences or before they were transferred to Ter Apel prison, and contrasted these experiences with their current situation.

These FNPs felt they did not receive the same treatment as Dutch prisoners, which they not only perceived as unfair, but also emphasised their feeling of otherness and reminded them they do not belong. They did not necessarily question the legitimacy of a separate prison for FNPs, but instead contested their own placement there. As Yusuf (Turkey), who had been living in the Netherlands for twenty-eight years, asserted:

> "I do not belong here. I have lived my whole life here [in the Netherlands, JB] and now I spend my days around illegals and I am being treated as an illegal."

As with the respondents in Hasselberg's (2014) study, most of these men accepted their time in prison as a punishment for their crimes. What they rejected was their categorisation as non-member, communicated through their imprisonment in Ter Apel (cf. Kaufman & Bosworth, 2013). Explaining his frustration about the way he was treated by the state, Hakim (Morocco) explained:

> "I didn't have that before. Before, when I get locked up for something, I was like: 'Hakim, you did it, done deal, shut up'. So you see, you just accept it."

FNPs who had grown up in the Netherlands or in exceptional cases where even born there, felt they did not belong in a prison for foreign nationals. In an all foreign prison, those who see themselves as citizen, end up feeling foreign.

6.6 Conclusion and discussion

This article has analysed the penal regime for FNPs in the Netherlands and examined how this is experienced and understood by both prison officers and FNPs. I have argued that this penal regime is very similar to what has been observed in Norway and England & Wales and constitutes a prime example of bordered penality. The most obvious expression of this is the crimmigration prison in Ter Apel, which is clearly aimed at deportation instead of resocialisation. The empirical data subsequently illustrated how both the characteristics of this specific institution and the wider penal regime play a key role in shaping the experiences of both prison officers and FNPs.

Prison officers struggled with their occupational identity and job satisfaction, finding it often hard to find real meaning in their work. Moreover, at time the exclusionary logic of immigration control collided with their belief in resocialisation and second chances. For FNPs, the prison in Ter Apel hampers the ability to stay in touch with loved ones, while the regime itself lacks meaningful activities. FNPs responded in different ways to the particularities of the crimmigration prison regime, reflecting the wide diversity within this group. Those who did not see themselves as legitimate residents of the Netherlands primarily contested the sober regime and lack of resocialisation activities available in Ter Apel, criticising the parallel penal system for FNPs. Respondents who perceived themselves as legitimate residents reacted in a different way to their imprisonment in a crimmigration prison. For these men, it challenged their very sense of identity and belonging.

The general absence of meaningful activities in Ter Apel prison and the lack of attention for resocialisation raises serious questions about the legitimacy of crimmigration prisons, especially because some FNPs serve very long prison sentences. Whereas the logic behind this approach is that FNPs do not return to Dutch society, they always do return to *a* society. As Boone and Kox (2012) note, the Dutch supreme court ruled already in 1987 that non-Dutch prisoners have the right to resocialisation, no matter which society they will return to. Moreover, a substantial number of FNPs are eventually released in the Netherlands again. More emphasis on resocialisation and preparing FNPs for their return to society would likely considerably improve the prison experiences of both FNPs and prison officers. At the same time, this would raise important questions about the difference in treatment between FNPs and other unauthorised migrants without a criminal conviction, as the latter group is generally totally exempt from any form of state support and immigration detention is very sober.

Bordered penality, and crimmigration in general, has often been critiqued on a fundamental level, as the blurring of two distinct legal domains is seen as undesirable on the ground of legal principles (Stumpf, 2006). It is argued that crimmigration leads to a more punitive approach towards migrants, while procedural protections embedded in the criminal justice system are often absent in the administrative migration control system. This is clearly visible in the bordered penality constellation: FNPs enjoy fewer rights than regular prisoners, resulting in a more sober prison regime and therefore an objectively harsher form of punishment. At the same time, not all elements of the crimmigration prison negatively affect FNPs. For many respondents, being placed in prison together with other FNPs helped to address some of the commonly identified pains experienced by FNPs, especially social isolation. Moreover, FNPs who are not opposed to return to their country of origin benefit on some levels from the far-reaching integration of punishment and migration control in Ter Apel prison, as it prevents uncertainty and unnecessary time in immigration detention. This is a nuance that has so far remained unexplored in the literature on bordered penality and crimmigration.

In today's globalising world, unless one entirely rejects the legitimacy of deporting FNPs, there will always be individuals falling simultaneously under the criminal justice system and the migration control system. This raises the question how these people should be treated by a state that seeks to both punish and deport them. While the bordered penality constellation in the Netherlands still exacerbates the pains of imprisonment for FNPs in several crucial ways, it might also offer some starting points for thinking about a better approach.

7 Can I stay or should I go?

The deportation of criminally convicted non-citizens in the Netherlands[1]

7.1 Introduction

In recent years many Western states have made what has been referred to as a 'deportation turn' (Gibney, 2008). As return of unauthorised migrants to their country of origin is increasingly seen as a crucial part of migration policy, many governments have strengthened their return enforcement (Rosenberger & Koppes, 2018). Besides rejected asylum seekers and unauthorised migrants, criminally convicted non-citizens (CCNCs)[2] are an important group targeted for return. Yet enforcing returns is often complicated, resulting in what is termed a deportation gap: a difference between the number of migrants targeted for return and those who actually leave the territory of the host country (Gibney, 2008). There are several reasons for this gap, which has been observed for decades: uncooperative countries of origin, concerns about the safety of migrants upon return, or difficulties with establishing a migrant's identity and nationality (Broeders & Engbersen, 2007). Migrants can also decide to resist their own return. In the absence of valid identity and travel documents, migrants who do not wish to return can try to obstruct their own deportation, by refusing to give up their identity and nationality or providing false information. As a result, many states are struggling with the existence of a group of so-called 'undeportable deportable migrants' (Leerkes & Broeders, 2010) or 'undesirable but unreturnable migrants' (Cantor, Van Wijk, Singer, & Bolhuis, 2017).

States have employed a range of tactics to increase the effectiveness of their return policies, ranging from trying to become more effective in their own organisational chain and making deals with countries of origin to policies aimed at increasing cooperation with return among unauthorised migrants (Rosenberger & Koppes, 2018). Regarding the latter, a range of policies have been adopted aimed at stimulating non-citizens to agree with their return

1 Under review for publication in Migration Studies, as: J. Brouwer. Can I stay or should I go? The deportation of criminally convicted non-citizens in the Netherlands.

2 In this paper, criminally convicted non-citizen (CCNC) refers to a non-citizen with a criminal conviction and without legal stay in the host country. This can be because he/she had no legal stay to begin with or because his/her legal stay was revoked as a consequence of his/her criminal conviction. It does not include legally staying foreigners with a criminal conviction.

decision and leave the country where they are staying, preferably without the use of force (Cleton & Chauvin, 2019). As Walters (2016, p. 438) suggests, the aim "is to provide a sufficient level of material inducement such that the migrant places themselves on the plane, without the need for guards, restraints or any spectacle of enforcement." Leerkes, Van Os & Boersema (2017, p. 8) refer to this as 'soft deportation' to acknowledge

> "that such return has deportation-like properties, while acknowledging that it depends less on force and deterrence, and more on perceived legitimacy and – should the return be 'assisted' – on payments."

States try to achieve soft deportation through both carrots, such as financial and reintegration assistance, and sticks, such as the threat of detention or policies aimed at making life in the host country as complicated as possible (Brouwer, 2018).

The incentives used to achieve cooperation with return can come from a variety of policy domains. For CCNCs, elements from the criminal justice system are increasingly employed to realise deportation. Such developments fit within the larger trend of crimmigration, a term used to refer to the merging of the previously largely separate systems of crime control and migration control (Stumpf, 2006; Van der Woude, Van der Leun, & Nijland, 2014). Not only have migratory acts increasingly been criminalised, the criminal justice system has also adopted practices and aims that are traditionally within the domain of migration control (Aas, 2014). In the area of punishment and deportation, two developments stand out: criminal convictions lead more easily to migration consequences, while criminal punishment is increasingly designed to result in deportation. The latter can be seen in the creation of special prisons and the adoption of specific release policies for CCNCs (Kaufman, 2014; Turnbull & Hasselberg, 2017; Ugelvik & Damsa, 2018).

To date very few studies have been conducted on the legal and social situation of criminal deportees in Europe (Cantor et al., 2017). And although there is a growing body of research on the determinants of return of a wide range of different migrant groups, empirical research into the experiences of CCNCs and how these experiences relate to return intentions is still limited. Yet, as Bosworth (2012, p. 127) argues, "first-hand accounts from detainees can flesh out the burden of living without citizenship while appreciating how these individuals try to assert alternative, identity-based claims." This article therefore aims to start filling this gap, by means of a case study of the Netherlands. In recent years, the country has not only repeatedly restricted its policy on deportations following a criminal conviction, but also introduced a variety of policies aimed at increasing the return rate of CCNCs. It has created a dedicated prison for CCNCs, embedded with so-called departure supervisors of the Repatriation and Departure Service (DT&V), the central government agency responsible for organising the return of unauthorised migrants. Despite these significant developments, empirical research on CCNCs in the Netherlands is non-existent (Bolhuis, Battjes, & van Wijk, 2017).

Drawing on extensive empirical research, this article seeks to provide insight into what policies aimed at the deportation of CCNCs look like, how they are implemented by departure supervisors, and what role they play in CCNCs' intentions and decisions regarding return. The first paragraph below discusses the Dutch criminal deportation regime, highlighting how over the last decade an increasing number of migrants have become subjected to criminal deportation and how the state is trying to achieve deportation. This is followed by a discussion of the available literature on return migration, including the various factors influencing return decisions. After a brief methodological paragraph, the empirical section of this paper examines how departure supervisors try to achieve return of CCNCs, how this is understood and experienced by CCNCs, and to what extent this affects their willingness to cooperate with return. The article finishes with a conclusion and a discussion of the effectiveness of increasingly restrictive policies dealing with CCNCs.

7.2 The Dutch criminal deportation regime

There are two elements to the Dutch criminal deportation regime: 1) the decision to revoke someone's right to stay following a criminal conviction, and 2) the policies aimed at effectuating return. Both elements underwent significant changes in recent years.

7.2.1 Losing your residence permit following a criminal conviction

In the Netherlands, whether a criminal conviction results in withdrawal of a residence permit is decided on the basis of a sliding scale policy that takes into account the seriousness of the offense and the duration of legal residence. The sliding scale is thus a balancing act between the interests of society and those of individual CCNCs. The basic presumption of this policy is that the longer someone lives in the Netherlands, the more serious the offense needs to be to terminate his/her legal stay. This stems from the idea that over time immigrants build up considerable social ties in their new country and deportation should therefore gradually warrant more serious criminal conduct (Stronks, 2013). In recent years the policy has repeatedly been restricted, most notably in 2002, 2010, and 2012 (Stronks, 2013; Van der Woude et al., 2014). The sliding scale policy has also become considerably more complicated, with separate scales for serious crimes and repeat offenders.

Until 2002, legally staying migrants living in the Netherlands for less than three years could lose their residence permit following a conviction for an offense punishable by nine months of imprisonment. Following the changes in 2012, this threshold has been lowered to one day of imprisonment.[3] And whereas previously anyone staying legally in the Netherlands for twenty years or more could no longer be deported, this is no longer the case, as the end term of the scale has been removed. After fifteen years of legal residence, non-citizens can lose their residence permit following repeated convictions or following a conviction to 65 months of imprisonment for a violent, sexual or drug offence.[4] This means that offenders who came to the Netherlands at a young age and never obtained Dutch citizenship, remain eligible for deportation later in life (Stronks, 2013). Denizens – lawful permanent residents who for whatever reason do not obtain legal citizenship (Golash-Boza, 2016) – are thus "eternal guests" (Kanstroom, 2000, p. 1907) with an interminable form of "probationary membership" (Stumpf, 2006, p. 401). These restrictions have been motivated by a clear crime control rationale. In a 2009 letter informing parliament about the second round of proposed restrictions, the Minister of Justice wrote:

> "Reducing crime and improving security in the Netherlands are important objectives of the government. In this letter, the government presents its vision on the migration law-based public order policy. (...) This vision is linked to the measure taken by the government to contribute to fighting crime among foreign nationals in the Netherlands."[5]

These repeated restrictions have not been without effect. An impact evaluation study in 2012 estimated that the percentage of foreigners with a criminal conviction falling within the scope of the sliding scale policy increased from 6.9% in 2009 to 35.1% in 2012, although this was partly driven by a growing number of foreigners convicted for serious crimes. The number of terminations of lawful residence are estimated to have increased from 69 in 2002 to 475 in 2012. This is an increase from 0.6% of the total population of foreigners with a criminal conviction to 3.4% of this population and includes a significant increase in the number of long-term legal residents. The increase is to a certain extent limited by the need for the state, arising from European human rights law and provisions, to prove in each individual case that the revocation is proportionate, balancing the interests of society with personal consequences for the concerned individual. This includes assessing the cultural and social

---

3 April 17, 2012, Official Gazette of the Kingdom of the Netherlands, no. 158.

4 Following Article 3.86 Alien Decree 2000, there are various reasons to withdraw the residence permit of a foreigner legally residing in the Netherlands for more than fifteen years. The first option is a conviction for at least 65 months for a violent, sexual or drug offense. The second option is a combined total of fourteen months if imprisonment for a repeat offender who committed at least three criminal offenses. The third option is 48 month of imprisonment for an offense qualified as 'serious crime'. This can be either drug trafficking or a serious violent or sexual offense.

5 Parliamentary Documents II 2009/2010, 19637, no. 1306.

connection with the Netherlands and the right to respect for private and family life (Berdowski & Vennekens, 2014).

Besides deportation, CCNCs are issued an entry ban for the entire EU/EEA and Switzerland for a period of five, ten, or twenty years.[6] Individuals who cannot be issued such an entry ban – in most cases because they are EU-citizens – are pronounced 'undesirable alien' and barred from entering the Netherlands for a period of time, usually five or ten years.[7] Whereas illegal stay in the Netherlands itself is not a criminal offense, article 197 of the Dutch criminal code does criminalise staying in the Netherlands after having been issued an entry ban or being pronounced an undesirable alien. This act is punishable with six months of imprisonment, but punishment can only be imposed when all return procedures have failed. In other words, deportation takes primacy over punishment. This highlights the instrumental nature of such crimmigration laws and policies (cf. Sklansky, 2012).

7.2.2 Ensuring the deportation of criminally convicted non-citizens

As CCNCs constitute a priority group in the Dutch return policy, the government puts in considerable efforts to ensure they are deported. To that end, a specialised department has been created within the DT&V that deals with CCNCs. Moreover, through the adoption of the so-called VRIS-protocol,[8] better cooperation has been established between the various agencies of the criminal justice system and migration control system, such as the Alien Police, the Immigration and Naturalisation Service (IND), the Custodial Institutions Agency (DJI) and DT&V. The main aim of this protocol is to more effectively detect criminal non-citizens and make sure they are deported immediately after they have served their criminal sentence.

One outcome of the VRIS-protocol has been the creation of a prison that exclusively holds CCNCs, also referred to as a 'crimmigration prison' (Ugelvik & Damsa, 2018). This prison is located in the small village of Ter Apel, in the somewhat remote northeast of the country (Di Molfetta & Brouwer, 2019). Ter Apel is primarily known for housing the country's central asylum reception centre. The prison is located on the same terrain as this reception centre, making Ter Apel not only a symbolic point of entry for asylum seekers, but also a symbolic point of exit for former asylum seekers and other foreigners who have been convicted of a criminal offense and lost their right to stay in the Netherlands. The prison's regime is specifically focussed on encouraging CCNCs to return to their country of origin. To that end, departure supervisors

6 Article 66A Alien Act 2000. This is the Dutch implementation of the 2008 EU Return Directive.

7 Article 67 Alien Act 2000.

8 VRIS stands for Alien in the Criminal Justice Chain (Vreemdeling in de Strafrechtsketen).

have their offices located inside the prison. Their aim is to organise the return of CCNCs, preferably directly upon completion of their prison sentence and without the use of force. To that end, they enjoy considerable discretionary freedom in dealing with CCNCs (Cleton & Chauvin, 2019). Departure supervisors do not have any decision-making power, as the decision to revoke someone's right to stay is made by the IND.

To stimulate CCNCs to cooperate with their own return, a new release policy was introduced in 2012. Since then, CCNCs are excluded from the regular procedures dealing with early release from prison. Instead, a separate system was introduced called 'sentence suspension' – *strafonderbreking*, or SOB in Dutch. Under this policy, CCNCs can be granted early release *only* when they agree to leave the Netherlands directly from prison. Moreover, if they subsequently return to the Netherlands, they will need to serve the remainder of their sentence. The government has repeatedly stated that the measure is aimed at increasing CCNCs' willingness to leave the Netherlands and to stimulate them to cooperate with their own identification and return.[9] Both the crimmigration prison and the SOB-measure are key examples of how the criminal justice system is increasingly being employed to achieve aims in the field of migration control.

7.3 THEORETICAL BACKGROUND

In recent years there has been a growing body of literature dealing with return migration, including research specifically focussing on return decisions (Brouwer, 2018; Koser & Kuschminder, 2015; Leerkes et al., 2017). Most of this research conceptualises return migration, like initial migration decisions, as the result of a combination of the aspiration and ability to return (Carling & Schewel, 2018). As Schewel (2019, p. 7) argues, "the aspiration-capability framework holds promise because it provides the conceptual tools to analyse processes that lead to both mobility and immobility outcomes." In this context, aspiration refers to the willingness of a migrant to return to his/her country of origin, while ability refers to the possibility to actually do so (Carling & Schewel, 2018). However, for migrants facing forced return, the conceptualisation of ability changes. As the host state intends to return them against their will if they do not leave the country on their own, it refers to the ability of the host state to return a migrant to his/her country of origin and not to a migrant's individual ability to move to another place.

Both aspiration and ability are the result of an interaction between individual characteristics and perceptions, and macro-level social, economic, cultural, and political factors (Brouwer, 2018; Schewel, 2019). When it comes

9 Parliamentary Documents 2016/2017, 19637, no. 2335

to forced return, migrants generally possess very little agency, rendering it questionable to use the term return 'decision'. Migrants might successfully resist their deportation, by refusing to cooperate with the state's identification proceedings, but the best possible outcome is continued illegal stay in the host country. Leerkes, Galloway and Kromhout (2010) therefore speak of having to choose between the lesser of two evils, while Klaver, Telli and Witvliet (2015) summarize this as a trade-off between the perceived life opportunities in the country of origin and the perceived life opportunities as an unauthorised migrant in the host country. This trade-off is informed by a wide array of different factors related to the personal situation of the migrant, current life in the destination country, and the perceived situation in the country of origin. Important factors that have been identified are the perceived risk of forced return, the perceived safety in the country of origin, and a migrants' social network, in particular direct family members (Brouwer, 2018; Leerkes et al., 2017). Research also finds that the longer someone lives in a place, the less likely it becomes they will leave, as people build up both social and economic connections (Schewel, 2019).

Particularly relevant for this article is a recent study by Leerkes and Kox (2017), who looked at the effect of deterrence and perceived legitimacy of immigration detention on continued illegal stay. They found that migrants made a sort of cost-benefit analysis to see whether immigration detention was worth continued stay in the Netherlands. However, migrants who developed more positive return intentions during their time in immigration detention not only mentioned the hardships of detention as an important reason to decide to return, but also perceived their detention as more legitimate. This led the authors to argue that compliance with return decisions is most likely "when the *product* of perceived severity, perceived certainty and perceived legitimacy reaches a kind of optimum (p. 904)." Translated to the situation of CCNCs, it could be argued that a similar kind of trade-off needs to be made. Because of the SOB-measure, they effectively have to make a trade-off between a longer time in prison and life as an unauthorised migrant on the one hand, and deportation on the other hand. The question is then which state intervention is perceived as more painful.

Regarding deterrence, criminological research has long stressed that imprisonment brings with it a set of distinct 'pains' in the form of a number of deprivations (Crewe, 2011; Sykes, 1958). Recent research has found that foreign prisoners often experience a distinct set of pains, which are related to their status as foreigner in the criminal justice system and their immigration status (Ugelvik & Damsa, 2018; Warr, 2016). Deportation, on the other hand, is legally speaking a preventive measure and not a form of punishment. The same applies to the entry ban and undesirable alien pronunciations. However, it has been argued that since it is so directly linked to a criminal conviction and often perceived as punishment, it cannot be seen as merely an administrative practice, but instead creates a form of double punishment (Di Molfetta &

Brouwer, 2019; Turnbull & Hasselberg, 2017). Kanstroom (2000) has in this regard argued for a distinction between deportation that is part of *border control* and deportation that is part of *social control.* He argues that the second form of deportation, based on post-entry criminal conduct, "is more analogous to criminal law and often seems more punitive than regulatory" (p. 1898).

Regarding legitimacy, criminal justice studies have long shown that the perceived legitimacy of the law, legal actors, and legal procedures is at least as important in achieving compliance as coercion and deterrence stemming from potential sanctions (Tyler, 2003). Studies focussing on return migration have also stressed the importance of fairness and legitimacy in order for migrants to cooperate with return (Van Alphen, Molleman, Leerkes, & Van Hoek, 2013). When people believe that rules are fair and that they are enforced in a just manner by trusted actors, they are more likely to follow these rules or accept the outcome of legal proceedings. A lack of perceived legitimacy, on the other hand, may result in resistance (Leerkes & Kox, 2017).

7.4 Methodology

This paper draws on data collected for a research project on the punishment and deportation of CCNCs in the Netherlands. Empirical data was collected between April and September 2016 and consists of 37 in-depth interviews with foreign national prisoners and seventeen interviews with departure supervisors.[10] All interviews with CCNCs were conducted in Ter Apel prison, whereas interviews with departure supervisors took place in both this prison and the prison at Schiphol International Airport. Nearly all CCNCs are imprisoned in these two prisons: the prison at Schiphol International Airport primarily houses foreigners in pre-trial detention, whereas convicted male FNPs are moved to Ter Apel prison. Departure supervisors of the DT&V have offices in both these prisons. Besides these formal interviews, for a period of about one and a half year (February 2015-September 2016) and on an irregular basis, I spent an average of one day per week at the offices of DT&V at Schiphol. Here I could read transcripts of departure talks between departure supervisors and CCNCs, observe everyday working activities, and hold informal conversations with departure supervisors and managers. I also observed several interviews of departure supervisors with CCNCs and a presentation of several men at a consulate aimed at establishing their nationality. This relatively long-term informal fieldwork period provided me with great insights in the day-to-day operations of organising return.

Formal semi-structured interviews with CCNCs and departure supervisors were conducted towards the end of this fieldwork period. CCNCs were sampled

10 I also conducted interviews with prison officers but have not used these for this specific paper.

with the aim of capturing as much diversity as possible in terms of nationality, age, prison sentence, remaining prison time left and time spent in the Netherlands. Every respondent signed an informed consent form before the interview started and was given the opportunity to ask questions about the interview, the research project or the researcher. Interviews lasted between twenty minutes and more than an hour. Where possible respondents were interviewed in their native language or another preferred language; translators were never used. To that end, the interviews were conducted by different researchers. Whereas this greatly increased the number of potential respondents and the diversity of the final sample, factors such as age, gender, nationality, and personality of the interviewers are likely to have influenced the interview and therefore the nature of the data. At the same time, recent research on CCNCs in Norway by two completely different researchers suggests that such differences do not necessarily lead to different findings (Damsa & Ugelvik, 2017). Moreover, findings that came back in interviews collected by different researchers can be said to be particularly strong.

Interviewed departure supervisors all worked for the team dealing with CCNCs. They differed in their years of experience and some also worked with other migrants groups, such as rejected asylum seekers. These interviews lasted between forty minutes and two hours. I conducted some of these interviews alone, while others were conducted together with another researcher. All of the interviews, both with CCNCs and departure supervisors, were recorded and transcribed verbatim, except for two CCNCs who preferred not to be recorded. In those cases notes were taken during the interview, which were turned into a detailed interview report immediately after the interview. Transcripts of interviews in another language than English have been translated by the interviewer. For the data analysis, all interview transcripts have been coded according to relevant research themes using the qualitative software program NVivo.

7.5 The implementation and lived experiences of criminal deportation

Compared to other migrant groups, the return rate for CCNCs in the Netherlands is relatively high and has slightly increased since 2012. In recent years, more than 75% of CCNCs who had completed their criminal sentence were subsequently deported. The slight decrease in 2015 is primarily the result of a dispute between the Netherlands and Morocco, as a result of which the Moroccan authorities refused to take back any citizens. To compare, for all unauthorised migrants combined the return rate was 52% in 2016 and 42% in 2017.[11] At the same time, this also means that around 25% of the CCNCs are eventually released into Dutch society again as unauthorised migrants.

11 Kerncijfers Asiel en Migratie.

Year	Total released	In the Netherlands	Deported	Deported (%)
2018	1.140	250	890	78%
2017	1.150	250	890	77%
2016	1.090	240	850	78%
2015	1.200	300	900	75%
2014	1.220	260	960	79%
2013	1.120	260	860	77%
2012	910	220	690	76%
2011	800	220	580	72%
2010	780	220	550	70%

Table 7.1 Release and return, 2010 – 2017, numbers rounded to tens[12]

7.5.1 When the state is able to deport: "I have little hope they will release me here"

Organising return involves first and foremost planning all practical arrangements necessary for departure. This can be a straightforward process when a CCNC possesses a valid travel document and is accepted by his/her country of origin. Departure supervisors indicated that this was often the case, which meant that organising return posed little problems. This means that for many CCNCs structural factors determine whether they will leave the Netherlands after completing their criminal sentence, and their agency is limited to the conditions of their return. Respondents who cooperated with their own return therefore showed different degrees of voluntariness, depending on the perceived painfulness of deportation.

Whereas most academic literature on deportation describes this as a painful and violent state interference (Turnbull & Hasselberg, 2017), a relatively large number of interviewed CCNCs actually did not perceive their deportation as such. Because these respondents often had family members in their country of origin, they wanted to leave prison as soon as possible and were sometimes explicitly looking forward to their return. Not surprisingly, this was especially the case for respondents who had no family or other social attachments in

12 Data about the return of unauthorised migrants is published on the website of the DT&V (http://www.dienstterugkeerenvertrek.nl/mediatheek/vertrekcijfers/index.aspx). The statistics for CCNCs come from the bi-annual Rapportage Vreemdelingenketen (Report of the Immigration Chain).

the Netherlands, as was often the case for CCNCs who had been arrested at the border or who had only been in the Netherlands for a relatively short period of time. Mario (Italy), for example, had been arrested two hours after arriving in the Netherlands. Since most of his social life was in Italy and he had no desire to stay in the Netherlands or return in the future, he was looking forward to leave prison and return to his country of origin:

> "I cannot wait more to come back to Italy. I told them to send me to Italy straight away and give me ten years of entry ban in the Netherlands. I don't care at all about staying in the Netherlands."

The same applied to various respondents who had been arrested at Schiphol International Airport for attempted drug smuggling and either had a family to support in their country of origin or had reasons to not be too worried about return. John (Suriname) was one of them, serving a prison sentence of thirty months for attempted drug smuggling – something he readily confessed he did. He had no desire to stay in the Netherlands and could return to his old job in Suriname, where he also still had an apartment. At the time of the interview, he was even considering giving up his ongoing appeal process so that he could return shortly with SOB (in order to qualify for SOB, the criminal process needs to be finalised). Such examples illustrate that whereas deportation is a painful state interference for those who have their loved ones in the country they are deported from, it can actually be a form of relief for those who are imprisoned and have family in their country of origin. In other words, the painfulness of deportation is highly subjective and dependent on a range of personal factors.

Whereas some respondents were actively looking forward to leaving the Netherlands, this was definitely not the case for all. One of the respondents who struggled with this was Milos (Bosnia and Herzegovina). As a child, he had been granted asylum in the Netherlands. Repeated convictions for minor offences meant he had never been able to obtain Dutch citizenship, but he was a legal permanent resident. Because his residence permit had been revoked following his last conviction for a violent crime, he now faced deportation to Bosnia and Herzegovina. Whereas he preferred to stay in the Netherlands, he still had family in Bosnia and Herzegovina who could accommodate him, making return slightly less daunting. As he was contemplating whether to cooperate with his own return, he took into account the possibility of early release with SOB and his chances of actually staying in the Netherlands if he would not cooperate:

> "Because on the other hand, I am thinking about it like this: my residence permit has been revoked and my appeal has been dismissed, so there is little left to do about that. And I have little hope that, even if I serve my full sentence, they will release me here. I don't think they will put someone without papers on the street. For all I know, you could serve your whole sentence and be deported anyway.

And I've nearly served half of my sentence now, so that's why I am thinking about SOB."

Quite importantly, Milos did not downright disagree with his deportation. Although he struggled with accepting this, he tried to understand the situation from the state's perspective. This seemed to help him to accept it.

> "I don't think it is really fair. But well, I have also done things that are unacceptable. So yes, I try to weigh this against each other. I have a long criminal record, I have been in prison before. (…) My mum always warned me: 'be careful, don't do all these crazy things'. But well, you hang out with the wrong people. You do things that are not okay. You get arrested, go to prison. And well, it did not happen once or twice. And that is what they look at."

It was clear that Milos had little hope that he would be able to avoid deportation, a sentiment echoed by many other CCNCs. The institutional setting of Ter Apel prison – with its remote location, sober regime without resocialisation activities, and especially the permanent presence of departure supervisors – played an important role in this. Speaking specifically about the remote location of the prison, Khalid (the Netherlands) said:

> "They did that on purpose. If you look closely, they did that on purpose, that you don't get any visits. You understand? You are being stressed and then you will give up. You understand?"

Several respondents believed the system to be designed as tough as possible on purpose to 'break their resistance' and make them cooperate with return. Departure supervisors generally believed that the institutional setting contributes to CCNCs believing that they are permanently excluded from the Dutch society and that deportation is inevitable, and therefore has a considerable deterrent effect. As one of them explained when asked what had changed with the creation of the crimmigration prison:

> "What I do feel, but I can't substantiate that, is that when people arrive here, they realize much more that it is really over."

This was also acknowledged by some of the CCNCs, who seemed to feel that there was little chance to be released in the Netherlands from Ter Apel prison. As Ermir (Albania) explained:

> "When you don't have a Dutch residence permit, you don't qualify for regular prisons. So you're transferred to Ter Apel, final destination."

Several other respondents equally indicated they felt they had nothing to win by trying to avoid their deportation and therefore pragmatically decided to cooperate with the state in order to qualify for SOB. For these respondents the accumulation of imprisonment and deportation was a matter of fact, and SOB at least provided the possibility to reduce their prison time. Whereas non-cooperation previously came with little extra risks – the worst-case scenario was deportation – the introduction of the SOB-measure means that successfully avoiding deportation results in serving a longer prison sentence, while one can never be entirely sure to not get deported anyway. In these cases, SOB thus only becomes a factor in the decision-making process of CCNCs because deportation is seen as unavoidable. However, even CCNCs who do not want to return are frequently deported with SOB. Although the government explicitly frames SOB as a favour and not a right, departure supervisors also apply for SOB for CCNCs who do not want to return. Obviously, granting SOB against someone's will seems to somewhat undermine the idea of a favour.

7.5.2 When the state is unable to deport: "I already planned to not cooperate anyway"

When a CCNC does not have a valid travel document, departure supervisors need to obtain a replacement document (a so-called laissez-passer) from the perceived country of origin. Usually a CCNC will be presented at an embassy or consulate, where the foreign authorities have to confirm his/her identity and nationality. However, there are a number of countries notoriously unwilling to cooperate with foreign authorities in order to take back their citizens, especially when these have a criminal conviction and/or are forcibly returned (Ellermann, 2008). For example, both Algeria and Morocco are countries that have been reluctant to cooperate with the Dutch authorities on forced return; the majority of CCNCs released without deportation come from these two countries. Ali (Morocco), who had come with his family to the Netherlands more than thirty years ago when he was a teenager, claimed that the Moroccan authorities simply refused to issue the necessary travel documents in order for him to be deported.

> "I arrive there and he [the Moroccan consul, JB] says: 'this man lives here since more than thirty years, he has a Dutch wife, a Dutch child, what is he supposed to do in Morocco? Because he has nobody there. His whole family is here, what should he do there?' (...) He told me: 'Listen, I can send you back to Morocco, but you have no money, you have no house, you have no family to support you. So what will you do? Commit crimes in order to survive.'"

Similarly, Karim (Morocco) had grown up in Amsterdam, where his wife and most of his family still lived. Therefore, being deported to Morocco seemed particularly painful to him. Although his departure supervisor had informed him that he could be released after serving half of his sentence if he agreed to leave the Netherlands, he said he preferred to just serve his full sentence and then either stay illegally in the Netherlands or try to move to Belgium or Germany with his wife on his own terms. He explained how he could easily avoid being deported by simply informing the Moroccan authorities that he did not want to return:

> "Maybe you have heard about that as well, that Morocco has problems with the Netherlands and they no longer cooperate. (...) They take people from here all the way to the consulate, but they are simply sent back, because Morocco no longer cooperates. (...) Anyway, I already planned to not cooperate anyway. Even if I go all the way with them to the consulate, I am just going to talk honestly to this head of the consulate. I am just going to tell him: 'I do not want to return.' Done."

Whenever the government is not able to deport a CCNC, departure supervisors' only choice is to try to motivate him to cooperate with return. To that end, they engage in various conversation techniques that are aimed at creating relationships with CCNCs and winning their trust (Cleton & Chauvin, 2019). To convince CCNCs to cooperate with return, they employ various incentives to try to change the mind of reluctant CCNCs and convince them that return would be better than staying.

The main stick to discourage CCNCs from staying in the Netherlands is the relatively tough circumstances they will encounter after their release. Since the early 1990s the Netherlands has a far-reaching 'discouragement policy' aimed at making life as an unauthorised migrant as unattractive as possible, by excluding them from legal work, housing, most medical help, and a range of social services (Leerkes & Broeders, 2010). Moreover, unauthorised migrants always run the risk of being arrested again and returned to prison. Departure supervisors tried to use these circumstances to convince CCNCs that their life upon release would be very tough.

> "I try to let the migrant explain what he will encounter as an illegal in Netherlands. So let him mention the downsides of illegality himself: 'You always have to look over your shoulder, you can't start a family, you can't work legally, can't build up an existence, will regularly return here to this prison.' (...) Let them describe it as extensively as possible, so that they become aware of what their future in the Netherlands really is like. Or rather, the lack of a future."

In terms of carrots, departure supervisors have rather limited possibilities for CCNCs, especially in comparison with other categories of unauthorised migrants. Rejected asylum seekers, for example, can receive substantial return and reintegration assistance, which includes both monetary support and skills development, but CCNCs are generally excluded from these programmes. However, the SOB-measure could be seen as both a carrot (offering early release from prison to cooperating CCNCs) and a stick (more time in prison for non-cooperative CCNCs). Most departure supervisors were positive about the SOB measure, although none of them thought it had a substantial effect on motivating foreign national prisoners to agree to return.

> "It is an incentive to cooperate with return, but I wonder if it also an incentive to cooperate if you first did not want to. Some people would not have cooperated without SOB, but I do not think it is a large percentage. I think it is only an incentive for a small percentage to finally give up who they are."

Departure supervisors usually spoke of a few people they believed had been convinced to leave due to the possibility of SOB, but generally indicated this was not a very substantial group. They believed many CCNCs would have been deported anyway – either because they want to leave the Netherlands or because they could be forcibly returned – and that it would not change the mind of CCNCs who desperately intend to stay in the Netherlands. Instead, nearly all of them believed the measure was primarily intended to save money on the imprisonment of CCNCs.

Indeed, despite the attempts of departure supervisors, many CCNCs preferred serving their full prison sentence and subsequently having to live as an unauthorised migrant over cooperating with their own return. Particularly noticeable among these respondents was that they explicitly challenged the legitimacy of their deportation. Two arguments were commonly used to substantiate their claim that they should be allowed to stay in the Netherlands, both of which stem directly from the two elements of the sliding scale policy: the lack of seriousness of their offense and the long time they had been living in the Netherlands. A similar result was found by Griffiths (2017, p. 536), who illustrated how foreign criminals in the United Kingdom "present themselves as either Almost Citizens or Good Migrants, reflecting the two categories – foreign and criminal – that produce the category."

Regarding the seriousness of their offense, several respondents believed their criminal history was not serious enough to warrant deportation from the Netherlands. Some of them denied having committed the crimes they had been convicted for; others readily admitted to committing these crimes, but argued they were not serious enough to justify deportation. These respondents generally did not challenge the legitimacy of deporting CCNCs (cf. Hasselberg, 2014a). Rather, they challenged their own position in it. As Ali (Morocco) said:

> "It is not the system. (…) As I already said, when you killed someone or you are a real big criminal, or a terrorist, then I can understand that you are not welcome, then you are a danger to society. But someone who has been a bit naughty in the past, doesn't matter what, as long as you don't kill someone, or whatever, then you have to give him a chance. You know, that's what I think. And not just for me, but for everyone. There are more people like me here."

Besides dismissing the seriousness of their crimes, another argument frequently invoked by CCNCs was related to the duration of stay in the Netherlands and the social life they had built up. Respondents drew on different reasons why they believed they had a legitimate claim to membership in the Netherlands: their long period of residence in the Netherlands, often including their formative years; the presence of Dutch family members, especially children; the lack of ties to their country of origin, which was often unknown to them; or long periods when they had been 'good citizens' holding legal jobs and paying their taxes, thus contributing to Dutch society. Respondents also frequently explained how they had become very Dutch over the years. For example, Juan (Ecuador) had been living in the Netherlands for more than thirty years. He had an extensive family in the Netherlands and that deporting him and separating him from his family for at least ten years was highly unfair. In explaining why he believed he was Dutch, he drew on ideas about Dutch culture as being progressive and the importance of arriving on time for an appointment.

> "There are people here who are not Dutch, but I call myself Dutch. Because of the small details about equality, but also I came here [for the interview, JB] and I knew that I had to be five minutes early."

Numerous authors have shown how deportation often exposes the tensions between legal citizenship and subjective sense of belonging (Golash-Boza, 2016; Griffiths, 2017; Kaufman & Bosworth, 2013). Long-term residents who had lost their right to stay in the Netherlands struggled with the erosion of a status they had held until their last conviction. For them, the migration-related consequences of their punishment constituted an attack on their sense of self, as they believed themselves to be insiders. Many of them felt they had more in common with prison officers than with other prisoners. Speaking about psychological issues that led him to be aggressive, Yusuf (Turkey) accepted that he could be a danger to others. However, as he claimed his problems were at least in part the result of his life trajectory in the Netherlands, he argued it would be unjust to deport him to Turkey.

> "This hits me hard, you know. It is not like I just arrived here, three years ago from Turkey and I have a huge criminal record. No, it is twenty-eight years, I already came here when I was four years old. So I have lived here, I am not born as a criminal, nobody is born like that. So everything that happened, happened here in the Netherlands. (…) I have had two businesses here. Everything happened here. I say, look at my body, all my traumas, it happened here, in the Netherlands. Here in this country I took, but I have also given."

This sentiment was echoed by Mohammed (Morocco), who after many years in the Netherlands felt different from most other CCNCs around him:

> "He is alien to me. I am not an alien, I have lived here all these years. And that is… I believe they should make a distinction there. But they don't. You know, and

then I think to myself: 'but you cannot compare me with him. You can't. He is completely different than me.'"

CCNCs who had been living in the Netherlands since a long time and had a family in the country, had considerably more to lose when they would be deported. They also generally considered their deportation as fundamentally unfair and illegitimate. As a result, there was little chance they would cooperate with their own return.

7.6 Conclusion and discussion

This article has looked at the deportation of CCNCs from the Netherlands, examining the deportation regime, its implementation in practice, and how this is experienced by CCNCs. The far-reaching integration of the criminal justice system and the migration control system, both in terms of processes and actors, has contributed to a relatively high return rate of this specific migrant population. For many CCNCs, structural factors determine whether they will leave the Netherlands after completing their criminal sentence. In other words, the ability of the state to move towards hard deportation is the most important factor in achieving soft deportation. As a result, CCNCs who 'cooperate' with their own return show different degrees of voluntariness, ranging from wishing to return to seeing no alternative than cooperation. For some CCNCs deportation felt like punishment, whereas for others it was a form of relief.

Nonetheless, there is a sizeable group of CCNCs who cannot be returned without their own cooperation. Aided by the specific institutional setting of Ter Apel prison, departure supervisors try to convince these CCNCs to cooperate with return through conversational techniques and various incentives. They primarily emphasise the hardships of life as an unauthorised migrant and the possibility of early release from prison. However, in many cases these 'decisions' of CCNCs are the result of factors that lie beyond the sphere of influence of departure supervisors. Interviews with CCNCs illustrate how deterrence and legitimacy interact with each other and other return-relevant factors to inform the willingness to cooperate with their own return. Personal circumstances – in particular the presence of family members and duration of stay in the Netherlands – heavily influenced the deterrent effect, as well as the perceived legitimacy, of deportation.

The decision on whether or not to cooperate was in essence the result of a trade-off between prolonged imprisonment followed by life as an unauthorised migrant and deportation. Not surprisingly, deportation was most painful for respondents who had been living in the Netherlands for a long time and had built up considerable relationships, whereas imprisonment was generally more painful for respondents who had little attachment to the Netherlands and had their loved ones in their country of origin. This is in line with the argument of Kanstroom (2000), who argues for a distinction between deportation as a form of border control and deportation as a form of social control, and claims the latter form should be seen as a form of punishment. This makes it questionable whether it is just that non-citizens are confronted with a second form of punishment after their prison sentence. It also raises the question what the justification is for the distinction between long-term legal residents and citizens, except for legal technicalities. Moreover, it has repeatedly been argued that criminal deportations are really only successful on a local level, especially in combination with the current specialised foreign national-prisons, as instead of addressing the criminal risk an individual poses, this risk is simply exported to elsewhere (Grewcock, 2011; Kanstroom, 2000).

Besides these normative arguments, this article has also suggested that the effectiveness of these measures is limited. Recently there has been growing attention for undesirable and unreturnable migrants, who frequently live in legal limbo and pose considerable challenges to national governments (Cantor et al., 2017). Whereas it was hoped that the SOB-measure would provide a motivation for these CCNCs to return to their country of origin, the percentage of deportations has risen only slightly since its introduction. Despite the combined threat of a longer prison sentence and life as an unauthorised migrant, around twenty-five percent of CCNCs are ultimately not deported. In part, this seems to stem from the government's own legal changes, which have resulted in a growing number of long-term residents losing their residence permit. As these CCNCs are generally less willing to return and countries of origin are hesitant to accept them back, it is considerably harder to deport this group. In light of the literature on so-called 'survival crime' by unauthorised migrants (Engbersen & van der Leun, 2001), the restrictions of the sliding scale policy might therefore even be counterproductive. Moreover, because all these CCNCs have been issued an entry ban or pronounced undesirable, their stay in the Netherlands constitutes a criminal act and they risk getting caught in a vicious circle of arrest, imprisonment and release. This illustrates the limits of crime control, migration control *and* crimmigration control in finding an acceptable solution for this group.

8 Conclusion

8.1 Introduction

Border control has significantly changed in recent decades. Whereas globalisation processes seem to have diminished the relevance of international borders, states have simultaneously sought ways to regain some form of control over cross-border mobility. In this process, alternative and novel means of border enforcement have emerged. This dissertation has studied some of these novel means of border enforcement, referred to here as bordering practices. Bordering practices are defined as all measures taken by a state to regulate and enforce its borders in order to determine who has the right to stay within its territory; this can be both at the external border and inside the national territory. The main aim of the dissertation is to provide an understanding of what these bordering practices actually look like in practice. In particular, it looked at bordering practices in the Netherlands through the lens of crimmigration. Defined as the intertwinement of migration control and the criminal justice system, the dissertation aims to provide insight into *how* bordering practices are conducted, as well as *where* and by *whom*. Moreover, the dissertation examines *who* are subjected to contemporary bordering practices. More specifically, two bordering practices were empirically examined: intra-Schengen migration policing and criminal deportations. Building on a recent surge in criminological scholarship that concerns itself with border and migration control (Aas, 2011, 2014; Bosworth, 2012), the different empirical chapters of this dissertation examined the various ways these bordering practices are shaped by, and shape the criminal justice system. This final chapter brings the findings of the two case studies together and discusses them in light of the overarching conceptual and theoretical framework. Paragraph 8.2 first summarizes the main findings of the different empirical chapters. After this, the main research question will be answered in paragraph 8.3, followed by a discussion of the theoretical reflections and implications in paragraph 8.4.

8.2 Summary of empirical findings

The first chapter after the introduction provided the broad discursive context for the two cases studies. Because public discourse is generally seen as influencing laws, policies, and practices, the chapter looked at media coverage of unauthorised migrants. It took as a starting point a bill introduced in 2010 to formally criminalise illegal stay in the Netherlands – generally seen as the most far-reaching example of crimmigration. Based on the notion that the media play a crucial role in putting issues on the public agenda and discursively constructing certain migrant groups as disproportionally criminal, the study examined whether this bill was preceded by increasing amounts of media attention for crime committed by unauthorised migrants. It did so by examining all newspaper articles about unauthorised migrants by Dutch national newspaper during the period 1999 – 2013.

Several interesting and unexpected findings of the study stood out. First, the bill to criminalise illegal stay was introduced at what was practically the lowest point with regard to media attention for unauthorised migrants. The annual number of newspaper articles on unauthorised migrants was relatively stable between 1999 and 2006, but subsequently strongly decreased for four years in a row. Following the introduction of the bill to criminalise illegal stay in 2010 the number of annual newspaper articles started to increase again, but not enough to reach the same numbers as before. Second, the terminology employed by Dutch newspapers was noteworthy. In many Anglo-Saxon countries there is much debate about using the term 'illegal', as it is seen as stigmatising and criminalising. It is often argued that whereas behaviour can be illegal, this does not apply to individuals. Various press agencies and news outlets have therefore decided not to use the terms illegal migrants anymore. This was not the case for Dutch newspapers, as in more than 95 percent of the instances they use the term illegal – instead of irregular, undocumented, or other alternatives – to denote unauthorised migrants. Moreover, in most cases newspaper articles used the term as a noun (illegals) and not as an adjective (illegal migrant). Finally, the core question of the chapter was how unauthorised migrants are described by Dutch newspapers and whether there were any changes over time. The results showed that numerical terms were often used to describe 'illegals'. This included both concrete numbers and more vague descriptions, such as 'thousands', 'many', and 'groups'. The most significant finding was that 'criminal' was one of the most prevalent adjectives for the noun 'illegals'. This signals that unauthorised migrants are relatively often described as criminals. However, most of these references occurred during the initial years that were studied and the number of times the term 'criminal illegals' surfaced gradually decreased over time. The conclusion of the study was therefore that the bill to criminalise illegal stay was not the result of growing and increasingly negative media coverage of unauthorised migrants. Instead, media attention on unauthorised migrants decreased in the years before the bill was introduced, while also focussing less and less on issues of crime. At the same time, media attention for other migrant groups, in particular from new EU countries such as Bulgaria and Romania, seemed to increase. It is likely that to a certain extent this has replaced news coverage of unauthorised migrants following the 2007 EU enlargement of the EU.

8.2.1 Intra-Schengen migration policing

The first case study focussed on the Mobile Security Monitor (MSM), a form of migration policing in Dutch border areas introduced followed the implementation of the Schengen agreement, illustrating how in the Netherlands intra-Schengen border controls have been replaced by highly discretionary border checks. The MSM has a complex legal framework combining migration control with elements of crime control. Initially the checks were aimed at preventing illegal immigration; if RNM officers happen to detect a criminal offense, they would have to hand over the case to the Dutch police. However, since 2006 the official aim of the MSM expanded and came to include the fight against migrant smuggling and identity fraud. Any other detected criminal offenses would still need to be handed over to the police. This was later matched with an informal name change in the policy discourse around the MSM; whereas previously the full name of the instrument was Mobile Alien Monitor, this was changed to Mobile Security Monitor. Moreover, official policy documents started to describe the aim of the MSM as preventing illegal immigration and fighting different forms of cross-border crime. It is for this reason that I have argued that at least the policy framework of the MSM in many ways fits within the trend of crimmigration.

RNM officers carrying out the MSM have a high level of discretionary freedom in deciding whom to stop, as they do not need to have a reasonable suspicion of illegal stay or a criminal offense. This discretionary freedom is further increased by the ambiguous policy aims of the MSM and the unofficial name change, since officers can pick and choose from a wider array of powers, navigating between migration control and criminal detection. It also allowed officers to let their own ideas and beliefs about the aim of the MSM and their own tasks play a role in their decisions. Officers differed in what they considered more important or interesting. Much like regular police officers, RNM officers have different styles of work. Some of them primarily focus on migration control, while others are more focussed on fighting crime. This last group was strongly driven by a desire to make the Netherlands safer. For these officers 'catching criminals' was not only more exciting, it was also perceived as more rewarding than finding possible unauthorised migrants.

Especially RNM officers who focussed more on fighting crime during the MSM often found their existing powers too limited to carry out their tasks. To deal with that they would regularly use their powers in what they called a 'creative manner', 'playing' with the different legal areas. In this way these street-level officers further contribute to the fading of the boundaries between migration control and crime control. This is in line with the notions of crimmigration and ad-hoc instrumentalism: officers make use of a range of tools that stem from both migration law and criminal law to target both undesirable migrants and criminals. They can first form a judgment about a certain individual or situation and subsequently find the most effective tool to base their decision on. The result is that it is not always transparent on which ground certain decisions are made, especially not for the individuals that are stopped. Moreover, criminal law based enforcement generally comes with considerably more procedural safeguards than administrative forms of enforcement, such as migration control.

The ambiguity regarding the objectives of the MSM, in combination with organisational policies and the prevailing social climate in the Netherlands, also had an influence on who were stopped during the MSM by RNM officers. As officers generally had very little time to decide whether to stop a vehicle or not, and rarely received concrete and useful prior information, they relied primarily on their own beliefs and experiences to make decisions about whom to stop. These beliefs were primarily the result of knowledge shared among street-level officers, as on an organisational level there was little guidance or instructions on how to select vehicles during the MSM. The dual aim of the MSM means that crime- and migration-related indicators often freely interacted with each other in selection decisions.

Officers invoked several factors to recognise potential unauthorised migrants, with skin colour being one of the most important ones. During the controls primarily black and Arab-looking people were stopped, as the mostly white male RNM officers saw this as an indicator of 'foreignness'. Officers were aware of the sensitivities of using racial or ethnic categories, but argued that when trying to identify unauthorised migrants they had little choice than to rely upon these indicators. They also frequently made clear that a stop was always based on a combination of several factors, which included the national origin of the license plate, the state of the vehicle, the number of passengers, and clothing. At the same time, during observations it regularly seemed that a stop was based on perceived foreign appearance alone.

Officers also regularly stopped people because they believed they might be involved in crime. Such stops were often based on perceptions about the disproportionate involvement in crime of certain ethnic or national groups. First, Moroccans, or more generally North Africans, who were primarily identified on the basis of their appearance. Second, people from Central and Eastern Europe were often seen as a risk, in particular Bulgarians and Romanians, reflecting some of the discourses that were found in the media study. In this case, the origin of the license plate of the vehicle was the main indicator officers relied on. These profiles were not necessarily static: a Polish license plate was for a long time considered to be a reason to stop a vehicle, but in recent years most officers believed there was little chance they would find something wrong. Most officers perceived such selection decisions on the basis of national categories as less controversial than selection decisions based on ethnic or racial categories.

The different ethnic and national groups that were stopped during the MSM experienced these controls in different ways. The vast majority of non-Dutch citizens had few problems with the MSM controls or even perceived them as positive. This included EU citizens from other countries, despite the fact that they believed they were stopped because they were foreign. The same was observed with Dutch majority group members, who on average perceived the MSM as even more positive than non-Dutch citizens. On the other hand, Dutch ethnic minority group members were considerably more critical about the MSM. This seemed to stem primarily from the perception that they were stopped on the basis of their skin colour and a lack of clarity about the reasons of the control. Although respondents in this group were generally not negative about their treatment by the RNM officers, this did not substantially effect their overall judgement of the MSM. These experiences occurred primarily among Dutch ethnic minority group members who self-identified as Dutch.

Officers emphasised the importance of treating the people they stop in a respectful and friendly manner, something generally corroborated by the observations. They were generally aware of the importance of explaining the aim of the MSM and the reasons for a specific stop. At the same time, our observations indicated that this was often done in such a brief way that people did not pick up on this, and respondents were often confused about whether this was a migration control or a police stop. Officers sometimes failed to take the communicative power of these controls into account. Whereas they saw the impact of being stopped in the context of the MSM as very limited, as it often took only a few minutes to carry out the check, for Dutch ethnic minority group members being selected for a stop, it felt like their status as a full citizen was denied. It was such contrasting perceptions that formed the basis of the negative legitimacy judgments of the Dutch minority group members.

8.2.2 Criminal punishment and deportation

The second case study focussed on the punishment and deportation of CCNCs. In the Netherlands, whether a criminal conviction results in withdrawal of a residence permit is decided on the basis of a sliding scale policy that takes into account the seriousness of the offense and the duration of legal residence. In recent years this sliding scale policy has repeatedly been restricted, generally motivated by an emphasis on crime control rationales. The most striking changes have been that migrants staying in the Netherlands for less than three years can lose their right to stay following a conviction to one day of imprisonment, and that there is no longer an end date when legally staying non-citizens cannot lose their residence permit anymore. Previously, anyone residing legally in the Netherlands for more than twenty years could no longer have their legal stay revoked. As a result, increasing numbers of legally residing migrants are targeted for deportation. This includes a growing number of long-term legal residents who have been living in the Netherlands for many years.

As CCNCs have been designated a priority group in the Dutch return policy, several policy measures have been adopted in the last year that are aimed at increasing their return rate. Better cooperation between various agencies working in the criminal justice chain and migration control chain is intended to result in the detection of CCNCs in an early phase and ensure they are deported following their criminal punishment. To achieve the latter, nearly all CCNCs are placed in the designated all-foreign national prison in Ter Apel. As CCNCs are not supposed to return into Dutch society after completing their sentence, rehabilitation activities are largely absent in Ter Apel prison and prisoners are not entitled to a range of common prison privileges. Instead, departure supervisors of the DT&V are embedded in the prison to work on organising CCNCs' return to their country of origin upon finishing their sentence. The concentration of more than sixty different nationalities in one prison, the lack of meaningful activities, and focus on deportation all impacted on the experiences of both prison officers and CCNCs in Ter Apel prison.

Most prison officers already worked in the prison in Ter Apel before it became a dedicated foreign national prison and were therefore used to working in a regular prison. Despite having no prior experience in dealing with this specific sub-group of prisoners, they received no training to equip themselves to deal with the new circumstances. Prison officers sometimes struggled to have good contact and build up relationships with prisoners, primarily because of language barriers. They also found it hard to find meaning and satisfaction in their work, as preparing prisoners for their life after release was generally seen as one of the most fulfilling parts of their work. With the lack of resocialisation activities in Ter Apel prison and prospect of deportation for CCNCs, there was little opportunity for that. In theory they could work on preparing CCNCs for return to their country of origin, but officers lacked the know-how to do so in a meaningful way.

For CCNCs the specific set-up and regime of Ter Apel prison had both positive and negative effects. Feelings of isolation and uncertainty about their migration status and possible deportation, which are commonly experienced by CCNCs, are to a certain extent mitigated by the presence of fellow prisoners who speak the same language and departure supervisors handling their migration case. At the same time, the relatively remote location of the prison exacerbate feelings of isolation. The fact that the prison acts as a precursor for deportation emphasises non-belonging, and CCNCs are constantly reminded of their permanent exclusion from society. How they responded to this depended largely on how they perceived themselves. Those who perceived themselves as foreigner primarily argued that all prisoners should enjoy the same rights, regardless of their citizenship status. However, they did not challenge their placement in an all-foreign prison in itself. Those who perceived themselves as legitimate members of Dutch society primarily felt foreign and alienated in an institution where they believed they did not belong.

For departure supervisors, the increasing cooperation between various agencies in the criminal justice and migration control systems, as well as their embeddedness in the all-foreign national prison, helped to organise the deportation of CCNCs more effectively. Because in many cases CCNCs possess valid travel documents, the return rate of this population is relatively high in comparison with other groups of unauthorised migrants. At the same time, there was still a considerable group of CCNCs who could not be easily deported without their own cooperation, mostly because their country of origin was reluctant to take them back. To convince these CCNCs to cooperate with their own return, departure supervisors highlighted the negative aspects of life as an unauthorised migrant and emphasised that CCNCs could reduce their prison time if they leave the Netherlands. The latter is as result of the so-called SOB-measure, which was introduced in 2012. Under this measure, CCNCs only qualify for early release – something readily available to regular prisoners – if they leave the Netherlands directly from prison. In all other cases, they will need to serve 100% of their sentence.CCNCs who possessed some agency over their deportation thus need to make a trade-off between a longer prison sentence and life as an unauthorised migrant on the one hand, and deportation on the other hand. Whether imprisonment or deportation was considered harsher depended on several factors that were generally beyond the sphere of influence of departure supervisors, in particular the presence of family members and duration of stay in the Netherlands. Many long-term residents perceived their deportation as illegitimate and therefore refused to cooperate and return to their country of origin. They relied on two broad arguments why they should be allowed to stay in the Netherlands: their criminal offense was not serious enough, or they had been living in the Netherlands for so long that they had a legitimate claim to membership. This illustrates the limitations of responding to criminal behaviour with migration control tools and the need for a distinction between deportation as a form of border control and deportation as a form of social control.

8.3 Answering the research question

The empirical findings of this dissertation have provided a rich insight in contemporary bordering practices in the Netherlands. The following section will use these findings to answer the overarching research question of this dissertation:

> *To what extent are contemporary bordering practices in the Netherlands characterised by crimmigration, who is targeted by these bordering practices, and how are they experienced and understood by those implementing them and those subjected to them?*

This research question essentially consists of three sub-questions, which will be dealt with separately.

8.3.1 To what extent are contemporary bordering practices in the Netherlands characterised by crimmigration?

In order to answer the first part of the research question, it is necessary to analyse the identified bordering practices within the context of crimmigration. Two case studies, focussing on the beginning and the end of the migration control chain, were studied in-depth, on both the legislative and policy level as well as in practice.

The first case study focussed on a form of intra-Schengen migration policing that came into existence following the lifting of internal border controls as a result of the 1994 Schengen agreement. On the policy level, this bordering practice was initially aimed at controlling migration. However, as it became apparent over time that RNM officers regularly found cases of migrant smuggling and identity fraud, eventually the scope of the MSM expanded and came to include these types of crime. Whereas previously they would have to refer such cases to the regular police, RNM officers gained additional powers to act and investigate when they detect particular types of crime. Besides this actual change on the policy level, there was also the more cosmetic name change of the MSM from Mobile Alien Monitor to Mobile Security Monitor, thus placing immigration control under the banner of security. In other words, an instrument that initially almost exclusively focussed on migration control over time became an instrument that combined this focus with at least a partial focus on crime control. Stumpf (2006) highlighted this development – immigration enforcement coming to resemble criminal law enforcement – as the second front of crimmigration.

The crime control powers of the RNM are officially still limited to two types of migration-related forms of crime. As such, it could be argued that the MSM in its current form fits only partially within the definition of crimmigration. Yet, as chapter two and three have illustrated, the focus on crime fighting during the MSM seems to be more significant in practice than on paper. The way officers operated and reasoned was a key example of Sklansky's (2012) ad hoc instrumentalism. With officers regularly interpreting their mandate as wider than it officially is, the integration of crime control and migration control went further than what could be deduced from the legal and policy framework. As such, although the legal and policy framework might create only a limited form of crimmigration, in practice the MSM can be fully characterised by crimmigration. Within the context of this particular bordering practice the conditions for crimmigration are created on the legislative and policy level, but ultimately crimmigration is further stimulated by the practices of street-level officers.

The second case study focussed on the end of the migration control chain, looking at the punishment and deportation of CCNCs. In particular, three recent policy changes were analysed, all of which came into existence during the last decade. These policy changes illustrated how migration status has a profound impact in the different phases of the criminal justice system, to the extent that an almost separate criminal justice system for non-citizens emerges. The first policy was discussed in both chapter six and chapter seven, and was the so-called sliding scale policy, which balances the duration of stay with the severity of a criminal offense to determine whether a CCNC loses his or her right to stay. The policy has repeatedly been restricted in recent years, making it much easier for immigrants to lose their residence permit. The main reason behind repeatedly restricting the sliding scale policy is to address crime by getting rid of individuals that are deemed to be a risk. As mentioned in the introduction, Stumpf (2006) herself highlighted the expansion of criminal grounds that are reason to deport non-citizens and the more general trend towards detention and deportation individuals that are deemed to be a particularly high risk as examples of the increasing overlap between criminal law and immigration law. The repeated restriction of the sliding scale policy is therefore a good example of this particular aspect of crimmigration. At the same time, the practical implementation of the policy is to a certain extent diminished by human rights protections.

The second policy was primarily discussed in chapter six and was the designation of the prison in Ter Apel as a dedicated all-foreign national prison, the first of its kind in the Netherlands. Two main rationales were given for the creation of this prison. First, CCNCs are not supposed to return to Dutch society after their criminal sentence and many of the provisions available to regular prisoners are therefore not applicable to this group. Second, it enables the departure supervisors of DT&V – whom are embedded in the prison – to work more effectively on realising the return of CCNCs upon completion of their imprisonment. Imprisonment for non-citizens thus takes on distinct migration control aims. Indeed, various authors have highlighted these prisons as a prime example of crimmigration (Pakes & Holt, 2017), with some even explicitly referring to them as crimmigration prisons (Ugelvik, 2017; Ugelvik & Damsa, 2018). It mostly fits in with the second front of crimmigration that Stumpf identified: immigration enforcement has come to resemble criminal law enforcement. Yet in the case of the prison in Ter Apel, it is not so much resembling, as fully overlapping: immigration enforcement *has become* criminal law enforcement, as the two types of enforcement occur simultaneously and have become almost indistinguishable.

The third and final policy was analysed in chapter seven of this dissertation. The SOB-measure was introduced in 2012 to increase the number of CCNCs that return to their country of origin following their imprisonment. To that end, they only qualify for early release when they leave the Netherlands directly from prison. The policy was specifically motivated by the aim to increase CCNCs willingness to cooperate with the authorities and return to their country of origin. This is a key example of using elements of criminal enforcement to achieve migration control related aims. It fits within the instrumentalistic logic of crimmigration described before.

8.3.2 Who is targeted by these bordering practices?

As noted in the introduction, Stumpf (2006) already warned that crimmigration ultimately leads to a growing group of outsiders and that race and class were important factors in delineating the borders of belonging. Aas (2011) subsequently further developed the consequences of crimmigration for four different social groups, depending on their citizenship status and moral worth. However, citizenship status in her classification exclusively related to national citizenship. In the discussion below on who is targeted by the two bordering practices analysed in this dissertation, the additional layer of EU citizenship will also be taken into account.

The discretionary and proactive nature of the MSM means that citizenship status means relatively little about whether one is targeted or not. Instead, how one is perceived is of crucial importance here. Those perceived as full citizen can pass freely, but those perceived as subcitizen, supracitizen, or non-citizen will have to prove that they are, in fact, bona fide citizen. As the MSM targets people both for potential illegal stay and criminal activities, the groups of people targeted by this bordering practice are wide-ranging and diverse. As discussed in more detail in chapter four, specific categories of non-white people could be perceived as all three types of outsiders. Individuals within these categories were frequently Dutch citizens, but because they were perceived as potential criminals or non-citizens, they were nonetheless targeted by this bordering practice. EU citizens from countries associated with high levels of cross-border crime were also frequently targeted. These people are not Dutch citizens, but as EU citizens they legally enjoy unrestricted travel within the Schengen area. However, because they were perceived as potential subcitizens, these legal rights did not always translate into practice. They thus constitute somewhat of a new category, in between supracitizens and citizens, further complicating the picture of rights and privileges connected to different levels of membership.

At the end of the migration control chain, the categories of people targeted by bordering practices differ substantially from the beginning. Here, legal status is of crucial importance, as exclusion is no longer decided on the basis on the perceptions of officials with high levels of discretionary freedom. In fact, the nature of who is targeted by the MSM and who is targeted for criminal deportation is so different, that a direct comparison between the two case studies is futile. Instead, they should be seen in conjunction, highlighting the outcomes of two different bordering practices at completely different stages of the migration control chain.

The individuals targeted for criminal deportation are all non-citizens in Aas' categorisation; they have neither citizenship status nor are they deemed morally worth to stay in the Netherlands. Some of them were previously supracitizens, or denizens: individuals who stay legally in the Netherlands, but without full citizenship status. These people are not fully part of the polity, but were allowed to stay on the basis of their moral worth. Following a conviction for a serious enough criminal offense, they became non-citizens. With the growing restrictions in the sliding scale policy, this group has considerably expanded in recent years. Chapter seven discussed in more detail which national groups are primarily targeted by this, which included some of the same ethnic groups targeted by the MSM. It demonstrated that EU citizenship is not enough to be exempt from this bordering practice, as citizens from other EU countries can still be targeted for deportation from the Netherlands. However, the consequences are less severe, as the entry ban only applies to the Netherlands and not the entire EU/EEA + Switzerland. Thus, criminal punishment and deportation exclusively targets non-citizens, but the bordering practice increasingly also targets supracitizens by removing their legal stay following a criminal conviction.

This illustrates that bordering practices at the beginning of the migration control chain cast a much wider net than bordering practices located at the end of the migration control chain. Much in line with the often used metaphor for the criminal justice, the migration control chain is characterised by a funnel model. Similarly to the criminal justice chain, the consequences become more severe further down the migration control chain. The biggest difference represents itself at the end of the chain: where the criminal justice chain ends with a return into society, the migration control chain ends with deportation.

8.3.3 How are these bordering practices experienced and understood by those implementing them?

This dissertation has looked at three different actors and how they deal with their mandates in light of a growing merger of crime control and migration control: RNM officers, prison officers, and departure supervisors. It is important to highlight the differences that existed within these groups of actors; while there was no general view that was shared by all, there were nonetheless broad trends discernible amongst all of them.

RNM officers often saw themselves as a special type of police officers and were generally less interested in purely combating unauthorised migration. Fighting crime was an important part of their motivation and as such, the gradual expansion of their mandate was generally welcomed, but for many officers this still did not go far enough. Perhaps not surprisingly, many officers believed there should be no limitations to the types of crimes they were allowed to act upon – they reasoned that if they were present anyway, it would make little sense to not counter other forms of non-migration related crimes. As such, these officers were generally in favour of crimmigration. As has been described above, in the case of the MSM the process of crimmigration was actually partly driven by the actions of street-level RNM officers.

Prison officers were most critical of the integration of crime control and migration control. Many of them had previously worked with regular prisoners and were used to work on preparing prisoners for their life after prison and their return into society. With the CCNC population, this element of their work has become practically irrelevant. What remained of their mandate was trying to keep order in the prison and ensuring that everyone made it through the day. Especially when they perceived a CCNC as Dutch, most prison officers perceived the system as unduly harsh and unfair. For some of them, an important reason for this was that they felt that Dutch society also had its obligations towards foreigners who had grown up in the country. As I explained in chapter six, this illustrates the fundamental difference between the two systems of social control.

Finally, the experiences and perceptions of the departure supervisors of DT&V were less explicitly addressed in the core chapters of this dissertation. However, especially in chapter seven their work was discussed in relation to the increasing reliance on the criminal justice system to effectuate return. In general, most departure supervisors did not see the far-reaching integration of punishment and migration control as something problematic. Whereas they were not convinced of the effectiveness of the SOB-measure in stimulating growing numbers of CCNCs to cooperate with their return, they perceived their placement inside the prison in Ter Apel as a key element to conduct their work in an effective way. The possibility to simply walk into the prison and engage with CCNCs in a more informal way was generally seen in very positive terms.

8.3.4 How are these bordering practices experienced and understood by those subjected to them?

The section above discussed who were targeted by the bordering practices studied in this dissertation. An important question for the impact and legitimacy of such practices is how they are experienced by those subjected to them. Although on many levels the two case studies are incomparable, they shared one important similarity. In both cases it was primarily individuals who perceived themselves as insiders who challenged the legitimacy of the bordering practice.

How the individuals targeted by the MSM understood and experienced this bordering practice was primarily discussed in chapter five. Respondents were divided between non-Dutch citizens and Dutch citizens. The results of the survey indicated that these people generally did not perceive it as problematic that they were stopped by the RNM for a check. As I argued, it is likely that this had to do with the fact that they did not see themselves as members of Dutch society and thus perceived it as reasonable that they were targeted by a form of border control upon entering the country. This was also the case for citizens from other EU countries, suggesting that freedom of movement within the EU is not perceived as an absolute right.

The respondents who were Dutch citizens were divided in two groups: majority group members and ethnic minority group members. The first group was very positive about the MSM and the RNM officers. Minority group members were therefore the only respondents who were in general outspokenly critical about this bordering practice. As I argued in chapter five, an important explanation for this might be a form of uncertainty about their status and inclusion in society. The fact that they were targeted for an immigration control seems to confirm that they are not perceived and treated as a full member. Nearly all these respondents described themselves as being Dutch, but felt they were not perceived and treated as such. Most of them believed their physical appearance, in particular their skin colour, was the main reason for this.

A somewhat similar distinction could be observed in the experiences of CCNCs in the Netherlands. As outlined in chapter six, all CCNCs were aware they enjoyed fewer rights and privileges as a result of their status as non-citizen. Not surprisingly, this was generally perceived as unfair. However, there was a difference in their response depending on how they perceived themselves: as a foreigner or as a Dutch citizen. Both groups found the constellation of migration control and punishment problematic. However, those who saw themselves as foreigners primarily problematised the lack of rights and privileges in the prison in Ter Apel. Those who thought of themselves as Dutch also challenged their place in this particular prison. For these respondents, the biggest problem was not the prison regime itself. Instead, it was the underlying logic that they were classified as non-members and were thus supposed to be deported. As further discussed in chapter seven, since they perceived their deportation as fundamentally unfair, this also meant they heavily resisted it. These findings are further discussed in paragraph 8.3.3.

8.4 Reflections and implications

This dissertation has illustrated how crimmigration proves to be a useful framework to understand contemporary bordering practices. It has highlighted the importance of empirical studies to account for the nuances and complexities of the macro-level conceptual framework of crimmigration. This final section offers some theoretical reflections and implications of the findings of this dissertation. It discusses what these findings mean for our understanding of the concept of crimmigration and what this implies for contemporary notions of membership and belonging.

8.4.1 Defining and understanding crimmigration

As already discussed in the introduction, research on crimmigration has really taken flight since Stumpf introduced the term more than ten years ago. Figure 8.1 shows the annual number of publications in google scholar that include the term 'crimmigration'. It illustrates how popular this framework has become in recent years to study practices of border and migration control.

Two important reasons can be identified to explain this increase. First, it is an attractive term that works as an excellent catchphrase for any work that sits at the edge of crime and migration. As a result, the term appears to have become somewhat overused in recent years. Second, by broadening the definition of crimmigration, a wide range of scholars from different academic disciplines have been able to frame their research in terms of crimmigration. These explanations serve to make two observations about our understanding of the concept of crimmigration: the importance of emphasizing the bi-directional nature of crimmigration, and the need to have a broad perspective on crimmigration, both in terms of the multiple levels in which it occurs and the way it manifests itself.

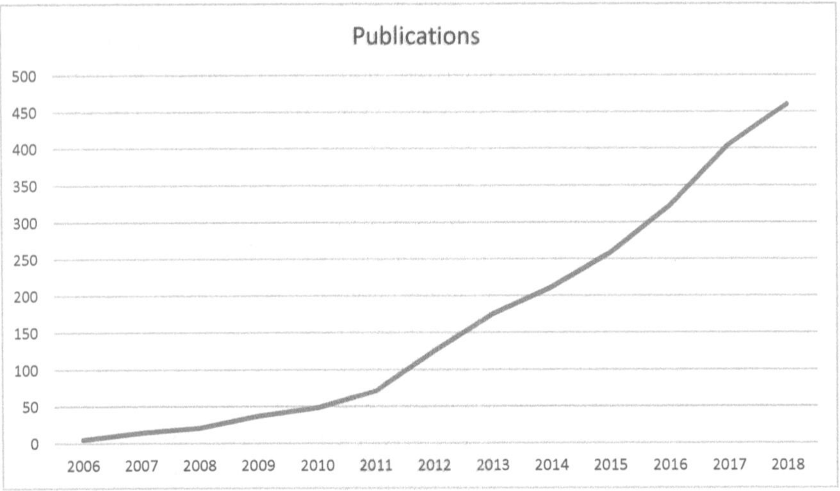

Figure 8.1 Crimmigration publications per year, 2006-2018 (source: own)

8.4.2 Crimmigration: a bi-directional process

Crimmigration has become somewhat of a buzzword in recent years, and the term has been widely used by scholars writing about migration. The downside of this is that the concept is frequently misunderstood and misused in the academic literature. In particular, many scholars reduce the term to simply mean the criminalisation of migration. As the abstract of a recent academic book (Atak & Simeon, 2018) read:

> "This book examines 'crimmigration' – the criminalization of migration – from national and comparative perspectives, drawing attention to the increasing use of criminal law measures, public policies, and practices that stigmatize or diminish the rights of forced migrants and refugees within a dominant public discourse that not only stereotypes and criminalizes but marginalizes forced migrants."

Other scholars have criticised crimmigration as a suitable lens to view contemporary developments in crime control and migration control. Writing about migration law enforcement inside UK prisons, Kaufman (2015, p. 174) argued that "by foregrounding the process of criminalisation, the crimmigration framework can suppress this crucially non-criminal element of the relationship between crime and border control." However, such a conclusion seems to be guided by an overemphasis on the criminalisation of migration, while neglecting the other important trend captured by the concept of crimmigration: the importation of migration control rationales into the criminal justice system. Many of the existing studies on crimmigration do tend to focus on the criminalisation of migration – perhaps also driven by the generally much larger body of research on this trend, even before the introduction of the concept of crimmigration. Indeed, even Stumpf (2006) herself in her seminal publication referred eight times to the 'criminalisation of migration', while only once mentioning the 'immigrationisation of criminal law' – in a footnote quoting Miller (2003). At least until recently, academic work exploring how criminals are cast into the net of migration control remained largely absent.

As this dissertation has shown in chapter six and seven, the enforcement of migration control during the punishment phase inside prisons can be seen as a key example of crimmigration. Indeed, the immigrationisation of crime control can have equally harsh consequences for unauthorised migrants as the much more discussed criminalisation of migration. The case studies in this dissertation thus illustrate that crimmigration should be understood as a bi-directional process, encompassing not only the importation of criminal law discourse and practices into migration control, but also the adoption of migration control rationales and aims by the criminal justice area. As Miller (Miller, 2003, pp. 617-618) already emphasised,

> "the 'criminalization' of immigration law fails to capture the dynamic process by which both systems converge at points to create a new system of social control that draws from both immigration and criminal justice, but it is purely neither."

It is for this reason that some authors have argued that we see the emergence of a novel system of 'crimmigration control' (Bowling & Westenra, 2018). In this dissertation this was particularly visible in the second case study, with non-citizens being exposed to an almost entirely separate criminal justice system.

8.4.3 Crimmigration: a broad concept

Another reason for the steep increase in publications on crimmigration is the evolution of the way the concept is understood by scholars. Whereas Stumpf (2006) merely spoke of the merger between criminal law and migration law, scholars nowadays see crimmigration as a much broader phenomenon, as evidenced by some of the definitions used: "the convergence between immigration and criminal justice policies" (Coutin, 2010, p. 357), "the convergence of the criminal justice and immigration enforcement systems" (Armenta, 2017, p. 82), "the growing interdependence between criminal justice and migration control" (Bosworth, Aas, & Pickering, 2017, p. 35), "the interconnections between crime and migration in the context of public authorities' responses to irregular migration" (Marin & Spena, 2016, p. 147), and "a merger of features that were traditionally and doctrinally squared within the separate domains of criminal justice and migration control" (Van Berlo, 2015, p. 78). This much wider interpretation of the term crimmigration has opened up the term to a wide range of academics from very different disciplines and backgrounds, examining trends on various levels and in different manifestations.

Crimmigration encompasses a wide range of policies and practices that would not be captured by adopting a strictly legal interpretation of the phenomenon. It plays a role in *shaping* the boundaries of belonging as well as *enforcing* these boundaries. Indeed, the examples of crimmigration discussed in this dissertation sit at various levels and are driven by different processes. The bill to criminalise illegal stay and the repeated restriction of the sliding scale policy are key examples of the legal definition of crimmigration. The designation of Ter Apel prison as an all-foreign national prison and the introduction of the SOB-measure sit more at the policy and administrative level. In these cases, crimmigration sometimes simply stemmed from administrative reforms or changes in internal procedures and street level actors had little discretionary freedom to make key decisions. Finally, crimmigration within the MSM is facilitated by decisions on the legal and policy level, but is also at least to a certain extent the result of the actions and decisions on the street level.

The examples discussed in this dissertation illustrate the diverse and sometimes complicated ways in which crimmigration manifests itself. In short: crimmigration during the MSM is different from crimmigration in the punishment of CCNCs, but they are both examples of the same concept. Crimmigration during the MSM stems from one agency broadening its aim to include also tasks that are traditionally located within another agency in the other chain. It is a key example of Sklansky's (2012) ad-hoc instrumentalism: officers rely on one of these powers to achieve their aims. This highlights that crimmigration is not always a *merger* or *convergence* of criminal law and migration law. Instead, in some cases the two legal frameworks are used *interchangeably* in an instrumental manner and decision makers employ whatever legal framework offer the best possibilities to achieve their intended result. As Moffette (2018, p. 2) has recently argued,

> "while much has been gained from researching where immigration law and criminal law converge to form a distinct realm of crimmigration law, we should pay more attention to where they diverge and how this separation is productive."

On the other hands, crimmigration in the punishment of CCNCs did not stem from one agency taking on additional powers, but from one migration agency (DT&V) seeking closer cooperation with another criminal one (DJI) and locating itself at its sites in order to establish migration control related goals. Here we can clearly observe how the criminal justice system has been put to use to achieve migration control related aims, through the establishment of the all-foreign national prison and the introduction of the SOB-measure. Except for the SOB-measure, the two legal frameworks are not so much used interchangeably, but rather applied simultaneously or consecutively. After all, deportation formally occurs after the criminal punishment, but its implementation already takes place during the punishment phase.

The two case studies thus highlight the importance of seeing crimmigration as more than a legal process and more than merely the criminalisation of migration. It covers a broad range of discourses, laws, policies, and practices. Moreover, crimmigration can be a merger of crime control and migration control, but the two domains can also be used interchangeably in highly instrumental manners. They can reinforce each other, but also used individually according to their own strengths. While this means it might be hard to define what crimmigration exactly entails, it is important to not only be thorough, but also precise. Whereas there is a tendency to frame every type of restrictive migration policy in the context of criminalisation of migration, it is important to stress the overlap or interchangeability of crime control and migration control as the defining feature of crimmigration. This means that while there might be plenty of grounds to criticize restrictive asylum policies, this does not automatically mean it fits within the definition of crimmigration – after all, there does not have to be a crime control logic to such policies. Similarly, while the introduction of internal border controls in the Schengen area can be seen as a violation of important fundamental rights, it is not necessarily a form of crimmigration – even if in practice it will often be.

8.4.4 The drivers of crimmigration

The examples of crimmigration studied in this dissertation showed significant differences in their political and public response. For example, the bill to criminalise illegal stay attracted much more political and public resistance than the repeated restrictions of the sliding scale policy. Perhaps not surprisingly, there appears to be considerably more resistance against using crime control techniques against immigrants than against deploying migration control techniques against criminals – both among the general public and government practitioners. Indeed, the creation of an all-foreign national prison and the introduction of the SOB-measure went largely beyond the public's eye. One of the reasons this might have generally escaped attention is that many of the developments in this area were the result of what Welch (2012) refers to as 'quiet manoeuvring' – as opposed to the 'loud panic' that sometimes accompanies law making in the areas of crime and migration. This is all the more surprising given that, as Pakes and Holt (2017) have previously noted, politicians tend to believe that being tough on crime and migration is a popular stance. It could therefore be expected that these developments were widely promoted among the general public. It illustrates the need for scholars to look beyond the criminalisation processes that are often at the forefront of political and public debates, and equally focus on the more administrative and technocrat processes that are implemented on the grounds of efficiency (Bowling & Westenra, 2018; Pakes & Holt, 2017). As this dissertation has shown, the impact of such processes can be equally punitive.

In seeking to explain the drivers of crimmigration, many scholars have looked at negative views and concerns about migrants. While this undoubtedly plays a role, the examples studied in this dissertation show that this alone cannot adequately explain *why* states resort to crimmigration policies. It especially does not provide a satisfying explanation for the immigrationalisation of the criminal justice system. Especially many of the non-legal forms of crimmigration stem from administrative or organisational changes that are aimed at efficiency and effectiveness. As Pakes and Holt (2017, p. 70) claim: "states revert to non-criminal justice modes of operating because it is easier." This point is convincingly illustrated by Aliverti (2012), who shows that criminal law for immigration-related crimes is only used when deportation is not feasible. A similar logic underlies for example the SOB measure. What drives crimmigration is an instrumental logic applied to exclude those deemed undesirable – with little regard for formal legal categories. This raises important questions about the value of legal protections and fundamental rights.

Crimmigration control benefits from the strengths of two different systems of social control. The criminal justice system is less exclusionary than migration control. The migration control system is less condemnatory than criminal justice. Immigration control is administrative and entails less formal individual rights. It also allows differential treatment on the basis of nationality and, although less explicitly because by proxy, on race or ethnicity. Criminal justice entails considerably more protections for the individuals it targets and explicitly prohibits differential treatment on any ground, especially race or ethnicity – although proactive profiling practices based on risk profiles are a grey area. Immigration control is based on privileges: no foreigner has the right to be included. Criminal justice is based on rights: citizens are free from its intervention, unless they misbehave. Yet exactly in these differences lies the strength of the crimmigration system. States can decide which legal framework to invoke depending on their own benefit. It highlights how the instrumental nature of crimmigration is of particular concern for issues of accountability and legitimacy.

In many cases there is a certain undeniable logic to crimmigration. After all, border policing officers ignoring any form of crime would appear to be a peculiar use of resources. Similarly, it makes sense than unauthorised migrants are not released back into society with a reintegration plan: this would undermine the state's migration control system. In some cases crimmigration even seems practically inevitable: CCNCs simply fall under both the criminal justice system and the migration control system. And as chapter six has highlighted, in some cases the application of crimmigration can even be beneficial for such individuals. This illustrates the complicated nature of contemporary governance of crime and migration and shows how assessments of crimmigration require careful analysis. And perhaps in some cases instead of outright rejection crimmigration, it is necessary to ask the question how to organise the simultaneous application of these two social control systems in a fair and just manner.

8.4.5 Borders, crimmigration, and membership

As noted in the introduction and throughout this dissertation, bordering practices play a key role in defining the boundaries of membership and shaping national identity, on both a symbolic level and the legal level. This dissertation has illustrated how these bordering practices in the Netherlands are increasingly characterised by crimmigration and take place at multiple 'sites of enforcement' (Weber & Bowling, 2004). Stumpf (2006) already highlighted that crimmigration results in growing numbers of excluded individuals, often based on factors such as class and race. As Barker (2013) argues, "membership matters most." This dissertation has highlighted how this comprises both *legal* membership and *perceived* membership. Not all migrants are targeted by the bordering practices studied in this dissertation, but only those classified or perceived as criminal or unauthorised. Through the integration of crime control rationales into these bordering practices, these categories are expanding and increasingly come to include long-term migrants and even citizens.

At the entrance of the migration control chain, exclusion primarily occurs on a symbolic and communicative level. Intra-Schengen borders did not so much disappear, but rather transform into highly selective border checks, targeting a very small percentage of the overall number of border-crossers (Van der Woude, Brouwer, & Dekkers, 2016). As noted, the highly discretionary nature of the MSM resulted in a range of different groups targeted for an identity control. Due to the infusion of the MSM with crime control rationales, this includes EU citizens from especially Eastern European countries and Dutch citizens from certain ethnic minority backgrounds, reflecting wider social attitudes about suspiciousness and belonging. Unless issues arise on the criminal level, these people are subsequently allowed to continue their journey and are thus formally recognised as insiders. Nonetheless, such an identity check is a clear signal that one is *perceived* as an outsider. In other words: their membership is questioned and this results in less rights and privileges than individuals whose membership is immediately accepted. As discussed in chapter five, such practices also have a communicative function, sending messages about who belongs. Experiencing such treatment can therefore reduce subjective feelings of inclusion and belonging. At the same time, and with the notable exception for individuals living in these border areas, in many cases this is likely to be a singular occurrence. As such, these practices are likely to be less harmful than repeated identity checks in one's own neighbourhood or city. Recent research confirms that especially experiencing *frequent* identity checks leads to decreased feelings of belonging and these feelings are most pertinent among people with a legal claim to membership, such as immigrant children born in the country or individuals from overseas territories (Terrasse, 2019). This is not surprising, as especially these individuals will experience such identity checks as a form of identity denial. The stops during the MSM should therefore rather be seen in a wider pattern of frequent identity checks by different policing actors, where crime control and migration control rationales have become blurred (Van der Leun & Van der Woude, 2011). Continuous differential treatment is a key example of a conceptual bordering practice, constructing boundaries for legitimate citizens (Weber, 2019).

At the end of the migration control chain, exclusion is much less symbolic, as migrants convicted of a serious enough criminal offense are formally excluded through deportation – arguably the most extreme form of exclusion. In particular, the restrictions in the sliding scale policy have a direct effect on the number of individuals permanently excluded from Dutch society – although this effect is somewhat diminished by the application of European human rights law. Nonetheless, increasingly long-term members are formally excluded from the Dutch polity. Anyone who is not a formal citizen can be permanently excluded and this has become increasingly common in recent years. In other words, non-citizens are 'probationary members', who can have their membership revoked following a criminal conviction (Stumpf, 2006). For a long time, legal permanent residents were exempt from legal precarity, as opposed to non-citizens and temporary legal residents (Ellermann, 2019). However, nowadays any legal migrant who does not obtain legal citizenship is never fully included in the polity. More recently, even citizens have had their inclusion revoked as a result of convictions for terrorism. Such practices seem to reflect societal notions about migrants who, despite having lived in the Netherlands for almost their entire life, are still perceived as foreign (Gibney, 2019). Exclusion is subsequently further institutionalised in the criminal justice system through differential treatment in terms of punishment. The different prison, prison regime, and release policies that are reserved for non-citizens add to the feeling of being an outsider.

Crimmigration blurs the boundaries between citizens and non-citizens and amplifies the impact of bordering practices on legal residents and citizens. The introduction of crime control elements in bordering practices means that denizens and even citizens are increasingly targeted by these practices, based on alleged or actual criminality. As Ellermann (2019, p. 2) claims,

> "far from reflecting a linear progression from alien to denizen to citizen, status can travel along downward trajectories that – even for permanent residents and certain citizens – can result in legal precarity and loss of status."

For some members of society, their access to full and equal citizenship is hampered on the basis of their identity. Ultimately this has an effect on the legitimacy and effectiveness of these bordering practices, when self-perceptions of people collide with how they are perceived and treated by authorities, especially in the absence of proper accountability and transparency. As chapter five discussed, legal citizens targeted by the MSM challenged the legitimacy of this bordering practice. Similarly, chapters six and seven highlighted how those migrants who perceived themselves as members were most critical of their classification and related treatment as outsiders. As a result, they were also less likely to cooperate with the authorities. Crimmigration thus creates a growing group of outsiders, who nonetheless feel like they should belong and often stay in society. This illustrates the problematic nature of using bordering practices in response to criminal behaviour.

As Bowling and Westenra (2018) argue, crimmigration "has the effect of widening the net of social control", as non-citizens are increasingly perceived and treated as criminals and criminals are increasingly perceived and treated as non-citizens. As has been illustrated by this dissertation, these processes intersect in familiar – and sometimes less familiar – "various axes of social stratification", in particular race/ethnicity, nationality, class, and gender, to "closely map onto social group membership" (Ellermann, 2019, pp. 3, 2). Benhabib (Benhabib, 2002, p. 37) already observed more than fifteen years ago, that "what is emerging in contemporary Europe is a mixed bag of rights, entitlements, and privileges, distributed quite unevenly across resident populations, in accordance with varying principles." The citizen and non-citizen are not binary categories, but rather two ends of a continuum with many different legal *and* social categories in between (Ellermann, 2019; Wonders & Jones, 2018). These different categories are shaped by practices of territorial, organisational, and conceptual bordering (Geddes, 2008; Weber, 2019). The case studies in this dissertation have illustrated what this means in practice. In particular, it matters whether one has national citizenship, EU citizenship, or legal membership, as all these categories come with a set of legally defined rights, entitlements, and privileges. It also matters whether one is *perceived* as having national citizenship, EU citizenship, legal membership, as this has an effect on how one is treated by authorities, and therefore also on one's rights, entitlements, and privileges. These different categories are increasingly shaped by the criminal justice system. What we are observing is a hierarchy of membership on the basis of citizenship and moral worth, as well as *perceived* citizenship and moral worth.

8.4.6 Globalisation, migration control, and criminology

As already noted in the introduction, globalisation forces criminologists to see beyond their traditional research sites and subjects. This dissertation has illustrated that it is not only desirable for the field of criminology to engage with questions of migration control and citizenship, but that it has become crucial to properly understand contemporary criminal justice systems and social control.

First, the case study of the MSM has illustrated how, in the absence of real border controls, novel forms of border policing have emerged around the intra-Schengen border areas. These practices are aimed at controlling migration as well as controlling criminal suspects and should therefore be of key interest to criminologists (Pickering, Bosworth, & Aas, 2014). Second, it barely needs to be argued that the punishment and deportation of CCNCs warrants attention from criminologists. Chapter six and seven have highlighted how contemporary criminal justice is crucially shaped by issues of citizenship and migration, as the nature and impact of criminal justice strongly depends on someone's legal status. With nearly one in every four prisoners being a foreigner, it is clear that penal scholars cannot study the prison anymore as a purely national institution. As processes of globalisation and increased international mobility are likely to keep presenting significant challenges to traditionally domestic criminal justice systems in the near future, we cannot understand the how and why of contemporary punishment practices without engaging with issues of citizenship and migration control (Bosworth, 2012; Kaufman & Bosworth, 2013; Turnbull & Hasselberg, 2017).

The recent criminological turn towards borders as a key site of engagement has raised the questions who should be included in criminological enquiries. Migrants and non-citizens have long been excluded from mainstream criminological research (Pickering et al., 2014; Wonders & Jones, 2018), but with growing numbers of migration related act being criminalised and increasing numbers of foreigners inside the prisons, at least in many western countries, this has started to change in recent years. This has also forced a reconceptualisation of who are seen as included and excluded. As Aas (2007, p. 289) notes, even those who are considered as outsiders by mainstream criminology "in many ways are still 'insiders' of the privileged club of western citizens." By opening up criminological analysis to include migrants, non-citizens, and foreigners, the contours of a more global system of crimmigration control start to emerge.

References

CHAPTER 1

Aas, K. F. (2007). Analysing a world in motion: Global flows meet 'criminology of the other'. *Theoretical Criminology, 11*(2), 283-303.

Aas, K. F. (2011). "Crimmigrant" bodies and bona fide travelers: surveillance, citizenship and global governance. *Theoretical Criminology, 15*(3), 331-346.

Aas, K. F. (2013). The ordered and the bordered society: migration control, citizenship, and the northern penal state. In K. F. Aas & M. Bosworth (Eds.), *The borders of punishment: migration, citizenship, and social exclusion* (pp. 21-39). Oxford: Oxford University Press.

Aas, K. F. (2014). Bordered penality: Precarious membership and abnormal justice. *Punishment & Society, 16*(5), 520-541.

Aliverti, A. (2012). Exploring the Function of Criminal Law in the Policing of Foreigners: The Decision to Prosecute Immigration-related Offences. *Social & Legal Studies, 21*(4), 511-527.

Aliverti, A., & Bosworth, M. (2017). Introduction: Criminal justice adjudication in an age of migration. *New Criminal Law Review, 20*(1), 1-11.

Aliverti, A., Milivojevic, S., & Weber, L. (2019). Tracing Imprints of the Border in the Territorial, Justice and Welfare Domains: A Multi-Site Ethnography. *The Howard Journal of Crime and Justice.*

Balibar, E. (2002). *Politics and the Other Scene.* London & New York: Verso.

Barbero, I. (2018). The European Union Never got Rid of Its Internal Controls. *European Journal of Migration and Law, 20*(1), 1-27.

Benhabib, S. (2002). In search of Europe's borders. The politics of migration in the European Union. *Dissent, 49*(4), 33-39.

Blackwood, L. (2015). Policing Airport Spaces: The Muslim Experience of Scrutiny. *Policing, 9*(3), 255-264.

Bloemraad, I. (2015). Theorizing and Analyzing Citizenship in Multicultural Societies. *Sociological Quarterly, 56*(4), 591-606.

Bosworth, M. (2012). Subjectivity and identity in detention: Punishment and society in a global age. *Theoretical Criminology, 16*(2), 123-140.

Bosworth, M. (2014). *Inside immigration detention: foreigners in a carceral age.* Oxford: Oxford University Press.

Bosworth, M., Aas, K. F., & Pickering, S. (2017). Punishment, globalization and migration control: "Get them the hell out of here." *Punishment & Society, 20*(1), 34-53.

Bosworth, M., & Guild, M. (2008). Governing Through Migration Control: Security and Citizenship in Britain. *British Journal of Criminology, 48*(6), 703-719.

Bosworth, M., Hasselberg, I., & Turnbull, S. (2016). Punishment, citizenship and identity: An Introduction. *Criminology and Criminal Justice, 16*(3), 257-266.

Bowling, B., & Westenra, S. (2018). 'A really hostile environment': Adiaphorization, global policing and the crimmigration control system. *Theoretical Criminology, Online fir*, 1-21.

Browne, S. (2006). Getting Carded: Border Control and the Politics of Canada's Permanent Resident Card. *Citizenship Studies, 9*(4), 423-438.

Casella Colombeau, S. (2019). Crisis of Schengen? The effect of two 'migrant crises' (2011 and 2015) on the free movement of people at an internal Schengen border. *Journal of Ethnic and Migration Studies, online fir*, 1-17.

Chacon, J. M. (2009). Managing Migration Through Crime. *Columbia Law Review, 109*, 135-148.

Cote-Boucher, K. (2011). Bordering citizenship in ' an open and generous society ' The criminalization of migration in Canada. In S. Pickering & J. Ham (Eds.), *The Routledge Handbook on Crime and International Migration* (pp. 75-90). London: Routledge.

Cote-Boucher, K., Infantino, F., & Salter, M. B. (2014). Border security as practice: an agenda for research. *Security Dialogue, 45*(3), 195-208.

De Vries, H. (2014). Uitzetting van criminele illegalen: procedures en ontwikkelingen. *Tijdschrift Voor Politie, 76*(3), 6-9.

Di Molfetta, E., & Brouwer, J. (2019). Unravelling the 'crimmigration knot': Penal subjectivities, punishment and the censure machine. *Criminology and Criminal Justice*, Online first, 1-17.

Diener, A. C., & Hagen, J. (2009). Theorizing borders in a "borderless world": Globalization, territory and identity. *Geography Compass, 3*(3), 1196-1216.

Downes, D., & Van Swaaningen, R. (2007). The road to dystopia: changes in the penal climate in the Netherlands. *Crime and Justice, 35*(1), 31-72.

Fabini, G. (2019). Internal bordering in the context of undeportability: Border performances in Italy. *Theoretical Criminology, Online fir*, 1-19.

Fassin, D. (2011). Policing borders, producing boundaries: The governmentality of immigration in dark times. *Annual Review of Anthropology, 40*, 213-226.

Feeley, M., & Simon, J. (1992). The New Penology: Notes of the Emerging Strategy for Corrections and its Implications. *Criminology, 30*(4), 449-474.

Garip, F., Gleeson, S., & Hall, M. (2019). How the State Criminalizes Immigrants and to What Effect: A Multidisciplinary Account. *American Behavioral Scientist*.

Garland, D. (2001). *The culture of control: crime and social order in contemporary society*. Chicago: University of Chicago Press.

Geddes, A. (2008). *Immigration & European Integration: Beyond Fortress Europe?* Manchester: Manchester University Press.

Gready, P. (2004). Conceptualising globalisation and human rights: boomerangs and borders. *International Journal of Human Rights, 8*, 345-354.

Green, P., & Grewcock, M. (2002). The War against Illegal Immigration: State Crime and the Construction of a European Identity. *Current Issues in Criminal Justice, 14*(1), 87-101.

Grewcock, M. (2011). Punishment, deportation and parole: The detention and removal of former prisoners under section 501 Migration Act 1958. *Australian & New Zealand Journal of Criminology, 44*(1), 56-73.

Hogg, R. (2002). Criminology beyond the Nation State: Global Conflict, Human Rights and the "New World Disorder." In K. Carrington & R. Hogg (Eds.), *Critical Criminology: Issues, Debates, Challenges* (pp. 185-217). Cullompton: Willan Publishing.

Huysmans, J. (2007). *The Politics of Insecurity: Fear, Migration and Asylum in the EU? JCMS: Journal of Common Market Studies* (Vol. 45).

Kanstroom, D. (2000). Deportation, social control, and punishment: Some thoughts about why hard laws make bad cases. *Harvard Law Review, 11*, 1889-1935.

Kaufman, E. (2014). Gender at the border: Nationalism and the new logic of punishment. *Punishment & Society, 16*(2), 135-151.

Kaufman, E. (2015). *Punish and Expel. Border Control, Nationalism, and the New Purpose of the Prison*. Oxford: Oxford University Press.

Leerkes, A., & Broeders, D. (2010). A case of mixed motives? Formal and informal functions of administrative immigration detention. *British Journal of Criminology, 50*(5), 830-850.

Leerkes, A., Engbersen, G., & Van der Leun, J. P. (2012). Crime among irregular immigrants and the influence of internal border control. *Crime, Law and Social Change, 58*(1), 15-38.

Leerkes, A., Leach, M. A., & Bachmeier, J. D. (2012). Borders Behind the Border: An Exploration of State-Level Differences in Migration Control and their Effects on US Migration Patterns. *Journal of Ethnic and Migration Studies, 38*(1), 111-129.

Legomsky, S. (2005). The Ethnic and Religious Profling of Noncitizens: National Security and International Human Rights. *Boston College Third World Law Journal, 25*(1), 161-196.

Legomsky, S. (2007). The new path of immigration law: asymmetic incorporation of criminal justice norms. *Washington and Lee University Law Review, 64*, 469-528.

Lipsky, M. (1980). *Street level bureaucracy: dilemmas of the individual in public services*. New York: Russel Sage Foundation.

Loader, I., & Sparks, R. (2002). Contemporary Landscapes of Crime, Order, and Control: Governance, Risk, and Globalization. In M. Maguire, R. Morgan, & R. Reiner (Eds.), *The Oxford Handbook of Criminology* (pp. 83-111). Oxford: Oxford University Press.

Loftus, B. (2015). Border regimes and the sociology of policing. *Policing and Society, 25*(1), 115-125.

Lyon, D. (2007). Surveillance, security and social sorting: emerging research priorities. *International Criminal Justice Review, 17*(1), 161-170.

Marin, L., & Spena, A. (2016). Introduction: The Criminalization of Migration and European (Dis)Integration. *European Journal of Migration and Law, 18*, 147-156.

Melin, R. (2016). 'Debordering' and 'rebordering': discriminatory and racial discourses of borders under globalisation. *International Journal of Migration and Border Studies, 2*(1), 59-76.

Menjívar, C., Gómez Cervantes, A., & Alvord, D. (2018). The expansion of "crimmigration", mass detention, and deportation. *Sociology Compass*, 1-15.

Miller, T. (2003). Citizenship and severity: recent immigration reforms and the new penology. *Georgetown Immigration Law Journal, 17*, 611-662.

Moffette, D. (2014). Governing immigration through probation: The displacement of borderwork and the assessment of desirability in Spain. *Security Dialogue, 45*(3), 262-278.

Moffette, D. (2018). The jurisdictional games of immigration policing: Barcelona's fight against unauthorised street vending. *Theoretical Criminology, Online fir*, 1-18.

Momen, M. (2005). Are you a Citizen? Insights from Borderlands. *Citizenship Studies, 9*(3), 323-334.

Monforte, P. (2015). The border as a space of contention: the spatial strategies of protest against border controls in Europe. *Citizenship Studies, 1025*(March), 1-16.

Motomura, H. (1993). Haitian asylum seekers: interdiction and immigrants' rights. *Cornell International Law Journal, 26*, 698-717.

Newman, D. (2006). The lines that continue to separate us: borders in our 'borderless' world. *Progress in Human Geography, 30*(2), 143-161.

Nijland, J. A. (2012). Vreemdelingenbewaring in crimmigratieperspectief. Over de rol van strafrechtelijke antecedenten en het ultimumremediumbeginsel voor de maatregel van bewaring in de rechtspraktijk. *Proces, 91*(6), 456-469.

Pakes, F. (2004). The politics of discontent: the emergence of a new criminal justice discourse in the Netherlands. *The Howard Journal of Criminal Justice, 43*(3), 284-298.

Pakes, F. (2013). Globalisation and criminology: an agenda of engagement. In F. Pakes (Ed.), *Globalisation and the challenge to Criminology* (pp. 1-9). New York: Routledge.

Pakes, F., & Holt, K. (2017). Crimmigration and the prison: Comparing trends in prison policy and practice in England & Wales and Norway. *European Journal of Criminology, 14*(1), 63-77.

Parmar, A. (2019). Arresting (Non)Citizenship: The Policing Migration Nexus of Nationality, Race and Criminalization. *Theoretical Criminology, Online fir*, 1-19.

Pickering, S., Bosworth, M., & Aas, K. F. (2014). The criminology of mobility. In S. Pickering & J. Ham (Eds.), *The Routledge Handbook on Crime and International Migration* (pp. 382-395). Oxford: Routledge.

Pickering, S., & Weber, L. (2006). *Borders, Mobility and Technologies of Control*. Dordrecht: Springer.

Pratt, A., & Thompson, S. K. (2008). Chivalry, "race" and discretion at the Canadian border. *British Journal of Criminology, 48*(5), 620-640.

Salter, M. B. (2008). When the exception becomes the rule: borders, sovereignty, and citizenship. *Citizenship Studies, 12*(4), 365-380.

Sklansky, D. A. (2012). Crime, immigration, and ad hoc instrumentalism. *New Criminal Law Review, 15*(2), 157-223.

Stanley, E. (2017). Expanding crimmigration: The detention and deportation of New Zealanders from Australia. *Australian & New Zealand Journal of Criminology*, 1-18.

Staring, R. (2012). Crimmigratie en de morele economie van illegale vreemdelingen. *PROCES, 91*(6), 396-407.

Stronks, M. (2013). Een bijna ongebreidelde beteugeling van de tijd. Een analyse van aanscherpingen van de glijdende schaal. *Nederlands Juristenblad, 34*, 2306-2314.

Stumpf, J. P. (2006). The crimmigration crisis: immigrants, crime, and sovereign power. *American University Law Review, 56*(2), 367-420.

Stumpf, J. P. (2013). Two profiles of crimmigration law: criminal deportation and illegal migration. In F. Pakes (Ed.), *Globalisation and the challenge to Criminology* (pp. 91-109). New York: Routledge.

Turnbull, S., & Hasselberg, I. (2017). From prison to detention: The carceral trajectories of foreign-national prisoners in the United Kingdom. *Punishment & Society, 19*(2), 135-154.

Ugelvik, T. (2017). The Limits of the Welfare State? Foreign National Prisoners in the Norwegian Crimmigration Prison. In P. Scharff Smith & T. Ugelvik (Eds.), *Scandinavia Penal History, Culture and Prison Practice: Embraced by the Welfare State* (pp. 405-423). London: Palgrave.

Ugelvik, T., & Damsa, D. (2018). The pains of crimmigration imprisonment: Perspectives from a Norwegian all-foreign prison. *The British Journal of Criminology, 58*(5), 1025-1043.

Van Berlo, P. (2015). Australia's Operation Sovereign Borders: Discourse, Power, and Policy from a Crimmigration Perspective. *Refugee Survey Quarterly, 34*(4), 75-104.

Van Berlo, P. (2017). The Protection of Asylum Seekers in Australian-Pacific Offshore Processing: the Legal Deficit of Human Rights in a Nodal Reality. *Human Rights Law Review, 17*(1), 33-71.

Van der Leun, J. P., & Van der Woude, M. A. H. (2012). A reflection on crimmigration in the Netherlands. On the cultural security complex and the impact of framing. In M. Joao Guia, M. Van der Woude, & J. Van der Leun (Eds.), *Social control and justice: crimmigration in the Age of Fear* (pp. 41-60). The Hague: Eleven International Publishing.

Van der Leun, J. P., Van der Woude, M. A. H., & De Ridder, S. (2013). Crimmigratie in de lage landen: smeltende grenzen? *Strafblad, 11*(3), 221-228.

Van der Woude, M. A. H., Barker, V., & Van der Leun, J. P. (2017). Crimmigration in Europe. *European Journal of Criminology, 14*(1), 3-6.

Van der Woude, M.A.H., & Brouwer, J. (2017). Searching for 'illegal' junk in the trunk. Underlying intentions of (cr)immigration controls in Schengen's border areas. *New criminal law review* 20 (1), 157-179.

Van der Woude, M. A. H., Brouwer, J., & Dekkers, T. J. M. (2016). *Beslissen in grensgebieden. Een onderzoek naar het Mobiel Toezicht Veiligheid zoals uitgevoerd door de Koninklijke Marechaussee.* Den Haag: Boom Juridische Uitgevers.

Van der Woude, M. A. H., Dekkers, T. J. M., & Brouwer, J. (2015). Over crimmigratie en discretionair beslissen binnen het Mobiel Toezicht Veiligheid ... of Vreemdelingen ... of Veiligheid? *Tijdschrift voor Veiligheid, 14*(2), 19-35.

Van der Woude, M. A. H., & Van Berlo, P. (2015). Crimmigration at the internal borders of Europe? Examining the Schengen governance package. *Utrecht Law Review, 11*(1), 61-79.

van der Woude, M. A. H., & van der Leun, J. P. (2017). Crimmigration checks in the internal border areas of the EU: finding the discretion that matters. *European Journal of Criminology, 14*(1), 27-45.

Van der Woude, M. A. H., Van der Leun, J. P., & Nijland, J. A. (2014). Crimmigration in the Netherlands. *Law & Social Inquiry, 39*(3), 560-579.

van Houtum, H., & van Naerssen, T. (2002). Bordering, Ordering and Othering. *Tijdschrift voor Economische en Sociale Geografie, 93*(2), 125-136.

Van Swaaningen, R. (2005). Public safety and the management of fear. *Theoretical Criminology, 9*(3), 289-305.

Vega, I. I. (2019). Toward a Cultural Sociology of Immigration Control: A Call for Research. *American Behavioral Scientist.*

Vollmer, B. (2017). A Hermeneutical Approach to European Bordering. *Journal of Contemporary European Studies, 25*(1), 1-15.
Walters, W. (2002). Deportation, Expulsion, and the International Police of Aliens. *Citizenship Studies, 6*(3), 265-292.
Weber, L. (2006). The shifting frontiers of migration control. In S. Pickering & L. Weber (Eds.), *Borders, Mobility and Technologies of Control* (pp. 21-43). Leiden: Springer.
Weber, L. (2011). 'It sounds like they shouldn't be here': immigration checks on the streets of Sydney. *Policing and Society, 21*(4), 456-467.
Weber, L. (2014). Deciphering deportation practices across the Global North. In S. Pickering & J. Ham (Eds.), *The Routledge Handbook on Crime and International Migration* (pp. 155-179). New York: Routledge.
Weber, L. (2018). From state-centric to transversal borders: Resisting the 'structurally embedded border' in Australia. *Theoretical Criminology, Online fir*, 1-19.
Weber, L. (2019). 'My kids won't grow up here': Policing, bordering and belonging. *Theoretical Criminology, Online fir*, 1-19.
Weber, L., & Bowling, B. (2004). Policing Migration: a Framework for Investigating the Regulation of Global Mobility. *Policing and Society, 14*(3), 195-212.
Weber, L., & McCulloch, J. (2018). Penal power and border control: which thesis? Sovereignty, governmentality, or the pre-emptive state? *Punishment & Society.*
Welch, M. (2004). Quiet constructions in the war on terror: subjecting asylum seekers to unnecessary detention. *Social Justice, 31*(1/2), 113-129.

CHAPTER 2

Aarts, K., & Semetko, H. A. (2003). The divided electorate: media use and political involvement. *Journal of Politics, 65*(2), 759-784.
Aas, K. F. (2011). "Crimmigrant" bodies and bona fide travelers: Surveillance, citizenship and global governance. *Theoretical Criminology, 15*, 331-346.
Allen, W., & Blinder, S. (2013). *Migration in the News: Portrayals of immigrants, migrants, asylum seekers and refugees in National British Newspapers, 2010-2012.*
Anderson, B. (2013). *Us and them? The dangerous politics of immigration control.* Oxford: Oxford University Press.
Anderson, B., & Ruhs, M. (2010). Researching illegality and labour migration. *Population, Space and Place, 16*(3), 175-179.
Baker, P. (2006). *Using corpora in discourse analysis*. London: Continuum.
Baker, P. (2012). Acceptable bias? Using corpus linguistics methods with critical discourse analysis. *Critical Discourse Studies, 9*(3), 247-256.
Baker, P., Gabrielatos, C., KhosraviNik, M., Krzyzanowski, M., McEnery, T., & Wodak, R. (2008). A useful methodological synergy? Combining critical discourse analysis and corpus linguistics to examine discourses of refugees and asylum seekers in the UK press. *Discourse & Society, 19*(3), 273-306.
Baker, P., Gabrielatos, C., & McEnery, T. (2013). *Discourse analysis and media attitudes: the representation of Islam in the British press.* Cambridge: Cambridge University Press.

Bakker, P., & Vasterman, P. (2007). The Dutch media landscape. In G. Terzis (Ed.), *European media governance: naitonal and regional dimensions* (pp. 145-157). Bristol: Intellect books.

Bauder, H. (2014). Why We Should Use the Term "Illegalized" Refugee or Immigrant: A Commentary. *International Journal of Refugee Law, 00*(00), 1-6.

Berezin, M. (2009). *Illiberal politics in neoliberal times: culture, security and populism in the new Europe*. Cambridge: Cambridge University Press.

Bleich, E., Bloemraad, I., & de Graauw, E. (2015). Migrants, minorities and the media: information, representations and participation in the public sphere. *Journal of Ethnic and Migration Studies, 41*(6), 857-873.

Bleich, E., Stonebraker, H., Nisar, H., & Abdelhamid, R. (2015). Media Portrayals of Minorities: Muslims in British Newspaper Headlines, 2001-2012. *Journal of Ethnic and Migration Studies, 41*(6), 942-962.

Blinder, S., & Allen, W. (2015). Constructing immigrants: portrayals of migrant groups in British national newspapers, 2010-2012. *International Migration Review*, 1-38.

Boomgaarden, H. G., & Vliegenthart, R. (2009). How news content influences anti-immigration attitudes: Germany, 1993-2005. *European Journal of Political Research, 48*(4), 516-542.

Bosworth, M., & Guild, M. (2008). Governing Through Migration Control: Security and Citizenship in Britain. *British Journal of Criminology, 48*(6), 703-719.

Broersma, M., & Graham, T. (2013). Twitter As a News Source. How Dutch and British newspapers used tweets in their news coverage, 2007-2011. *Journalism Practice, 7*(4),

Caviedes, A. (2015). An emerging "European" portrayal of immigration? *Journal of Ethnic and Migration Studies, 41*(6), 897-917.

Chacon, J. M. (2009). Managing Migration Through Crime. *Columbia Law Review, 109*, 135-148.

Cohen, S. (1972). *Folk devils and moral panics. The creation of the mods and rockers.* London: McGibbon and Kee.

Cohen, S. (2002). *Folk Devils and Moral Panics (third edition)*. London: Routledge.

Duffy, B., & Frere-Smith, T. (2014). *Perceptions and reality. Public attitudes to immigration.*

Dunaway, J., Branton, R. P., & Abrajano, M. A. (2010). Agenda setting, public opinion, and the issue of immigration reform. *Social Science Quarterly, 91*(2), 359-378.

Düvell, F. (2011). Paths into irregularity: the legal and political construction of irregular migration. *European Journal of Migration and Law2, 13*(1), 275-295.

Entman, R. M. (1993). Framing: towards clarification of a fractured paradigm. *Journal of Communication, 43*(4), 51-58.

Fairclough, N. (1989). *Language and power*. London: Longman.

Gabrielatos, C. (2007). Selecting query terms to build a specialised corpus from a restricted-access database. *ICAME Journal, 31*(5), 5-43.

Gabrielatos, C., & Baker, P. (2008). *Fleeing, Sneaking, Flooding: A Corpus Analysis of Discursive Constructions of Refugees and Asylum Seekers in the UK Press, 1996-2005. Journal of English Linguistics* (Vol. 36).

Gerard, A., & Pickering, S. (2013). Crimmigration. Criminal justice, refugee protection and the securitisation of migration. In B. Arrigo & H. Bersot (Eds.), *The Routledge Handbook of International Crime and Justice Studies* (pp. 587-611). New York: Routledge.

Goffman, E. (1974). *Frame analysis: An essay on the organization of experience*. Cambridge, MA: Harvard University Press.
Goode, E., & Ben-Yehuda, N. (2009). *Moral panics: the social construction of deviance (2nd edition)*. Malden: Wiley-Blackwell.
Grimmer, J., & Stewart, B. M. (2013). Text as data: the promise and pitfalls of automatic content analysis methods for political texts. *Political Analysis, 21*(3), 295-314.
Guild, E. (2004). Who is an irregular migrant? In B. Bogusz, R. Cholewinski, A. Cygan, & E. Szyszak (Eds.), *Irregular migration and human rights: theoretical, European and international perspectives*. Leiden: Martinus Nijhoff Publishers.
Hall, S., Critcher, C., Jefferson, T., Clarke, J., & Roberts, B. (1978). *Policing the crisis: mugging, the state, and law and order*. London: MacMillan.
Hallin, D. C. (2015). The Dynamics of Immigration Coverage in Comparative Perspective. *American Behavioral Scientist, 59*(7), 876-885.
Hartry, A. S. (2012). Gendering crimmigration: the intersection of gender, immigration and the criminal justice system. *Berkeley Journal of Gender, Law & Justice*, 2(8), 1-27.
Hauptman, S. (2013). *The criminalization of immigration: the post 9/11 moral panic*. El Paso: LFB Scholarly Publishing.
Helbling, M. (2013). Framing immigration in Western Europe. *Journal of Ethnic and Migration Studies, 40*(1), 101-122.
Hier, S. P. (2009). Beyond vernacular commentary: a response to Minelle Mahtani. *Canadian Journal of Communication, 35*, 173-178.
Kim, S., Carvalho, J. P., Davis, A. G., & Mullins, A. M. (2011). The view of the border: news framing of the definition, causes, and solutions to illegal immigration. *Mass Communication and Society, 14*(3), 292-314.
Kinney, E. (2015). Victims, villains, and valiant rescuers: unpacking sociolegal constructions of human trafficking and crimmigration in popular culture. In M.J. Guia (Ed.), *The illegal business of human trafficking* (pp. 87-108). New York: Springer.
Knoll, B. R., Redlawsk, D. P., & Sanborn, H. (2012). Framing labels and immigration policy attitudes in the Iowa Caucuses: "Trying to Out-Tancredo Tancredo." *Political Behavior, 33*(3), 433-454.
Koller, V., & Mautner, G. (2004). Computer applications in Critical Discourse Analysis. In C. Coffin, A. Hewings, & K. O'Halloran (Eds.), *Applying English grammar: corpus and functional approaches* (pp. 216-228). London: Arnold.
Lakoff, G., & Ferguson, S. (2006). *The framing of immigration*. Berkeley.
Lawlor, A. (2015). Local and national accounts of immigration framing in a cross-national perspective. *Journal of Ethnic and Migration Studies, 41*(6), 918-941.
Leerkes, A., & Broeders, D. (2010). A case of mixed motives? Formal and informal functions of administrative immigration detention. *British Journal of Criminology, 50*(5), 830-850.
Legomsky, S. (2007). The new path of immigration law: asymmetic incorporation of criminal justice norms. *Washington and Lee University Law Review, 64*, 469-528.
Lesisnka, M. (2014). The European backlash against immigration and multiculturalism. *Journal of Sociology, 50*(1), 37-50.
Maneri, M. (2011). Media discourse on immigration: control practices and the language we live. In S. Palidda (Ed.), *Racial criminalization of migrants in the 21st century* (pp. 77-93). Farnham: Ashgate.

Maneri, M., & Wal, J. (2005). The Criminalisation of Ethnic Groups?: An Issue for Media Analysis. *Forum: Qualitative Social Research*, *6*(3).

Mautner, G. (2009). Checks and balances: how corpus linguistics can contribute to CDA. In R. Wodak & M. Meyer (Eds.), *Methods of Critical Discourse Analysis* (pp. 122-143). London: Sage.

Mawby, R. C., & Gisby, W. (2009). Crime, Media and Moral Panic in an Expanding European Union. *The Howard Journal of Criminal Justice*, *48*(1), 37-51.

McCombs, M. E., & Shaw, D. L. (1972). The agenda-setting function of the press. *Public Opinion Quarterly*, *36*(176-187).

McEnery, A., & Wilson, A. (1996). *Corpus Linguistics*. Edinburgh: Edinburg University Press.

Merolla, J., Ramakrishnan, S. K., & Haynes, C. (2013). "Illegal," "Undocumented," or "Unauthorised": Equivalency frames, issue frames and public opinion on immigration. *Perspectives on Politics*, *11*(3), 789-807.

Mountz, A. (2010). *Seeking asylum: human smuggling and bureaucracy at the border*. Minneapolis: University of Minnesota Press.

Mutsaers, P. (2014). An ethnographic study of the policing of internal borders in the Netherlands. Synergies between criminology and anthropology. *British Journal of Criminology*, *54*(5), 831-848.

Orpin, D. (2005). Corpus linguistics and critical discourse analysis: examining the ideology of sleaze. *International Journal of Corpus Linguistics*, *10*(1), 37-61.

Pakes, F. (2006). The ebb and flow of criminal justice in the Netherlands. *International Journal of the Sociology of Law*, *34*(2), 141-156.

Palidda, S. (2009). *Criminalization and victimization of immigrants in Europe*.

Parkin, J. (2013). *The criminalisation of migration in Europe: a state-of-the-art of the academic literature and research* (No. 61).

Pinker, S. (2007). *The stuff of thought: language as a window into human nature*. New York: Viking.

Ruhs, M., & Anderson, B. (2010). Semi-compliance and illegality in migrant labour markets: an analysis of migrants, employers and the state in the UK. *Population, Space and Place*, *16*(1), 195-212.

Schuster, L. (2011). Turning refugees into "illegal migrants": Afghan asylum seekers in Europe. *Ethnic and Racial Studies*, *34*(8), 1392-1407.

Sciortino, G., & Colombo, A. (2004). The flows and the flood: the public discourse on immigration in Italy 1969-2001. *Journal of Modern Italian Studies*, *9*(1), 94-113.

Sklansky, D. A. (2012). Crime , Immigration , and Ad Hoc Instrumentalism. *New Criminal Law Review*, *15*(2), 157-223.

Sniderman, P., & Hagendoorn, L. (2007). *When ways of life collide: multiculturalism and its discontents in the Netherlands*. Princeton: Princenton University Press.

Spena, A. (2014). Iniuria Migrandi: Criminalization of Immigrants and the Basic Principles of the Criminal Law. *Criminal Law and Philosophy*, *8*(3), 635-657.

Stubbs, M. (1994). Grammar, text and ideology: computer-assisted methods in the linguistics of representation. *Applied Linguistics*, *15*(2), 201-223.

Stumpf, J. P. (2006). The crimmigration crisis: immigrants, crime, and sovereign power. *American University Law Review*, *56*(2), 367-420.

Thorbjornsrud, K. (2015). Framing Irregular Immigration in Western Media. *American Behavioral Scientist*, *59*(7), 771-782.

Thredgold, T. (2009). *The media and migration in the United Kingdom, 1999 to 2009*. Washington, DC.

Tolley, E. (2015). Racial mediation in the coverage of candidates' political viability: a comparison of approaches. *Journal of Ethnic and Migration Studies, 41*(6), 963-984.

Tsoukala, A. (2005). Looking at immigrants as enemies. In D. Bigo & E. Guild (Eds.), *Controlling frontiers. Free movement into and within Europe* (pp. 161-192). Aldershot: Ashgate.

van Berlo, P. (2015). Australia's Operation Sovereign Borders: discourse, power, and policy from a crimmigration perspective. *Refugee Survey Quarterly, 34*(4), 75-104.

Van der Heijden, P. G. M., Cruyff, M., & van Gils, G. H. C. (2011). *Schattingen illegaal in Nederland verblijvende vreemdelingen 2009*. Den Haag.

van der Leun, J. P. (2006). Excluding illegal migrants in the Netherlands: between national policies and local implementations. *West European Politics, 29*(2), 304-320.

van der Leun, J. P. (2010). *Crimmigratie*. Apeldoorn/Antwerpen: Maklu.

van der Leun, J. P., & Ilies, M. (2010). The Netherlands: assessing the irregular population in a restrictive setting. In A. Triandafyllidou (Ed.), *Irregular migration in Europe. Myths and realities* (pp. 187-206). Aldershot: Ashgate.

van der Leun, J., & van der Woude, M. (2012). A Reflection on Crimmigration in the Netherlands On the Cultural Security Complex and the Impact of Framing. In M. Joao Guia, M. van der Woude, & J. van der Leun (Eds.), *Social control and justice: crimmigration in the Age of Fear* (pp. 41-60). The Hague: Eleven International Publishing.

van Eijl, C. (2008). Tracing back "illegal aliens" in the Netherlands, 1850-1940. In M. Schrover, J. van der Leun, & C. Quispel (Eds.), *Illegal Migration and Gender in a Global and Historical Perspective* (pp. 39-56). Amsterdam: Amsterdam University Press.

van Liempt, I. (2007). *Navigating borders. Inside perspectives on the process of human smuggling into the Netherlands*. Amsterdam: Amsterdam University Press.

van Meeteren, M. (2010). *Irregular migrants in Belgium and the Netherlands; Aspirations and Incorporation*. Amsterdam: Amsterdam University Press.

Vliegenthart, R., & Boomgaarden, H. G. (2007). Real-World Indicators and the Coverage of Immigration and the Integration of Minorities in Dutch Newspapers. *European Journal of Communication, 22*(3), 293-314.

Vollmer, B. a. (2011). Policy Discourses on Irregular Migration in the EU – "Number Games" and "Political Games." *European Journal of Migration and Law, 13*(3), 317-339.

Wansink, H. A. (2007). Tussen populisme en rechtsradicalisme: overeenkomsten en verschillen tussen de Leefbaren, de fortuynisten en Wilders. *Justitiele Verkenningen, 5*(2), 68-74.

Welch, M. (2004). Quiet constructions in the war on terror: subjecting asylum seekers to unnecessary detention. *Social Justice, 31*(1/2), 113-129.

Welch, M. (2012). The Sonics of Crimmigration in Australia: Wall of Noise and Quiet Manoeuvring. *British Journal of Criminology, 52*(2), 324-344.

Welch, M., & Schuster, L. (2005). Detention of asylum seekers in the UK and USA. Deciphering noisy and quiet constructions. *Punishment & Society, 7*(4), 397-417.

Woude, M. van der, van der Leun, J. P., & Nijland, J.-A. A. (2014). Crimmigration in the Netherlands. *Law & Social Inquiry, 39*(3), 560-579.

CHAPTER 3

Aas, K. F., & Gundhus, H. O. I. (2015). Policing humanitarian borderlands: Frontex, human rights and the precariousness of life. *British Journal of Criminology, 55*(1), 1-18.

Alpert, G. P., Macdonald, J. M., & Dunham, R. G. (2005). Police suspicion and discretionary decision making during citizen stops. *Criminology, 43*(2), 407-434.

Bastien, J. (2009). Goal ambiguity and informal discretion in the implementation of public policies: the case of Spanish immigration policy. *International Review of Administrative Sciences, 75*(4), 665-685.

Brouwer, J., Van der Woude, M. A. H., & Van der Leun, J. P. (2017). (Cr)immigrant framing in border areas: decision making processes of Dutch border police officers. *Policing and Society, Online fir*, 1-16.

Brown, M. K. (1981). *Working the Street: Police Discretion and the Dilemmas of Reform.* New York: Russell Sage Found.

Casella Colombeau, S. (2017) Policing the internal Schengen borders – managing the double bind between free movement and migration control. Policing and Society, 14(1), 63-77.

Corstens, G. J. M., & Borgers, M.J. (2014). *Het Nederlands strafprocesrecht* (8th ed.). Deventer: Kluwer.

Cote-Boucher, K., Infantino, F., & Salter, M. B. (2014). Border security as practice: an agenda for research. *Security Dialogue, 45*(3), 195-208.

De Maillard, J., Hunold, D., Roché, S., & Oberwittler, D. (2016). Different styles of policing: discretionary power in street controls by the public police in France and Germany. *Policing and Society*, 1-14.

Dekkers, T. J. M., & Van der Woude, M. A. H. (2014). Staring at the felony forest. De complexiteit van risicoprofilering nader in kaart gebracht. *Proces, 93*(93), 52-70.

Dunham, R. G. (2005). Transforming citizens into suspects: factors that influence the formation of police suspicion. *Police Quarterly, 8*, 366-393.

Finch, H., Lewis, J., & Turley, C. (2013). Focus Groups. In J. Richtie, C. Lewis, N. McNaughton, & R. Ormston (Eds.), *Qualitative Research Practice: A Guide for Social Science Students and Researchers* (pp. 211-242). Thousand Oaks, CA: Sage.

Halderen, R. C. Van, & Lasthuizen, K. (2013). Creatief gebruik van bevoegdheden. *Tijdschrift voor Veiligheid, 2013*(12), 16-36.

Hawkins, K. (2014). Order rationality and silence: some reflections on criminal justice decision-making. In L. Gelsthorpe & N. Padfield (Eds.), *Exercising discretion: some reflections on criminal justice decision-making* (pp. 186-219). London: Routledge.

Johnson, R. R., & Morgan, M. A. (2013). Suspicion formation among police officers: an international literature review. *Criminal Justice Studies: A Critical Journal of Crime, Law and Society, 26*(1), 99-114.

Kleijer-Kool, L. (2010). Politiestijlen en conflictpotentieel in multiculturele achterstandswijken. In F. Bovenkerk, M. Easton, P. Ponsaers, & L. G. Moor (Eds.), *Policing multiple communities (Cahiers Politiestudies 15)* (pp. 69-86). Gent: Maklu.

Kleijer-Kool, L., & Landman, W. (2016). "Boeven vangen". Het spel tussen politieagenten en de Ander. *Tijdschrift over Cultuur & Criminaliteit, 6*(1), 42-65.

Krueger, R. A., & Casey, M. A. (2014). *Focus groups: A practical guide for applied research.* Thousand Oaks, CA: Sage.

Landman, W. (2015). *Blauwe patronen. Betekenisgeving in politiewerk.* Den Haag: Boom Lemma.

Ley, D. (1988). Interpretive social research in the inner city. In J. Eyles (Ed.), *Research in Human Geography. Introductions and Investigations.* (pp. 121-138). Oxford: Blackwell.

Lipsky, M. (1980). *Street level bureaucracy: dilemmas of the individual in public services.* New York: Russel Sage Foundation.

Loftus, B. (2015). Border regimes and the sociology of policing. *Policing and Society?: An International Journal of Research and Policy, 25*(1), 115-125.

Maynard-Moody, S., & Musheno, M. (2000). State Agent or Citizen Agent?: Two Narratives of Discretion. *Journal of Public Administration Research and Theory, 10,* 329-358.

Mendias, C., & Kehoe, E. J. (2006). Engagement of policing ideals and their relationship to the exercise of discretionary powers. *Criminal Justice and Behavior, 33*(1), 70-92.

Motomura, H. (2011). The discretion that matters: federal immigration enforcement, state and local arrests, and the civil-criminal line. *UCLA Law Review, 58,* 1819-1858.

Phillips, S. W. (2015). Police Discretion and Boredom: What Officers Do When There Is Nothing to Do. *Journal of Contemporary Ethnography,* 1-22.

Portillo, S., & Rudes, D. S. (2014). Construction of Justice at the Street Level. *Annual Review of Law and Social Science, 10,* 321-334.

Pratt, A. (2010). Between a hunch and a hard place: making suspicion reasonable at the Canadian border. *Social & Legal Studies, 19*(4), 461-480.

Pratt, A., & Thompson, S. K. (2008). Chivalry, "race" and discretion at the Canadian border. *British Journal of Criminology, 48*(5), 620-640.

Quinton, P. (2011). The formation of suspicions: police stop and search practices in England and Wales. *Policing and Society, 21*(4), 357-368.

Reiss, A. J. (1971). *The Police and the Public.* New Haven: Yale University Press.

Schneider, C. E. (1992). Discretion and Rules: A Lawyer's View. In K. Hawkins (Ed.), *The Uses of Discretion* (pp. 47-88). Oxford: Clarendon.

Sklansky, D. A. (2012). Crime, immigration, and ad hoc instrumentalism. *New Criminal Law Review, 15*(2), 157-223.

Spano, R. (2005). Potential sources of observer bias in police observational data. *Social Science Research, 34*(3), 591-617.

Staring, R. (2012). Crimmigratie en de morele economie van illegale vreemdelingen. *PROCES, 91*(6), 396-407.

Stroshine, M., Alpert, G. P., & Dunham, R. G. (2008). The influence of "working rules" on police suspicion and discretionary decision making. *Police Quarterly, 11*(3), 315-337.

Stumpf, J. P. (2006). The crimmigration crisis: immigrants, crime, and sovereign power. *American University Law Review, 56*(2), 367-420.

Terpstra, J., & Schaap, D. (2011). Politiecultuur: een empirische verkenning in de Nederlandse context. *Proces, 90*(4), 183-196.

Van der Leun, J. P. (2010). *Crimmigratie.* Apeldoorn/Antwerpen: Maklu.

Van der Leun, J. P., & Van der Woude, M. A. H. (2012). A reflection on crimmigration in the Netherlands. On the cultural security complex and the impact of framing. In M. Joao Guia, M. Van der Woude, & J. Van der Leun (Eds.), *Social control and*

justice: crimmigration in the Age of Fear (pp. 41-60). The Hague: Eleven International Publishing.
Van der Leun, J. P., Van der Woude, M. A. H., & De Ridder, S. (2013). Crimmigratie in de lage landen: smeltende grenzen? *Strafblad, Juli*, 221-228.
Van der Torre, E. J. (1999). *Politiewerk. Politiestijlen, community policing, professionalisme.* Alphen aan den Rijn: Samsom.
Van der Woude, M. A. H., Brouwer, J., & Dekkers, T. J. M. (2016). *Beslissen in grensgebieden. Een onderzoek naar het Mobiel Toezicht Veiligheid zoals uitgevoerd door de Koninklijke Marechaussee.* Den Haag: Boom Juridische Uitgevers.
Van der Woude, M. A. H., Dekkers, T. J. M., & Brouwer, J. (2015). Over crimmigratie en discretionair beslissen binnen het Mobiel Toezicht Veiligheid ... of Vreemdelingen ... of Veiligheid? *Tijdschrift voor Veiligheid, 14*(2), 19-35.
Van der Woude, M. A. H., Van der Leun, J. P., & Nijland, J. A. (2014). Crimmigration in the Netherlands. *Law & Social Inquiry, 39*(3), 560-579.
Van Gestel, B., & De Poot, C. (2014). Acute dreigingen, vage geruchten. *Tijdschrift voor Criminologie, 56*(4), 71-86.
Weber, L. (2011). "It sounds like they shouldn't be here": immigration checks on the streets of Sydney. *Policing and Society, 21*(4), 456-467.
Wilson, J. (1978). *Varieties of Police Behavior: The Management of Law and Order in Eight Communities.* Cambridge, MA: Harvard University Press.

Chapter 4

Aas, K.F., 2011. 'Crimmigrant' bodies and bona fide travelers: surveillance, citizenship and global governance. *Theoretical criminology*, 15, 331-346.
Alpert, G.P., Macdonald, J.M., and Dunham, R.G. 2005. Police suspicion and discretionary decision making during citizen stops. *Criminology*, 43 (2), 407-434.
Amnesty International. 2013. *Proactief politieoptreden vormt risico voor mensenrechten.* Amsterdam: Etnisch profileren onderkennen en aanpakken.
Atget, A.F., 2008. *The abolition of internal border checks in an enlarged Schengen area: freedom of movement or a web of scattered security checks?* (Challenge Research Paper No. 8). Brussels: The Challenge Observatory.
Bonnet, F. and Caillault, C., 2014. The invader, the enemy within and they-who-must-not-be-named: how police talk about minorities in Italy, the Netherlands and France. *Ethnic and racial studies*, 38 (7), 1-17.
Boomgaarden, H.G. and Vliegenthart, R., 2007. Explaining the rise of anti-immigrant parties: the role of news media content. *Electoral studies*, 26 (2), 404-417.
Bowling, B. and Phillips, C., 2007. Disproportionate and discriminatory: reviewing the evidence on police stop and search. *Modern law review*, 70, 936-961.
Brouwer, J., Van der Woude, M.A.H., and Van der Leun, J.P. 2017. Framing migration and the process of crimmigration: a systematic analysis of the media representation of unauthorised immigrants in the Netherlands. *European Journal of Criminology*, 14 (1), 100-119.
Buvik, K., 2016. The hole in the doughnut: a study of police discretion in a nightlife setting. *Policing and society*, 26 (7), 771-788.

Carrera, S., 2005. What does free movement mean in theory and practice in an enlarged EU? *European law journal*, 11 (6), 699-721.

Casella Colombeau, S., 2010. Border guards as an 'alien police': usages of the Schengen agreement in France. *Les Cahiers Européens de Sciences Po*, 4, 1-14.

Casella Colombeau, S. (2017) Policing the internal Schengen borders – managing the double bind between free movement and migration control. Policing and Society, 14(1), 63-77.

Cote-Boucher, K., Infantino, F., and Salter, M.B. 2014. Border security as practice: an agenda for research. *Security dialogue*, 45 (3), 195-208.

De Maillard, J., *et al.*, 2016. Different styles of policing: discretionary power in street controls by the public police in France and Germany. *Policing and society*, 9463 (June), 1-14.

Dekkers, T.J.M., Van der Woude, M.A.H., and Van der Leun, J.P. 2016. Exercising discretion in border areas: on the changing social surround and decision field of internal border control in the Netherlands. *International journal of migration and border studies*, 2 (4), 382-402.

Dunham, R.G., 2005. Transforming citizens into suspects: factors that influence the formation of police suspicion. *Police quarterly*, 8, 366-393.

Eijkman, Q., 2010. Has the genie been let out of the bottle? Ethnic profiling in the Netherlands. *Public space: the journal of law and social justice*, 5 (3692), 1-21.

Engel, R.S. and Johnson, R., 2006. Toward a better understanding of racial and ethnic disparities in search and seizure rates. *Journal of criminal justice*, 34, 605-617.

Fallik, S.W. and Novak, K.J., 2012. The decision to search: is race or ethnicity important? *Journal of contemporary criminal justice*, 28, 146-165.

Fan, M., 2013. The case for crimmigration reform. *North Carolina law review*, 92, 75-148.

Garland, D., 2001. *The culture of control: crime and social order in contemporary society*. Chicago: University of Chicago Press.

Gehring, J.S., 2013. Roma and the limits of free movement in the European Union. *In*: *Democratic citizenship and the free movement of people*. Leiden: Martinus Nijhoff, 143-174.

Gilboy, J.A., 1991. Deciding who gets in: decision making by immigration inspectors. *Law & society review*, 25 (3), 571-599.

Graham, S. and Lowery, B.S., 2004. Priming unconscious racial stereotypes about adolescent offenders. *Law and human behavior*, 28 (5), 483-504.

Groenendijk, K., 2003. New borders behind old ones: post-Schengen controls behind the internal borders and inside the Netherlands and Germany. *In*: K. Groenendijk, E. Guild, and P. Minderhoud, eds. *In search of Europe's borders*. The Hague: Kluwer Law International, 131-146.

Guild, E. and Zwaan, K., 2014. Does Europe still create refugees? Examining the situation of the Roma. *Queen's law journal*, 40 (1), 142-164.

Hawkins, K., 2014. Order rationality and silence: some reflections on criminal justice decision-making. *In*: L. Gelsthorpe & N. Padfield, eds. *Exercising discretion: some reflections on criminal justice decision-making*. London: Routledge, 186-219.

Holmberg, L., 2000. Discretionary leniency and typological guilt: results from a Danish study of police discretion. *Journal of scandinavian studies in criminology and crime prevention*, 1, 179-194.

Johnson, R.R. and Morgan, M.A., 2013. Suspicion formation among police officers: an international literature review. *Criminal justice studies: a critical journal of crime, law and society*, 3, 249-268.

Jorgensen, C.W. and Sorensen, K.E., 2012. Internal border controls in the European Union: recent challenges and reforms. *European Law Review*, 3, 249-268.

Lipsky, M., 1980. *Street level bureaucracy: dilemmas of the individual in public services.* New York: Russel Sage Foundation.

Loftus, B., 2007. Policing the 'irrelevant': class, diversity and contemporary police culture. *In:* M. O'Neill, M. M. Marks & A. Singh, eds. *Police occupational culture: new debates and directions*. Oxford: Elsevier, 181-204.

Loftus, B., 2010. Police occupational culture: classic themes, altered times. *Policing and society*, 20 (1), 1-20.

Loftus, B., 2015. Border regimes and the sociology of policing. *Policing and society: an international journal of research and policy*, 25 (1), 115-125.

Lyon, D., 2007. National ID cards: crime-control, citizenship and social sorting. *Policing*, 1 (1), 111-118.

Maas, W., 2014. The origins, evolution, and political objectives of EU citizenship. *German law journal*, 15 (5), 797-820.

Miller, J., *et al.*, 2008. Racism and police stops: adapting US and British debates to continental Europe. *European journal of criminology*, 5 (2), 161-191.

Miller, K., 2009. The institutionalization of racial profiling policy: an examination of antiprofiling policy adoption among large law enforcement agencies. *Crime & delinquency*, 59 (1), 32-58.

Motomura, H., 2011. The discretion that matters: federal immigration enforcement, state and local arrests, and the civil- criminal line. *Ucla law review*, 58, 1819-1858.

Mutsaers, P., 2014. An ethnographic study of the policing of internal borders in the Netherlands. Synergies between criminology and anthropology. *British journal of criminology*, 54 (5), 831-848.

Nanz, P., 2009. Mobility, migrants, and solidarity: towards an emerging European citizen regime. *In*: S. Benhabib and J. Resnik, eds. *Migrations and mobilities. Citizenship, borders, and gender*. New York: New York University Press, 410-438.

Pakes, F., 2006. The ebb and flow of criminal justice in the Netherlands. *International journal of the sociology of law*, 34 (2), 141-156.

Parker, O. & Catalan, O.L., 2014. Free movement for whom, where when? Roma EU citizens in France and Spain. *International political sociology*, 8, 379-395.

Parmar, A., 2011. Stop and search in London: counter-terrorist or counter-productive? *Policing and society*, 21 (4), 369- 382.

Pickering, S. and Ham, J., 2013. Hot pants at the border: sorting sex work from trafficking. *British journal of criminology*, 54 (1), 2-19.

Pickett, J.T., 2016. On the social foundations for crimmigration: Latino threat and support for expanded police powers. *Journal of quantitative criminology*, 32 (1), 103-231.

Pijpers, R., 2006. Help! The Poles are coming: narrating a contemporary moral panic. *Geografiska annaler*, 88 (1), 91-103.

Pratt, A. and Thompson, S.K., 2008. Chivalry, 'race' and discretion at the Canadian border. *British journal of criminology*, 48 (5), 620-640.

Quinton, P., 2011. The formation of suspicions: police stop and search practices in England and Wales. *Policing and society*, 21 (4), 357-368.

Rosmalen, F. Van and van Es, A., 2014. Criminele bendes of hardwerkende arbeidsmigranten? Het mediadiscours ten aanzien van Midden- en Oost-European in Nederland. *Proces*, 93, 229-244.

Satzewich, V. and Shaffir, W., 2009. Racism versus professionalism: claims and counter-claims about racial profiling. *Canadian journal of criminology and criminal justice*, 51 (2), 199-226.

Schafer, J.A., *et al.*, 2006. Decision making in traffic stop encounters: a multivariate analysis of police behavior. *Police quarterly*, 9, 184-209.

Schwell, A., 2010. The iron curtain revisited: the 'Austrian way' of policing the internal Schengen border. *European security*, 19, 317-336.

Sklansky, D.A., 2012. Crime, immigration, and ad hoc instrumentalism. *New criminal law review*, 15 (2), 157-223.

Skolnick, J., 1966. *Justice without trial*. New York: Wiley.

Smith, M.R., 2004. Depoliticizing racial profiling: suggestions for the limited use and management of race in police decision-making. *George mason university civil rights law journal*, 15, 219-260.

Stroshine, M., Alpert, G.P., and Dunham, R.G. 2008. The influence of 'working rules' on police suspicion and discretionary decision making. *Police quarterly*, 11 (3), 315-337.

Stumpf, J.P., 2006. The crimmigration crisis: immigrants, crime, and sovereign power. *American university law review*, 56 (2), 367-420.

Svensson, J.S. and Saharso, S., 2014. Proactive policing and equal treatment of ethnic-minority youths. *Policing and society*, 25 (4), 393-408.

Tillyer, R., 2012. Opening the black box of officer decision-making: an examination of race, criminal history, and discretionary searches. *Justice quarterly*, 31 (6), 961-985.

Tillyer, R. and Hartley, R.D., 2010. Driving racial profiling research forward: learning lessons from sentencing research. *Journal of criminal justice*, 38 (4), 657-665.

Van Hulst, M., 2013. Storytelling at the police station. The canteen culture revisited. *British journal of criminology*, 53 (4), 624-642.

Van Maanen, J., 1979. The fact of fiction in organizational ethnography. *Administrative science quarterly*, 24 (4), 34-41.

Van Swaaningen, R., 2005. Public safety and the management of fear. *Theoretical criminology*, 9 (3), 289-305.

Van der Leun, J.P. and Van der Woude, M.A.H., 2011. Ethnic profiling in the Netherlands? A reflection on expanding powers, ethnic profiling and a changing social and political context. *Policing and society*, 21 (4), 444-455.

Van der Woude, M.A.H. and Brouwer, J., 2017. Searching for 'illegal' junk in the trunk. Underlying intentions of (cr)immigration controls in Schengen's border areas. *New criminal law review* 20 (1), 157-179.

Van der Woude, M.A.H., Brouwer, J., and Dekkers, T.J.M., 2016. *Beslissen in grensgebieden. Een onderzoek naar het Mobiel Toezicht Veiligheid zoals uitgevoerd door de Koninklijke Marechaussee*. Den Haag: Boom Juridische Uitgevers.

Van der Woude, M.A.H. and Van Berlo, P., 2015. Crimmigration at the internal borders of Europe? Examining the Schengen governance package. *Utrecht law review*, 11 (1), 61-79.

Van der Woude, M.A.H. and Van der Leun, J.P., 2017. Crimmigration checks in the internal border areas of the EU: Finding the discretion that matters. *European journal of criminology*, 14 (1), 27-45.

Van der Woude, M.A.H., Van der Leun, J.P., and Nijland, J.A., 2014. Crimmigration in the Netherlands. *Law and social inquiry*, 39 (3), 560-579.

Waddington, P.A.J., Stenson, K., and Don, D. 2004. In proportion: race, and police stop and search. *British journal of criminology*, 44 (6), 889-914.

Weber, L., 2011. 'It sounds like they shouldn't be here': immigration checks on the streets of Sydney. *Policing and society*, 21 (4), 456-467.

Weber, L. and Bowling, B. 2004. Policing migration: a framework for investigating the regulation of global mobility. *Policing and society*, 14 (3), 195-212.

Wilson, G., Dunham, R.G., and Alpert, G.P. 2004. Prejudice in police profiling: assessing an overlooked aspect in prior research. *American behavioral scientist*, 47 (7), 896-909.

CHAPTER 5

Aas, K. F. (2011). "Crimmigrant" bodies and bona fide travelers: surveillance, citizenship and global governance. *Theoretical Criminology, 15*(3), 331-346.

Antrobus, E., Bradford, B., Murphy, K., & Sargeant, E. (2015). Community norms, procedural justice, and the public's perceptions of police legitimacy. *Journal of Contemporary Criminal Justice, 31*(2), 151-170.

Atget, A. F. (2008). *The abolition of internal border checks in an enlarged Schengen area: freedom of movement or a web of scattered security checks?* Challenge Research Paper No. 8. Brussels: CEPS.

Blackwood, L. (2015). Policing Airport Spaces: The Muslim Experience of Scrutiny. *Policing, 9*(3), 255-264.

Blackwood, L., Hopkins, N., & Reicher, S. D. (2015). "Flying While Muslim": Citizenship and Misrecognition in the Airport. *Journal of Social and Political Psychology, 3*(2), 148- 170.

Blader, S. L., & Tyler, T. R. (2009). Testing and extending the group engagement model: linkages between social identity, procedural justice, economic outcomes, and extrarole behavior. *Journal of Applied Psychology, 94*, 445-464.

Bradford, B. (2014). Policing and social identity: procedural justice, inclusion and cooperation between police and public. *Policing and Society, 24*(1), 22-41.

Bradford, B., Hohl, K., Jackson, J., & MacQueen, S. (2015). Obeying the rules of the road: Procedural justice, social identity and normative compliance. *Journal of Contemporary Criminal Justice, 31*(2), 171-191.

Bradford, B., Murphy, K., & Jackson, J. (2014). Officers as mirrors. Policing, procedural justice and the (re)production of social identity. *British Journal of Criminology, 54*(4), 527-550.

Brouwer, J., Van der Woude, M.A.H., & Van der Leun, J.P. (2018). (Cr)immigrant framing in border areas: decision making processes of Dutch border police officers. *Policing and Society, 28*(4), 448-463.

Casella Colombeau, S. (2017). Policing the internal Schengen borders – managing the double bind between free movement and migration control. *Policing and Society, 14*(1), 63 – 77.

Cherney, A., & Murphy, K. (2011). Understanding the contingency of procedural justice outcomes. *Policing, 5*(3), 228-235.

Crewe, B. (2011). Soft power in prison: Implications for staff-prisoner relationships, liberty and legitimacy. *European Journal of Criminology, 8*(6), 455-468.

Davies, S. G., Meliala, A., & Buttle, J. (2016). Gangnam Style versus Eye of the Tiger: people , police and procedural justice in Indonesia. *Policing and Society, 26*(4), 453-474.

Dekkers, T.J.M., Van der Woude, M.A.H., & Van der Leun, J.P. (2016). Acceptance denied. Intelligence-led Immigration Checks in Dutch Border Areas. *European Journal of Policing Studies, 4,* 242-264.

Griffiths, C. E. (2018). The disjuncture between confidence and cooperation: Police contact amongst Polish migrants and established residents. *European Journal of Criminology 15*(2), 197-216.

Harkin, D. (2015a). Police legitimacy, ideology and qualitative methods: a critique of procedural justice theory. *Criminology and Criminal Justice, 15*(5), 594-612.

Harkin, D. (2015b). The police and punishment: Understanding the pains of policing. *Theoretical C riminology, 19*(1), 43-58.

Hasisi, B., & Weisburd, D. (2011). Going beyond ascribed identities: the importance of procedural justice in airport security screening in Israël. *Law and Society Review, 45*(4), 867-892.

Hunold, D., Oberwittler, D., & Lukas, T. (2016). "Id like to see your identity cards please" – Negotiating authority in police-adolescent encounters: Findings from a mixed-method study of proactive police practices towards adolescents in two German cities. *European Journal of Criminology, 13*(5), 590-609.

Jackson, J., & Bradford, B. (2009). Crime, policing and social order: On the expressive nature of public confidence in policing. *British Journal of Sociology, 60*(3), 493-521.

Jonathan-Zamir, T., Mastrofski, S. D., & Moyal, S. (2013). Measuring Procedural Justice in Police-Citizen Encounters. *Justice Quarterly, 32*(5), 845-871.

Liebling, A. (2004). *Prisons and their moral performance. A study of values, quality and prison life.* Oxford: Oxford University Press.

Litmanovitz, Y., & Montgomery, P. (2015). On the borders of legitimacy. Procedural justice training in the Israeli border police. *European Journal of Policing Studies, 3*(2), 184- 203.

Lyon, D. (2007). National ID cards: crime-control, citizenship and social sorting. *Policing, 1*(1), 111- 118.

Madon, N. S., Murphy, K., & Cherney, A. (2017). Promoting community collaboration in counterterrorism: do social identities and perceptions of legitimacy mediate reactions to procedural justice policing? *British Journal of Criminology, 57,* 1144-1164.

Mastrofski, S. D., Jonathan-Zamir, T., Moyal, S., & Willis, J. J. (2016). Predicting Procedural Justice in Police-Citizen Encounters. *Criminal Justice and Behavior, 43,* 119-139.

Muller, B. J. (2010). Unsafe at any speed? Borders, mobility and "safe citizenship." *Citizenship Studies, 14*(1), 75-88.

Murphy, K., Sargeant, E., & Cherney, A. (2015). The importance of procedural justice and police performance in shaping intentions to cooperate with the police: Does social identity matter? *European Journal of Criminology, 12*(6), 719-738.

Pallitto, R., & Heyman, J. (2008). Theorizing Cross-Border Mobility: Surveillance, Security and Identity. *Surveillance & Society, 5*(3), 315-333.

Pickering, S., & Ham, J. (2013). Hot pants at the border: sorting sex work from trafficking. *British Journal of Criminology, 54*(1), 2-19.

Pickett, J. T., & Ryon, S. B. (2017). Procedurally just cooperation: Explaining support for due process reforms in policing. *Journal of Criminal Justice, 48*, 9-20.

Radburn, M., Stott, C., Bradford, B., & Robinson, M. (2016). When is policing fair? Groups, identity and judgements of the procedural justice of coercive crowd policing. *Policing and Society*, Online First, 1-18.

Shamir, R. (2005). Without Borders? Notes on Globalization as a Mobility Regime. *Sociological Theory, 23*(2), 197-217.

Stumpf, J. P. (2006). The crimmigration crisis: immigrants, crime, and sovereign power. *American University Law Review, 56*(2), 367-420.

Sunshine, J., & Tyler, T. R. (2003). The Role of Procedural Justice and Legitimacy in Shaping Public Support for Policing. *Law and Society Review, 37*(3), 513-548.

Tyler, T. R. (2003). Procedural justice, legitimacy, and the effective rule of law. *Crime and Justice, 30*, 283-357.

Tyler, T. R. (2005). Policing in Black and White: Ethnic Group Differences in Trust and Confidence in the Police. *Police Quarterly, 8*, 322-342.

Tyler, T. R., & Blader, S. L. (2003). The group engagement model: procedural justice, social identity, and cooperative behavior. *Personality and Social Psychology Review, 7*(4), 349-361.

Tyler, T. R., & Wakslak, C. J. (2004). Profiling and police legitimacy: procedural justice, attributions of motive, and acceptance of police authority. *Criminology, 42*(2), 253 – 281.

Van der Woude, M.A.H., & Van Berlo, P. (2015). Crimmigration at the Internal Borders of Europe? Examining the Schengen Governance Package. *Utrecht Law Review, 11*, 61-79.

Van der Woude, M.A.H., Brouwer, J., & Dekkers, T.J.M. (2016). *Beslissen in Grensgebieden. Een onderzoek naar het Mobiel Toezicht Veiligheid zoals uitgevoerd door de Koninklijke Marechaussee [Decision-making in border areas. A study of the Mobile Security Monitor as conducted by the Royal Netherlands Marechaussee]. The Hague: Boom Legal Publishers.*

Van der Woude, M.A.H., & Brouwer, J. (2017). Searching for "illegal" junk in the trunk: underlying intentions of (cr)immigration controls in Schengen's border areas. *New Criminal Law Review, 20*, 157-179.

Villegas, P. E. (2015). Moments of Humiliation, Intimidation and Implied "Illegality": Encounters with Immigration Officials at the Border and the Performance of Sovereignty. *Journal of Ethnic and Migration Studies, 41*(14), 2357-2375.

Waddington, P. A. J. (1999). *Policing Citizens*. London: Routledge.

Waddington, P. A. J., Williams, K., Wright, M., & Newburn, T. (2015). Dissension in public evaluations of the police. *Policing and Society, 25*(2), 212-235.

Weitzer, R., & Tuch, S. A. (2002). Perceptions of racial profiling: race, class and personal experience. *Criminology, 40*(2), 435-455.

CHAPTER 6

Aas, K. F. (2014). Bordered penality: Precarious membership and abnormal justice. *Punishment & Society, 16*(5), 520-541.

Bhui, H. S. (2007). Alien experience: Foreign national prisoners after the deportation crisis. *Probation Journal, 54*(4), 368-382.

Bolhuis, M. P., Battjes, H., & van Wijk, J. (2017). Undesirable but Unreturnable Migrants in the Netherlands. *Refugee Survey Quarterly, 36,* 61-84.

Boone, M. (2012a). *Our Own Rascals First: Inclusion and Exclusion in the Use of Sanctions.* The Hague: Eleven International Publishing.

Boone, M. (2012b). Rehabilitation perspectives for irregular migrants: Belgium, England & Wales, Greece and the Netherlands. *European Journal of Probation, 4*(3), 1-3.

Boone, M., & Kox, M. (2012). What works for irregular migrants in the Netherlands? *European Journal of Probation, 4*(3), 54-68.

Bosworth, M. (2011a). Deportation, detention and foreign-national prisoners in England and Wales. *Citizenship Studies, 15*(5), 583-595.

Bosworth, M. (2011b). Human rights and immigration detention in the United Kingdom. In M. Dembour & T. Kelly (Eds.), *Are Human Rights for Migrants? Critical Reflections on the Status of Irregular Migrants in Europe and the United States.* (pp. 165-183). Abingdon: Routledge.

Bosworth, M., Aas, K. F., & Pickering, S. (2017). Punishment, globalization and migration control: "Get them the hell out of here." *Punishment & Society, 20*(1), 34-53.

Bosworth, M., Hasselberg, I., & Turnbull, S. (2016). Punishment, citizenship and identity: An Introduction. *Criminology and Criminal Justice, 16*(3), 257-266.

Cavadino, M., & Dignan, J. (2006). *Penal systems. A comparative approach.* London: Sage.

Crewe, B. (2011a). Depth, weight, tightness: Revisiting the pains of imprisonment. *Punishment & Society, 13*(5), 509-529.

Crewe, B. (2011b). Soft power in prison: Implications for staff-prisoner relationships, liberty and legitimacy. *European Journal of Criminology, 8*(6), 455-468.

Crewe, B. (2015). Inside the Belly of the Penal Beast: Understanding the Experience of Imprisonment. *International Journal for Crime, Justice and Social Democracy, 4*(1), 50-65.

Damsa, D., & Ugelvik, T. (2017). A Difference That Makes a Difference? Reflexivity and Researcher Effects in an All-Foreign Prison. *International Journal of Qualitative Methods, 16,* 1-10.

Di Molfetta, E., & Brouwer, J. (2019). Unravelling the 'crimmigration knot': Penal subjectivities, punishment and the censure machine. *Criminology and Criminal Justice.*

Downes, D., & Van Swaaningen, R. (2007). The road to dystopia: changes in the penal climate in the Netherlands. *Crime and Justice, 35*(1), 31-72.

Feeley, M., & Simon, J. (1992). The New Penology: Notes of the Emerging Strategy for Corrections and its Implications. *Criminology, 30*(4), 449-474.

Fekete, L., & Webber, F. (2010). Foreign nationals, enemy penology and the criminal justice system. *Race & Class, 51*(4), 1-25.

Goffman, E. (1961). *Asylums: Essays on the social situation of mental patients and other inmates*. Garden City: Anchor Books.

Hasselberg, I. (2014). Balancing Legitimacy, Exceptionality and Accountability: On Foreign-national Offenders' Reluctance to Engage in Anti-deportation Campaigns in the UK. *Journal of Ethnic and Migration Studies, 41*(4), 563-579.

Kaufman, E. (2014). Gender at the border: Nationalism and the new logic of punishment. *Punishment & Society, 16*(2), 135-151.

Kaufman, E. (2015). *Punish and Expel. Border Control, Nationalism, and the New Purpose of the Prison*. Oxford: Oxford University Press.

Kaufman, E., & Bosworth, M. (2013). The prison and national identity: citizenship, punishment and the sovereign state. In D. Scott (Ed.), *Why prison?* (pp. 170-188). Cambridge: Cambridge University Press.

Kox, M., Ridder, S. De, Vanhouche, A. S., Boone, M., & Beyens, K. (2014). Detentiebeleving van strafrechtelijk gedetineerden zonder verblijfsrecht. *Tijdschrift voor Criminologie, 56*(2), 31-47.

Liebling, A. (2011). Distinctions and distinctiveness in the work of prison officers: Legitimacy and authority revisited. *European Journal of Criminology, 8*(6), 484-499.

Molleman, T., & Van Ginneken, E. (2013). We moeten samen het dansje afmaken. PIW'ers aan het woord over belastende en motiverende aspecten van hun werk. *Justitiele Verkenningen, 3*, 28-40.

Pakes, F. (2004). The politics of discontent: the emergence of a new criminal justice discourse in the Netherlands. *The Howard Journal of Criminal Justice, 43*(3), 284-298.

Pakes, F., & Holt, K. (2017). Crimmigration and the prison: Comparing trends in prison policy and practice in England & Wales and Norway. *European Journal of Criminology, 14*(1), 63-77.

Stumpf, J. P. (2006). The crimmigration crisis: immigrants, crime, and sovereign power. *American University Law Review, 56*(2), 367-420.

Sykes, G. (1958). *The Society of Captives: A Study in a Maximum Security Prison*. Princeton: Princenton University Press.

Turnbull, S., & Hasselberg, I. (2017). From prison to detention: The carceral trajectories of foreign-national prisoners in the United Kingdom. *Punishment & Society, 19*(2), 135-154.

Ugelvik, T. (2011). The hidden food: mealtime resistance and identity work in a Norwegian prison. *Punishment Society, 13*(1), 47-63.

Ugelvik, T. (2014). The incarceration of foreigners in European prisons. In S. Pickering & J. Ham (Eds.), *The Routledge Handbook on Crime and International Migration* (pp. 107-121). New York: Routledge.

Ugelvik, T., & Damsa, D. (2018). The pains of crimmigration imprisonment: Perspectives from a Norwegian all-foreign prison. *The British Journal of Criminology, 58*(5), 1025-1043.

Van Swaaningen, R. (2005). Public safety and the management of fear. *Theoretical Criminology, 9*(3), 289-305.

Warr, J. (2016). The deprivation of certitude, legitimacy and hope: Foreign national prisoners and the pains of imprisonment. *Criminology & Criminal Justice, 16*(3), 301-318.

CHAPTER 7

Aas, K. F. (2014). Bordered penality: Precarious membership and abnormal justice. *Punishment & Society, 16*(5), 520-541.

Berdowski, Z., & Vennekens, A. (2014). *Aanscherpingen glijdende schaal. Geschatte resultaten van recente en voorgenomen aanscherpingen*. Zoetermeer: Panteia.

Bolhuis, M. P., Battjes, H., & van Wijk, J. (2017). Undesirable but Unreturnable Migrants in the Netherlands. *Refugee Survey Quarterly, 36*, 61-84.

Bosworth, M. (2012). Subjectivity and identity in detention: Punishment and society in a global age. *Theoretical Criminology, 16*(2), 123-140.

Broeders, D., & Engbersen, G. (2007). The fight against illegal migration: Identification policies and immigrants' counterstrategies. *American Behavioral Scientist, 50*(12), 1592-1609.

Brouwer, J. (2018). *Family Matters: A Study into the Factors Hampering Voluntary Return of Migrants Residing at Family Locations*. Geneva: International Organization for Migration.

Cantor, D. J., Van Wijk, J., Singer, S., & Bolhuis, M. P. (2017). The Emperor's New Clothing: National Responses to "Undesirable and Unreturnable" Aliens under Asylum and Immigration Law. *Refugee Survey Quarterly, 36*, 1-8.

Carling, J., & Schewel, K. (2018). Revisiting aspiration and ability in international migration. *Journal of Ethnic and Migration Studies, 44*(6), 945-963.

Cleton, L., & Chauvin, S. (2019). Performing freedom in the Dutch deportation regime: bureaucratic persuasion and the enforcement of 'voluntary return.' *Journal of Ethnic and Migration Studies, 0*(0), 1-17.

Crewe, B. (2011). Depth, weight, tightness: Revisiting the pains of imprisonment. *Punishment & Society, 13*(5), 509-529.

Damsa, D., & Ugelvik, T. (2017). A Difference That Makes a Difference? Reflexivity and Researcher Effects in an All-Foreign Prison. *International Journal of Qualitative Methods, 16*, 1-10.

Di Molfetta, E., & Brouwer, J. (2019). Unravelling the 'crimmigration knot': Penal subjectivities, punishment and the censure machine. *Criminology and Criminal Justice*, Online first, 1-17.

Ellermann, A. (2008). The limits of unilateral migration control: Deportation and inter-state cooperation. *Government and Opposition, 43*(2), 168-189.

Engbersen, G., & van der Leun, J. P. (2001). The social construction of illegality and criminality. *European Journal on Criminal Policy and Research, 9*, 51-70.

Gibney, M.J. (2008). Asylum and the Expansion of Deportation in the United Kingdom. *Government and Opposition, 43*(2), 146-167.

Golash-Boza, T. (2016). Feeling Like a Citizen, Living As a Denizen: Deportees Sense of Belonging. *American Behavioral Scientist, 60*(13), 1575-1589.

Grewcock, M. (2011). Punishment, deportation and parole: The detention and removal of former prisoners under section 501 Migration Act 1958. *Australian & New Zealand Journal of Criminology, 44*(1), 56-73.

Griffiths, M. (2017). Foreign, criminal: a doubly damned modern British folk-devil. *Citizenship Studies, 21*(5), 527-546.

Hasselberg, I. (2014). Balancing Legitimacy, Exceptionality and Accountability: On Foreign-national Offenders' Reluctance to Engage in Anti-deportation Campaigns in the UK. *Journal of Ethnic and Migration Studies, 41*(4), 563-579.

Kanstroom, D. (2000). Deportation, social control, and punishment: Some thoughts about why hard laws make bad cases. *Harvard Law Review, 11*, 1889-1935.

Kaufman, E. (2014). Gender at the border: Nationalism and the new logic of punishment. *Punishment & Society, 16*(2), 135-151.

Kaufman, E., & Bosworth, M. (2013). The prison and national identity: citizenship, punishment and the sovereign state. In D. Scott (Ed.), *Why prison?* (pp. 170-188). Cambridge: Cambridge University Press.

Klaver, J., Telli, S., & Witvliet, M. (2015). *Terugkeer van vertrekplichtige vreemdelingen. Een verkenning van interventies om zelfstandige terugkeer te stimuleren*. Amsterdam: Regioplan.

Koser, K., & Kuschminder, K. (2015). *Comparative Research on the Assisted Voluntary Return and Reintegration of Migrants*. Geneva: International Organization for Migration.

Leerkes, A., & Broeders, D. (2010). A case of mixed motives? Formal and informal functions of administrative immigration detention. *British Journal of Criminology, 50*(5), 830-850.

Leerkes, A., Galloway, M., & Kromhout, M. (2010). *Kiezen tussen twee kwaden. Determinanten van blijf- en terugkeerintenties onder (bijna) uitgeprocedeerde asielmigranten*. Den Haag: Wetenschappelijk Onderzoek- en Documentatiecentrum.

Leerkes, A., & Kox, M. (2017). Pressured into a Preference to Leave? A Study on the "Specific" Deterrent Effects and Perceived Legitimacy of Immigration Detention. *Law and Society Review, 51*(4), 895-929.

Leerkes, A., van Os, R., & Boersema, E. (2017). What drives 'soft deportation'? Understanding the rise in Assisted Voluntary Return among rejected asylum seekers in the Netherlands. *Population, Space and Place, 23*(8), 1-11.

Rosenberger, S., & Koppes, S. (2018). Claiming control: cooperation with return as a condition for social benefits in Austria and the Netherlands. *Comparative Migration Studies, 6*(26), 1-18.

Schewel, K. (2019). Understanding Immobility: Moving Beyond the Mobility Bias in Migration Studies. *International Migration Review*.

Sklansky, D. A. (2012). Crime, immigration, and ad hoc instrumentalism. *New Criminal Law Review, 15*(2), 157-223.

Stronks, M. (2013). Een bijna ongebreidelde beteugeling van de tijd. Een analyse van aanscherpingen van de glijdende schaal. *Nederlands Juristenblad, 34*, 2306-2314.

Stumpf, J. P. (2006). The crimmigration crisis: immigrants, crime, and sovereign power. *American University Law Review, 56*(2), 367-420.

Sykes, G. (1958). *The Society of Captives: A Study in a Maximum Security Prison*. Princeton: Princenton University Press.

Turnbull, S., & Hasselberg, I. (2017). From prison to detention: The carceral trajectories of foreign-national prisoners in the United Kingdom. *Punishment & Society, 19*(2), 135-154.
Tyler, T. R. (2003). Procedural justice, legitimacy, and the effective rule of law. *Crime and Justice, 30*, 283-357.
Ugelvik, T., & Damsa, D. (2018). The pains of crimmigration imprisonment: Perspectives from a Norwegian all-foreign prison. *The British Journal of Criminology, 58*(5), 1025-1043.
Van Alphen, B., Molleman, T., Leerkes, A., & Van Hoek, J. (2013). *Van bejegening tot vertrek. Een onderzoek naar de werking van vreemdelingenbewaring*. Den Haag: Wetenschappelijk Onderzoek- en Documentatiecentrum.
Van der Woude, M. A. H., Van der Leun, J. P., & Nijland, J. A. (2014). Crimmigration in the Netherlands. *Law & Social Inquiry, 39*(3), 560-579.
Walters, W. (2016). The flight of the deported: Deportation, aviation and politics. *Geopolitics*, 1-24.
Warr, J. (2016). The deprivation of certitude, legitimacy and hope: Foreign national prisoners and the pains of imprisonment. *Criminology & Criminal Justice, 16*(3), 301-318.

Chapter 8

Aas, K. F. (2007). Analysing a world in motion: Global flows meet 'criminology of the other'. *Theoretical Criminology, 11*(2), 283-303.
Aas, K. F. (2011). "Crimmigrant" bodies and bona fide travelers: surveillance, citizenship and global governance. *Theoretical Criminology, 15*(3), 331-346.
Aas, K. F. (2014). Bordered penality: Precarious membership and abnormal justice. *Punishment & Society, 16*(5), 520-541.
Aliverti, A. (2012). Exploring the Function of Criminal Law in the Policing of Foreigners: The Decision to Prosecute Immigration-related Offences. *Social & Legal Studies, 21*(4), 511-527.
Armenta, A. (2017). Racializing Crimmigration: Structural Racism, Colorblindness, and the Institutional Production of Immigrant Criminality. *Sociology of Race and Ethnicity, 3*(1), 82-95.
Atak, I., & Simeon, J. (2018). *The Criminalization of Migration. Context and Consequences*. Montreal: Mcgill-Queen's University Press.
Barker, V. (2013). Democracy and deportation: why membership matters most. In K. F. Aas & M. Bosworth (Eds.), *The borders of punishment: Migration, citizenship, and social exclusion* (pp. 237-254). Oxford: Oxford University Press.
Benhabib, S. (2002). In search of Europe's borders. The politics of migration in the European Union. *Dissent, 49*(4), 33-39.
Bosworth, M. (2012). Subjectivity and identity in detention: Punishment and society in a global age. *Theoretical Criminology, 16*(2), 123-140.
Bosworth, M., Aas, K. F., & Pickering, S. (2017). Punishment, globalization and migration control: "Get them the hell out of here." *Punishment & Society, 20*(1), 34-53.

Bowling, B., & Westenra, S. (2018). 'A really hostile environment': Adiaphorization, global policing and the crimmigration control system. *Theoretical Criminology*, 1-21.

Coutin, S. B. (2010). Confined within: national territories as zones of confinement. *Political Geography, 29*, 200-208.

Ellermann, A. (2019). Discrimination in migration and citizenship. *Journal of Ethnic and Migration Studies, Online fir*, 1-17.

Geddes, A. (2008). *Immigration & European Integration: Beyond Fortress Europe?* (Manchester). Manchester.

Gibney, M.J. (2019). Denationalisation and discrimination. *Journal of Ethnic and Migration Studies, 0*(0), 1-18.

Kaufman, E. (2015). *Punish and Expel. Border Control, Nationalism, and the New Purpose of the Prison*. Oxford: Oxford University Press.

Kaufman, E., & Bosworth, M. (2013). The prison and national identity: citizenship, punishment and the sovereign state. In D. Scott (Ed.), *Why prison?* (pp. 170-188). Cambridge: Cambridge University Press.

Marin, L., & Spena, A. (2016). Introduction: The Criminalization of Migration and European (Dis)Integration. *European Journal of Migration and Law, 18*, 147-156.

Miller, T. (2003). Citizenship and severity: recent immigration reforms and the new penology. *Georgetown Immigration Law Journal, 17*, 611-662.

Moffette, D. (2018). The jurisdictional games of immigration policing: Barcelona's fight against unauthorised street vending. *Theoretical Criminology, Online fir*, 1-18.

Pakes, F., & Holt, K. (2017). Crimmigration and the prison: Comparing trends in prison policy and practice in England & Wales and Norway. *European Journal of Criminology, 14*(1), 63-77.

Pickering, S., Bosworth, M., & Aas, K. F. (2014). The criminology of mobility. In S. Pickering & J. Ham (Eds.), *The Routledge Handbook on Crime and International Migration* (pp. 382-395). Oxford: Routledge.

Sklansky, D. A. (2012). Crime, immigration, and ad hoc instrumentalism. *New Criminal Law Review, 15*(2), 157-223.

Stumpf, J. P. (2006). The crimmigration crisis: immigrants, crime, and sovereign power. *American University Law Review, 56*(2), 367-420.

Terrasse, M. (2019). Dimensions of belonging: relationships between police identity checks and national identity in France. *Journal of Ethnic and Migration Studies, 0*(0), 1-22.

Turnbull, S., & Hasselberg, I. (2017). From prison to detention: The carceral trajectories of foreign-national prisoners in the United Kingdom. *Punishment & Society, 19*(2), 135-154.

Ugelvik, T. (2017). The Limits of the Welfare State? Foreign National Prisoners in the Norwegian Crimmigration Prison. In P. Scharff Smith & T. Ugelvik (Eds.), *Scandinavia Penal History, Culture and Prison Practice: Embraced by the Welfare State* (pp. 405-423). London: Palgrave.

Ugelvik, T., & Damsa, D. (2018). The pains of crimmigration imprisonment: Perspectives from a Norwegian all-foreign prison. *The British Journal of Criminology, 58*(5), 1025-1043.

Van Berlo, P. (2015). Australia's Operation Sovereign Borders: discourse, power, and policy from a crimmigration perspective. *Refugee Survey Quarterly, 34*(4), 75-104.

Van der Leun, J. P., & Van der Woude, M. A. H. (2011). Ethnic profiling in the Netherlands? A reflection on expanding preventive powers, ethnic profiling and a changing social and political context. *Policing and Society, 21*(4), 444-455.

Van der Woude, M. A. H., Brouwer, J., & Dekkers, T. J. M. (2016). *Beslissen in grensgebieden. Een onderzoek naar het Mobiel Toezicht Veiligheid zoals uitgevoerd door de Koninklijke Marechaussee.* Den Haag: Boom Juridische Uitgevers.

Weber, L. (2019). 'My kids won't grow up here': Policing, bordering and belonging. *Theoretical Criminology, Online fir*, 1-19.

Weber, L., & Bowling, B. (2004). Policing Migration: a Framework for Investigating the Regulation of Global Mobility. *Policing and Society, 14*(3), 195-212.

Welch, M. (2012). The Sonics of Crimmigration in Australia: Wall of Noise and Quiet Manoeuvring. *British Journal of Criminology, 52*(2), 324-344.

Wonders, N. A., & Jones, L. C. (2018). Doing and undoing borders: The multiplication of citizenship, citizenship performances, and migration as social movement. *Theoretical Criminology*, 1-20.

Annex

Aas, K. F. (2014). Bordered penality: Precarious membership and abnormal justice. *Punishment & Society, 16*(5), 520-541.

Alpert, G. P., Macdonald, J. M., & Dunham, R. G. (2005). Police suspicion and discretionary decision making during citizen stops. *Criminology, 43*(2), 407-434.

Coutin, S. B. (2000). *Legalizing moves: Salvadoran immigrants' struggle for U.S. residency.* Ann Arbor: University of Michigan Press.

Crewe, B. (2015). Inside the Belly of the Penal Beast: Understanding the Experience of Imprisonment. *International Journal for Crime, Justice and Social Democracy, 4*(1), 50-65.

Damsa, D., & Ugelvik, T. (2017). A Difference That Makes a Difference? Reflexivity and Researcher Effects in an All-Foreign Prison. *International Journal of Qualitative Methods, 16*, 1-10.

De Genova, N. (2002). Migrant "illegality" and de- portability in everyday life. *Annual Review of Anthropology, 31*, 419-447.

De Ridder, S. (2016). *Foreign national prisoners facing expulsion. The percolation of migration law enforcement into sentence implementation decision-making on release in Belgium.*

Denzin, N. (1989). *The Research Act: A Theoretical Introduction to Sociological Methods.* Englewood Cliffs, NJ: Prentice Hall.

Di Molfetta, E., & Brouwer, J. (2019). Unravelling the 'crimmigration knot': Penal subjectivities, punishment and the censure machine. *Criminology and Criminal Justice.*

Düvell, F., Triandafyllidou, A., & Vollmer, B. (2009). Ethical issues in irregular migration research in Europe. *Population, Space and Place, 16*(3), 227-239.

Eastmond, M. (2007). Stories as lived experience: Narratives in forced migration research. *Journal of Refugee Studies, 20*(2), 248-264.

Hasselberg, I. (2016). *Enduring uncertainty. Deportation, punishment and everyday life.* New York: Berghahn Books.

Jacobsen, K., & Landau, L. B. (2003). The dual imperative in refugee research: some methodological and ethical considerations in social science research on forced migration. *Disasters, 27*(3), 185-206.

Kaufman, E. (2015). *Punish and Expel. Border Control, Nationalism, and the New Purpose of the Prison*. Oxford: Oxford University Press.

Moffette, D. (2018). The jurisdictional games of immigration policing: Barcelona's fight against unauthorised street vending. *Theoretical Criminology, Online fir*, 1-18.

Peutz, N. (2006). Embarking on an Anthropology of Removal. *Current Anthropology, 47*(2), 217-241.

Turnbull, S., & Hasselberg, I. (2017). From prison to detention: The carceral trajectories of foreign-national prisoners in the United Kingdom. *Punishment & Society, 19*(2), 135-154.

Van der Woude, M. A. H., Brouwer, J., & Dekkers, T. J. M. (2016). *Beslissen in grensgebieden. Een onderzoek naar het Mobiel Toezicht Veiligheid zoals uitgevoerd door de Koninklijke Marechaussee*. Den Haag: Boom Juridische Uitgevers.

Van Hulst, M. (2013). Storytelling at the police station. The canteen culture revisited. *British Journal of Criminology, 53*(4), 624-642.

Van Staa, A. L., & Evers, J. (2010). 'Thick analysis': Strategie om de kwaliteit van kwalitatieve data-analyse te verhogen. *Tijdschrift voor Kwalitatief Onderzoek in Nederland, 43*(1), 5-12.

Annex
Research methodologies

This dissertation studies bordering practices in the Netherlands from a crimmigration perspective. The empirical core of the dissertation consists of two case studies: one on intra-Schengen migration policing and one on the punishment and deportation of criminally convicted migrants (CCNCs). As an empirical examination of the broadly defined concept of crimmigration, the choice for a case study approach was the result of several contemplations. When research for this dissertation commenced, most of the existing crimmigration literature consisted of legal scholarship and was normative and theoretically oriented. This body of work generally described macro-level developments on a global scale – with a strong focus on the United States. While such macro-level accounts are particularly valuable in painting broad patterns that occur in multiple settings around the globe, they fail to account for considerable differences in how such global trends materialise at the national or local level (Crewe, 2015). Moreover, they say little about how such developments are interpreted, experienced, and understood 'on the ground' (Turnbull & Hasselberg, 2017). In order to avoid descriptions that are too generic and understand what these developments actually mean in practice, it is essential to study these theoretical constructs in specific national and local contexts (Aas, 2014). Empirical case studies are particularly suitable to do so and to answer questions related to the how and why of certain phenomena. The aim of such studies is not to achieve generalisability, although the analytical findings can often be applicable in other contexts as well, but rather to add depth and nuance to more abstract accounts (Moffette, 2018).

The choice for these specific two case studies was motivated by several factors. First, both case studies are interesting examples of novel bordering practices that have come into existence relatively recently. The MSM was created in response to the lifting of internal border controls following the implementation of the Schengen agreement, while the policy framework regarding CCNCs has seen considerable changes in recent years. Second, while there is a rich body of criminological research on policing and punishment in the Netherlands, neither the MSM nor the punishment and deportation of CCNCs had been the subject of empirical research. Third, besides different forms of social control, the two case studies are situated at different ends of the chains of social control. As such, they enable insights into both the front and the back of the criminal justice and migration control chain [see De Ridder]. Fourth, the case studies incorporate originate in the two different chains of social control. Whereas the first case study focusses on an actor situated in the migration control chain, the second case study primarily focusses on a setting located in the criminal justice system. This has the added benefit that the case studies address both directions of the crimmigration spectrum: the criminalisation of migration control and the immigrationalisation of the criminal justice system. Of course, the choice for these two case studies automatically means that other potentially interesting cases and actors have not been studied for this dissertation. In particular, studies into the migration control activities of police officers and the overlap between immigration detention and crime control rationales are potentially interesting avenues to pursue.

This annex will elaborate upon the methodological approach of these two case studies, including the choices, challenges, and limitations experienced before and during the fieldwork. Besides these two case studies, this dissertation also contained a contextual chapter on the media discourse on unauthorised migrants. Because the methodology of this study has already been discussed in detail in that chapter, it will not be discussed again here. Furthermore, both case studies also involved a significant amount of desk study: collecting, reading, and analysing academic literature, relevant and publicly available official documents, and some limited case law. Because this was not done in any structured way on the basis of a predetermined methodology, it will also not be discussed here. Instead, this annex will focus on the different types of empirical research that have been carried out through extensive (semi-)structured fieldwork.

Case study I: Intra-Schengen migration policing

The first case study examined intra-Schengen migration policing by means of a case study of the Mobile Security Monitor (MSM) carried out by the Royal Netherlands Marechaussee (RNM). The data used for this part of the dissertation was collected in the context of a larger research project on discretionary decision-making in border contexts (Van der Woude, Brouwer, & Dekkers, 2016). Empirical data for the larger research project was collected between November 2013 and March 2015. The research project was set up and coordinated by prof. Maartje van der Woude, at that time Associate Professor in criminal law, but nowadays Professor of Law and Society at Leiden Law School. She had also arranged fieldwork access to the MSM through existing contacts at the RNM by the time joined Leiden Law School as a PhD-Candidate. The fieldwork was carried out by prof. van der Woude, Tim Dekkers, junior researcher and later PhD-Candidate at Leiden Law School, and myself. Moreover, in the planning phase of the research several colleagues from the Department of Criminology at Leiden Law School provided helped with the research design and creating the different research instruments.

The data used for this dissertation consist of observational data, transcripts of focus group discussions with officers, and semi-structured interviews or surveys with people who have been stopped. For the larger research project we also analysed quantitative data provided by the RNM and conducted in-depth interviews with senior policy officials, but these data have not been used for this dissertation. By combining these different research methodologies, also referred to as methodological triangulation, the data collected is enriched and improved (Van Staa & Evers, 2010). This triangulation included in some cases verifying the findings from one methodology through another methodology. Further triangulation was established by the fact that the fieldwork was carried out by three researchers. In this way, observations and interpretations could be cross-checked and validated amongst each other (Denzin, 1989).

Participant observation

The first part of the empirical data for this case study was collected through participant observation. During a period of roughly fifteen months – between November 2013 and March 2015 – the three researchers carried out participant observations during a total of 57 MSM controls, always in duos. This amounted to over 800 individual hours of observation. I was present at 53 of the observed MSM control. All researchers completed a two-day training in participatory observation before the beginning of the fieldwork.

In order to build up trust and acceptance and get a comprehensive understanding of the MSM controls, all six brigades that carry out the MSM were visited at least six times. The duration of the controls varied, depending on the number of RNM officers and the events during the control. For example, during one of the first controls we observed there was a small team of RNM officers and one of the first vehicles immediately led to a 'case'. As a result, all officers went back to the brigade and the control was over after less than an hour. However, on average the controls lasted between six and eight hours. A regular shift started with a briefing and included plenty of time drinking coffee in the canteen; both function as important sites for storytelling, briefings in a more factual manner and the canteen as a place of informal conversation (Van Hulst, 2013). When it was the first time we visited a certain brigade, this was usually also the moment where we introduced ourselves and the research project and gave officers the opportunity to ask questions. This approach helped to create some trust among the research participants and frequently one of the officers would approach us after the briefing to discuss some elements of the MSM.

Most of the controls were so-called 'static' controls, meaning that one or several officers on motorbikes would stand just after the border to select vehicles for a check. He or she then directed the vehicle to a control location further inland, where other officers carried out the actual control by checking the identity papers of the persons stopped. Researchers usually spent most of the day on the control location, where they could observe the selected vehicles and the actual control, ask about the reasons behind a specific stop and chat with officers during the sometimes long periods waiting for a new vehicle. However, sometimes the RNM carried out so-called 'dynamic' MSM controls, usually when capacity was relatively low. This meant officers would drive around in the border area and stop vehicles to subsequently carry out the control themselves. In this case, the researchers would usually sit in the back of the vehicle, from where they could chat with the RNM officers and observe their decisions. This included cases where both researchers joined the same vehicle and cases where they went separately in different vehicles. During the observations, researchers were always clearly distinguishable from RNM officers. Whereas the officers always wore their official uniform, researchers were dressed in regular clothes and wore a reflective vest.

Besides observing the MSM controls, there was also ample opportunity for conversations with the RNM officers. These conversations were generally very informal and were often about the events taking place during the control. The nature of these conversations also depended on how busy it was during a control. Because of the informal nature of these conversations and the fact that they took place in a familiar setting, RNM officers often appeared to be very honest and open. More generally, most RNM officers were very welcoming and open towards the researchers. Whereas there has been no doubt somewhat of an observer effect, it did not appear as if officers radically altered their behaviour because of the presence of the researcher. In that regard, the fact that we usually observed for many hours and repeatedly visited the same brigades was a distinct advantage. This helped us to build up trust and acceptance, as we regularly saw the same officers during different controls.

During the observations a so-called observation form was used to note the characteristics of stopped vehicles and individuals, the reasons for this particular stop, the overall process during the stop, and the interaction between the officer(s) and the individual(s) who were stopped. Before we started using this form in practice, it had been tested several times to see if all relevant data was accurately captured with and whether researchers interpreted and filled out the forms in a similar manner. In case we also conducted an interview with one of the stopped individuals (see below) the forms were numbered in order to link them. A total of 330 of these forms were filled out during the observations. Researchers also wrote down short notes about their observations and impressions, which were turned into extensive fieldnote reports after the end of each shift. Researchers drew up individual fieldnotes, giving the opportunity to cross-check certain observations. Moreover, to ensure the overall quality and consistency of these fieldnotes we regularly read and discussed each other's fieldnotes.

Focus group discussions

Towards the end of the period of participant observations, we started with the second type of data collection: focus group discussions. Focus groups are structured discussions with a relatively small number of participants, guided by the researcher. They allow researchers to capture prevailing collective opinions and views within a social group. The group in this case is a homogenous population, usually consisting of about seven to ten individuals who discuss their ideas, beliefs, and thoughts about a specific topic. The questions that are asked are usually aimed at retrieving harder to get phenomena that play at the group level and topics that are normatively charged. The aim of these specific focus groups was to gain insight into how officers themselves interpreted and used their role and task. The data collected through the observations was used to inform the focus group discussions, considerably improving the discussions and enriching the data. This strategy also allowed for further reflection and validation of the findings from the observations.

A total of thirteen focus group discussions were organised with street-level officers between October 2014 and January 2015. Questions were structured around several topics that had either been part of the research from the start or had emerged as particularly interesting during the observations. Two sessions were organised at each brigade, except for one larger brigade where we held four sessions, and one smaller brigade where we only had one session. Twelve out of thirteen focus groups were conducted by the three researchers, with prof. van der Woude, who had completed a training in leading focus groups, generally taking the lead in asking the questions. One focus group was conducted by Tim Dekkers and myself. A previously created topic list was used to make sure the same issues were discussed during all focus groups. The number of respondents varied between eight and ten, with differences in experience, rank and age. The majority of respondents were men, in line with overall male-female ratio within the RNM. Participants were encouraged to react and disagree with each other, in order to create dynamic discussions and obtain rich data. The discussions lasted anywhere between 1,5 and 3,5 hours and all of them were recorded.

Interviews with people who are stopped

Besides data on the RNM officers, we also collected data among people who were stopped during the MSM. Collecting data on the perceptions of individuals who were stopped during the MSM proved to be a challenging task. In previous studies used for the design of this study, researchers asked people whether they were willing to answer a number of questions over the phone in a later stage (Alpert, Macdonald, & Dunham, 2005). Many people responded negatively to this request or gave false phone numbers, resulting in a very low response rate. For our research project we therefore decided to directly approach the people during the controls and ask whether they were willing to participate in a short interview or fill out a brief survey. During the actual controls, one researcher would focus on the characteristics of the vehicle and persons and reasons for the stop, while the other asked people if they were willing to participate in an academic study. This made it possible to link the observation data to the data on people's perceptions about the controls, which enriched the overall picture of what exactly happened during the controls and how this is perceived by different parties involved.

Before the start of the fieldwork, a survey was created on the basis of the main research and theoretical concepts regarding perceptions of law enforcement. After an explanatory text in the beginning of the survey, it contained a set of open questions about people's perceptions regarding the fact that they had been stopped, why they thought they had been stopped, whether they trusted the RNM officers had done the right thing and if the reason for the stop had been explained to them. It also asked people's country of birth, the country of birth of both their parents and, in order to capture their own sense of social identity, to what ethnic or national group they felt they belonged most. To measure legitimacy, two sets of five-point Likert-type scale ranging from 1 (strongly disagree) to 5 (strongly agree) were included. The first set of five statements focussed on the perceived effectiveness and acceptability of the instrument, while the second set of four questions focussed on treatment by the officers.

Initially the idea was to conduct the survey orally and fill in the answers people gave. However, it became quickly apparent that many of the potential respondents did not speak any of the languages the researchers spoke. It was therefore decided to translate the survey into eleven different languages, for which we used friends and acquaintances who upon completion of the fieldwork also translated the answers.[1] This greatly enhanced the number of respondents, including groups otherwise completely missed. However, whereas the interviews sometimes resulted in lively conversations, respondents filling out the survey themselves inevitably led to more basic information.

Vehicles were approached while RNM officers were checking the papers, as at this time there was usually no interaction between the officers and the stopped persons. RNM officers also agreed to give the researcher space to conduct the interview. The researcher was clearly distinguishable from RNM officers and always stressed before an interview that he or she did not work for the RNM but was part of an independent academic research team. He or

1 The survey was translated into Albanian, Bulgarian, Czech, German, French, Hungarian, Italian, Polish, Romanian, Russian, and Spanish. I want to thank Rogier Vijverberg for his assistance with designing the survey and thank the following persons for the translations: Francesco Cacciola, Sarah Castéran, Theodora Petrova, Benjamin Kiebeler, Ekaterina Kopylova, Bogdan Popescu, Silvia Rodriguez Rivero, Marie Skálová, Magdalena Szmidt, Burbuqe Thaci, Luca Valente, and Andrea Varga.

she also emphasised that all information would be treated anonymously and confidentially. Depending on the origin of the vehicles' license plate and the language proficiency of the researcher, people were approached in Dutch, English, French or German. If it became clear a language barrier prevented an actual interview, the researcher tried to identify the preferred language of the potential respondent and handed her/him the survey. In the end, a total of 167 respondents were interviewed or filled out a survey. A table with the breakdown of the different respondents can be found in chapter 5.

Analysis of the data

Prior to the data analysis phase, all researchers took a course in qualitative data analysis. The fieldnotes and transcripts of the focus group discussions were analysed with AtlasTi, a software package for qualitative data analysis. Prior to starting these materials, a list of different codes was created based on the main research questions and overarching themes of the research. This list was drawn up together by the three researchers involved. While this list formed the basis of the coding exercise, it was constantly updated and amended during the coding process, according to relevant topics that emerged. All three researchers were involved in the coding of the data. As this creates the risk of inconsistencies in the way the raw data is coded, we ran a test round before the actual coding started. All researchers coded the same piece of data, which was subsequently checked for crucial differences. The results of this test demonstrated general uniformity in the way we coded. Upon completion of the coding, all the relevant excerpts for specific research questions and topics were extracted, providing a good overview of the different situations, decisions, and perceptions regarding certain topics. It is important to note that, although this way of analysing the data helps to reduce the risk of researcher biases informing the outcomes of the research, his or her interpretation of the data and the analysis still plays an important role in the final reporting. Moreover, the decisions around the coding process are not objective in nature and therefore shape to a certain extent the focus of the analysis. However, this is to a certain extent inevitable in any form of qualitative research.

The data in the observation forms was put in an excel document, providing a good overview of the characteristics of the different vehicles and individuals that were stopped. Similarly, the data from the interviews and surveys with stopped people was also put in excel. Responses to the open questions were subsequently categorised in 'positive', 'negative', and 'neutral', making it possible to move beyond the quotes and get a broader idea of the overall perception of the RNM and the MSM. We also categorised and counted the closed questions with yes or no as possible answers. For the analysis of the Likert-type scale questions, we only used the surveys that responded to all statements in the concerned set. We calculated the two sets of questions as well as all questions individually. Finally, we categorised the survey results in different groups. For example, we looked at whether people were stopped for the first or had already been stopped before. As further elaborated on in chapter five, we also categorised respondents in 'non-Dutch citizens', 'Dutch majority citizens' and 'Dutch ethnic minority citizens'. The responses of the different groups were then analysed and compared to gain insight into noteworthy differences in overall perceptions. Moreover, the relatively small group of outspoken negative respondents was analysed separately to see whether they differed from the other respondents on other parts of the survey as well.

Ethical considerations

The first case study raised several ethical issues, although considerably less than the second case study. On a general level, the research has adhered to the 'code of conduct for scientific practice' and the 'code of use of personal data in research' of the Association of Universities in the Netherlands (VSNU). The large number of officers present during the MSM prevented the possibility of obtaining individualised written informed consent of all participants. However, officers were informed about the research project and the researchers before the observations and focus group interviews. It was during these introductions that the officers were informed that they were not obligated to participate by interacting with the researchers and also that all the collected information would be processed anonymously and no information would be traceable to an individual or even a brigade. Officers also had the opportunity to ask questions, which many of them did. The overall openness of almost all officers during the fieldwork could be seen as an indication of the willingness to engage with the research project.

The interviews with people who were stopped raised more questions about ethical issues, in particular voluntariness and written informed consent. Researchers always stressed that respondents were not obliged to participate and that all information would be anonymous. Moreover, it was emphasised that it was an independent academic study and that none of the surveys would be shared with the RNM. It was agreed with the RNM officers that they would give us space to approach a vehicle while they were carrying out their control. However, there were some instances where RNM officers told people they had stopped that we wanted to conduct a brief interview or survey, which could have given the impression we were part of the RNM and participation was not really optional. After all, during the interview or survey, the officers often still had the documents of people they were controlling. However, at least one good indicator of the fact that in general it will have been clear for people that participation was entirely on a voluntary basis, was the relatively high rate of people who did not want to participate.

Finally, the sensitivity of at least some of the data collected required a careful approach to data storage and sharing. Digital data was only stored on password-protected USB sticks and a folder on the university's network that was only accessible by the researchers. All physical data – primarily the observation forms and surveys – were stored in a locked closet with one key, that was kept by one of the researchers.

CASE STUDY II: PUNISHMENT AND DEPORTATION OF CRIMINALLY CONVICTED NON-CITIZENS

For this research project, I designed the research approach and methodologies, arranged access to research sites, and coordinated all of the fieldwork myself. Although various types of data were collected for this study, the most important empirical data for this study consists of semi-structured interviews with CCNCs, departure supervisors of DT&V, and prison officers in Ter Apel prison. Interviews are a particularly valuable method to capture people's experiences and feelings, enabling in-depth assessments and resulting in relatively 'thick' descriptive data (Jacobsen & Landau, 2003). More than for example questionnaires or surveys, they allow for a rich understanding of how people interpret and negotiate their experiences. The focus is not necessary on what exactly happened, but rather on how something is experienced, perceived, and understood (Kaufman, 2015; Turnbull and Hasselberg, 2016). Respondents' narratives are not objective versions of an absolute truth; instead, the aim is to portray one version of the experience of punishment and deportation and interpret these stories in the wider social and political contexts that have shaped the circumstances of respondents' lives (Eastmond, 2007; Kaufman, 2015). As Eastmond (2007, p. 253) suggests, "by juxtaposing individual accounts, we may glean the commonalities in the experiences of a particular group of forced migrants, as well as understand the internal variation among them." Analysing these narratives can therefore reveal diversity in seemingly similar accounts that make it possible to move beyond a generalised and homogenous understanding of imprisonment and deportation. Besides being a suitable methodology to achieve the envisaged aims of the research, it was also out of practical considerations that I opted for individual interviews. As Ter Apel prison is a relatively inaccessible research site, more ethnographic methodologies, such as long-term participant observation, were complicated or even impossible to organise.

Access 1: DT&V

Because of the two governmental agencies involved in the punishment and deportation of CCNCs – DT&V and DJI – access had to be ensured to both of these. Access to DT&V was established through already existing contact with the agency of one my supervisors. Following an initial e-mail exchange to indicate our interest in carrying out a research project on the deportation of

CCNCs, a brief research proposal was shared with the organisation in February 2014. This proposal provided a short background to the proposed study and outlined the main research questions, proposed data collection methods, and envisaged deliverables of the research project. This proposal elicited a positive response from DT&V and eventually full access and cooperation with the research project was granted in May 2014.

The department of DT&V that deals with CCNCs operates at two locations: Ter Apel prison, where the vast majority of CCNCs are incarcerated, and the relatively newly built multipurpose Judicial Complex Schiphol (JCS), which houses a tribunal, asylum application centre, immigration detention centre, and a prison. The latter location houses primarily CCNCs in pre-trial detention or with a relatively short sentence. For practical reasons, in particular the relatively short distance from my home and the university, it was decided that I would be able to access data at the offices of DT&V at JCS. I did bring a visit to the office in Ter Apel prison, during which I also got a tour of the prison and was able to see the different living and work areas.

Starting in February 2015, for a period of roughly one and a half year and on an irregular basis, I spent about one day per week at the offices of DT&V at JCS. I had access to the office building through a personal badge, could use one of the many empty work stations, and had login details for the computer system. Here, I could access digital files of CCNCs, which contained a wealth of information on their background, as well as written transcripts of so-called 'departure talks' between departure supervisors and CCNCs. I could also observe everyday working activities and hold informal conversations with departure supervisors and managers. I attended several departure talks and a presentation of several men at the Turkish consulate, aimed at confirming their identity and nationality. Although I did not use any of this data directly in this dissertation, this relatively long period of informal fieldwork did provide me with valuable insights in the day-to-day operations of organising the return of CCNCs. I did not take structured field notes during these observations and conversations, but I did write the most interesting observations down in a dedicated word file.

I was also provided with a dataset containing the characteristics of the population of CCNCs being managed by DT&V. This dataset contained information about the nationality, country of origin, age, crime committed, prison sentence, and current location of imprisonment. This enabled me to get a rough picture of the overall population. As further discussed below, I also used this dataset for the sampling of respondents.

Access 2: DJI and Ter Apel prison

As noted above, the majority of CCNCs are imprisoned in Ter Apel prison and it was there that I intended to conduct my interviews. As the prison falls under the authority of DJI, and I also wanted to interview prison officers working there, I had to get approval of DJI in order to carry out this part of the fieldwork. In order to get access to the research site and research participants, a formal request was sent to the Director of DJI. The application described the aim of the research and the research questions, the envisaged data collection activities and respondents, and the period of fieldwork. It also included the more detailed research proposal that had been written for DT&V. The application relied on the earlier established cooperation agreement between DJI and the Institute of Criminal law and Criminology of Leiden University for the period 2015 – 2020, which intended to advance knowledge about detention and imprisonment in the Netherlands through research activities and knowledge exchange. Several weeks after the formal application was lodged, an official letter was received granting permission to carry out the fieldwork. Following this, I got in touch with the administration of Ter Apel prison to organise the logistics and practical arrangements for the interviews.

Interviews with criminally convicted non-citizens

For the interviews with CCNCs, I worked together with four students from the Criminal Justice Master's programme at Leiden University.[2] This approach had several benefits, while simultaneously posing a couple of challenges. The main benefit of this approach was that I could recruit participants who only spoke languages I do not speak myself. Especially the ability to conduct interviews in Spanish and Italian greatly enhanced the diversity of the final sample. Moreover, by being able to interview respondents in their native or preferred language, it was generally easier to build up trust and rapport, thus improving the overall quality of the data. A second benefit of this approach was that it enabled us to conduct several interviews at the same time, thus increasing the number of interviews per day. Considering the significant travel time to Ter Apel and as the limited number of days we were allowed to come to the prison to conduct the fieldwork, this was an efficient way to collect as much data as possible within a relatively short period of time. A final benefit of this approach, although not directly related to this research project itself, was that it exposed students to the experience of conducting research and doing fieldwork. For all students involved in the project this possibility was a unique opportunity and generally perceived as adding considerable value to their regular education. In one case, it even resulted in a peer-reviewed publication in a criminological journal (Di Molfetta & Brouwer, 2019).

Conducting the interviews by different researchers also posed several challenges. Whereas I had been trained in qualitative interviews through a two-day training and had some experience from previous research projects, none of the students had significant training or experience in conducting

2 I would like to thank Arturo Alberto Muñoz, Eleonora di Molfetta, Karola Kolomainen, and Nadja Holfelder for their valuable assistance in data collection.

qualitative interviews. To somewhat compensate for this, and ensure consistency in the interviews, a training day was organised where we discussed what to expect, interview techniques, and the topic list for the interviews. Different interviewers also raises questions about the consistency of the data collected, since factors such as age, gender, nationality, and personality of the interviewers are likely to have influenced the interview process and therefore also the collected data. Although a topic list was used to make sure all relevant themes were raised during the interviews, the relatively open nature of the interviews also meant that they could result in very different conversations depending on the follow-up questions and discussions. Fortunately, in practice these differences turned out to be relatively small. This is in line with recent research on Romanian prisoners in Norway conducted by two very different researchers in terms of age, gender, nationality, and linguistic capabilities (Damsa & Ugelvik, 2017). Whereas Damsa is a young woman of Romanian origin, Ugelvik is a slightly older Norwegian man who does not speak Romanian. Whereas these differences did have an effect on how they experienced their fieldwork, the substantial findings of their research turned out to be very similar, leading them to argue that "our colleagues should not simply take researcher field effects in ethnographic studies for granted in future research (p. 2)". Indeed, it could even be argued that some of the findings that surfaced in interviews conducted by a number of different researchers – as was often the case with the data collected for this dissertation – can be considered stronger than findings on the basis of one interviewer only.

Sampling of respondents was a combination of purposive sampling and convenience sampling (cf. De Ridder, 2016). Potential respondents were identified through the list of current CCNCs provided by DT&V, with the aim to capture as much diversity as possible in terms of nationality, age, prison sentence, remaining prison time left, and time spent in the Netherlands. They were also sampled on the basis of their language skills, as this was a necessary requirement to conduct an interview. Whereas the list provided by DT&V did not include information on the languages spoken by CCNCs, their digital files did. Although departure supervisors informed me this was not always accurate, this was the only source of information and it eventually turned out to be very reliable. Eventually there were also respondents who were not deliberately sampled, but nonetheless offered to participate. As I will further discuss below, recruiting respondents was rather challenging and it was long uncertain whether it would be possible to conduct a reasonable amount of interviews. For this reason, these 'spontaneous respondents' were also included in the final sample.

Recruiting potential respondents was quite a challenging task, as I could not go around the prison to approach CCNCs myself. Instead, an information letter was drawn up to invite potential respondents to participate in an academic research project, providing some background and outlining the main purpose of the research. It also emphasised the independent nature of the study and that all interviews would be anonymously and confidential. The letter stressed the voluntary nature of participating and informed potential respondents that they could stop with the interview whenever they wanted, in which case all information provided so far would be deleted. They were also invited to let me know if they wanted more information about the study, the researchers, or anything else. The letter was translated in six languages (matching the language skills of the different interviewers) to reach as many potential respondents as possible. These were subsequently shared with the contact person in Ter Apel prison, who ensured distribution to the identified potential respondents via the prison staff at the different prison wings.

This approach was obviously not ideal, as I had little control over the actual information provided to CCNCs. Indeed, during the interviews it became apparent that various respondents had never seen the invitation letter, but had merely been asked by a prison officer whether they wanted to participate in a study. This might have also had an impact on the response rate, as positive responses were more likely when potential respondents had been able to read the invitation letter. The approach to already identify potential respondents had also had its downsides. One of the eventual respondents told me that he saw other prisoners at his wing being asked to participate in the study and believed they deliberately excluded him because of his outspoken criticism of the prison. He had therefore proactively ensured that the prison officer put his name on this list of interested CCNCs. Indeed, several of the eventual respondents had not been identified as potential respondents on the basis of the list of DT&V. This might have had an impact on the data collected, as these respondents might have been extra critical of the prison and the migration system. However, during the interviews a wide diversity of voices was apparent and not all respondents were critical of the prison or the regime.

The list of CCNCs provided by DT&V was not a real-time reflection of the population of CCNCs and sometimes potential respondents were no longer imprisoned in Ter Apel. Among those who were approached for participation, positive responses varied greatly between prison wings, with sometimes around eighty percent positive responses and other times less than twenty percent. This suggests that there was something of a 'negative snowballing' effect, with prisoners telling each other not to participate. This suggestion was supported by the time that an expected respondent decided at the last moment not to do the interview anymore. When the next respondent also no longer wanted to participate, I was informed by one of the prison guards that they had their cells next to each other and were good friends. It was therefore suggested that they had influenced each other's' decision not to participate.

Based on the responses I received from the contact person in Ter Apel prison, I made a list of respondents we would like to interview on each fieldwork day, primarily based on the languages spoken by respondents and interviewers. The contact person subsequently made a planning, taking into account the part of the day respondents did not work. Prisoners in Ter Apel work one part of the day, either the morning or the afternoon; the other part of the day is for broadly defined recreation. Despite this planning and the initial consent of respondents to participate in the research, interviews regularly did not go through in the end, either because a respondent was no longer available at a given time or because he decided at the last moment to not participate after all. Eventually, 37 CCNCs were interviewed over a period of four days in April and May 2016, with the final list of respondents displaying considerable diversity on all factors mentioned above. The exact breakdown of respondents can be found in table A1.

The interviews took place in the building of the Repatriation and Departure Service, as this was one of the few places inside the prison where one can establish an acceptable level of privacy. These offices are located within a small separate building on the prison grounds, but outside the main prison building. This building is separated in two parts: one part with the offices of staff members of DT&V and one part with five 'conversations rooms' where they hold departure talks with CCNCs; the two parts are separated by a locked door. The part with the conversation rooms also has a counter where a prison officer is working. Prisoners who have an appointment with someone from DT&V enter the building in this part and then give their personal card to the prison officer, in order to keep track of their whereabouts. The conversation rooms themselves are relatively sober rooms, installed with little more than a desk with a phone that is used for translation services and two chairs. Underneath the desk was an emergency button, which would alert the prison officer located just outside the room. The rooms had one window and a window in the door, so that if needed people could look inside to see what happened. This also meant other people – such as departure supervisors looking for an empty room – would generally not disturb the interview.

For the interviews, some respondents came over spontaneously, as they were aware of their appointment for an interview. Other times respondents were not aware they were expected for an interview and the prison officer at the counter would contact a colleague at the relevant prison wing to ask a respondent to come over; in those cases there was frequently some initial confusion, as respondents believed they were called for a meeting with their departure supervisor. Indeed, conducting the interviews in the rooms of DT&V sometimes generated some issues of distrust, this could quickly be addressed when researchers explained who they were and what the interview was for. For example, during one interview a respondent came into the room with a clear hostile attitude and refused to sit down, saying that he preferred to keep standing and had nothing to say anyway. After I made clear that I did not work for DT&V but was a researcher for Leiden University he relaxed and sat down. Eventually, this was one of the most engaging respondents.

Creating rapport and trust during the interviews was crucial and several steps were taken in order to achieve this. Once respondents arrived in the building of DT&V, the interviewer would welcome him and shake hands to introduce her- or himself. The respondent was then invited into one of the rooms and asked to take the seat he preferred; it was interesting to note that all respondents chose the seat normally used for CCNCs and not the one normally used by the departure supervisors. The interviewer also asked whether the respondent preferred to have the door open or closed, with nearly all respondents preferring to have the door closed. In many cases the interviewer also tried to make some small talk to further lighten the mood and decrease any tensions.

	Interviewer	*Country of origin*	*Language*	*Transcript*
Mar-22	Jelmer	Algeria	Dutch	Yes
	Jelmer	Bosnia and Herzegovina	Dutch	Yes
	Jelmer	Morocco	Dutch	Yes
	Jelmer	Ecuador	English	Yes
	Karola	Surinam	English	Yes
	Karola	Albania	English	Yes
	Karola	China	English	No
	Karola	Iraq	English	Yes
	Nadja	Lithuania	English	Yes
	Nadja	Canada/Angola	English	Yes
	Nadja	Tunisia	English	Yes
Apr-05	Jelmer	Albania	English	Yes
	Jelmer	Turkey	Dutch	Yes
	Jelmer	Morocco	Dutch	Yes
	Jelmer	Morocco	Dutch	Yes
	Arturo	Colombia	Spanish	Yes
	Arturo	Colombia	Spanish	Yes
	Arturo	Colombia	Spanish	Yes
	Arturo	Colombia	Spanish	Yes
	Eleonora	Albania	Italian	Yes
	Eleonora	Bosnia and Herzegovina	English	Yes
	Eleonora	Serbia	English	Yes
	Eleonora	Costa Rica	English	Yes
Apr-12	Jelmer	France	Dutch	Yes
	Jelmer	Surinam	Dutch	Yes
Apr-20	Jelmer	Morocco	Dutch	Yes
	Jelmer	Kosovo	Dutch	Yes
	Jelmer	Israel	Dutch	Yes
	Jelmer	Guinea	Dutch	No
	Jelmer	Albania	Dutch	Yes

Interviewer	*Country of origin*	*Language*	*Transcript*
Arturo	Morocco	French	Yes
Arturo	Colombia	Spanish	Yes
Arturo	Ecuador	Spanish	Yes
Eleonora	Serbia	English	Yes
Eleonora	China	English	Yes
Eleonora	Italy	Italian	Yes
Eleonora	Algeria	English	Yes

Table A1 Interviewed CCNCs

Before the start of the actual interview, respondents were clearly informed about the purpose of the research, the role and position of the interviewer, the main topics and expected duration of the interview, the voluntary nature of their participation, including the possibility to stop with the interview, and the anonymous and confidential nature of the interview. As CCNCs experience frequent interviews by a range of state actors, it was deemed especially important to emphasise our position as independent researchers affiliated with Leiden University. It was also stressed that none of the information they provided would be share with DJI, DT&V, or any other government bodies in a way that would enable identification of the source. Respondents were also given the opportunity to ask any questions, which regularly resulted in questions about the eventual purpose of the overall research. At the end of the interview, they were again explicitly asked whether they had any questions left. As respondents had volunteered to be interviewed, they were generally very willing to talk about their experiences. Indeed, several respondents indicated they were pleased to be able to talk with an outsider about their experiences in Ter Apel prison, a sentiment that seemed to be broadly shared among respondents. This obviously helped improve the overall richness and quality of the interview data.

Respondents were also asked whether they agreed to recording the interview in order to transcribe it later. They were informed that the interviews would be transcribed by the interviewer or by a professional transcription service, which had signed a confidentially agreement. It was also mentioned that the transcripts would be anonymised and that the audio recording would be deleted afterwards. Moreover, all recordings and transcripts would be stored in a secure location only accessible by myself or my supervisors, and the latter only if needed. Respondents could also stop the audio recordings at any point during the interview. Only two respondents did not consent to recording the interview. In those cases, notes were taken during the interview and reworked into an interview report as soon as possible. During all other interviews, a recording device was visibly located at the table. On the first day of fieldwork, some of the researchers recorded the interview with their phone. However, this created some unrest among both respondents and staff and it was therefore decided – upon request of the contact person in the prison – to subsequently only use recording devices.

Interviews lasted anywhere between twenty minutes and more than an hour, largely depending on how talkative a respondent was. Where possible, respondents were interviewed in their native language or another preferred language; translators were never used. All interviews conducted for this research were semi-structured, informed by the main concepts and topics discussed in existing literature and issues that arose during the relatively long period I spent at the offices at DT&V. A topic list was used to conduct the interviews, reflecting the main research questions of the study. The main topics discussed were life before coming to the Netherlands, life in the Netherlands before their current imprisonment period, experiences in Ter Apel prison, experiences with the criminal justice and migration control systems more broadly, and how they saw the future. Depending on the respondent, some of the interviews neatly followed this topic list, whereas others were much more jumbled. Indeed, during some of the interviews it was barely necessary to ask a question, as the respondent simply kept talking about his experiences and telling stories. More generally, the flexibility allowed by the semi-structured nature of the interviews and the open questions meant that respondents were able to share their experiences in their own way with as little pressure as possible to use certain narratives.

Interviewing prisoners generally provided rich and thick narrative data on the subjective experiences of CCNCs, perceptions of imprisonment in Ter Apel, and the impact this had on their life and future. At the same time, it is important to stress the limitations of primarily relying on verbal exchange, and for example not include participatory observation or other more ethnographic research methods. Respondents no doubt had their own agendas during the interviews and might exaggerate or even make up certain claims. Whereas this is perhaps less relevant when studying prisoners' experiences, particularly critical accounts of prison life in Ter Apel were always corroborated with other respondents, prison officers, and other staff members for accuracy.

Interviews with departure supervisors

A total of seventeen departure supervisors working specifically with CCNCs were interviewed, accounting for more than 80% of the total number of departure supervisors dealing with CCNCs at the time of research. For these interviews, I cooperated with dr. Steven de Ridder, who had previously conducted similar research in Belgium and was at that time employed as a postdoctoral researcher at the Vrije Universiteit Brussel. Departure supervisors at JCS were recruited by asking them personally, after they had already been informed about the research by the manager of the unit. The interviews with departure supervisors in Ter Apel prison were arranged via one of the senior departure supervisors, who acted as my primary contact person for this team. The interviews took place between April and October 2016, and were conducted by myself, by Steven de Ridder, or by the two of us. A topic list consisting of clusters of questions dealing with a specific topic was drawn up beforehand, but during the interviews the conversation often flowed freely to other issues. All interviews took place in the offices of DT&V, either at JCS or in Ter Apel Prison. Interviewed departure supervisors differed in their years of experience and some also worked with other migrant groups, such as rejected asylum seekers. However, all had at least some CCNCs among their current cases.

Before the start of the interview, the aim of the research and the interview were explained and participants were given the opportunity to ask any questions. Respondents were also asked whether the interview could be recorded and subsequently transcribed verbatim, something all respondents agreed upon. The interviewer also stressed the anonymity of the respondents, emphasizing that none of the information would be used in a way that it could be traced back to specific individuals, although most departure supervisors indicated they would not find it problematic if the interviews were not anonymised. Departure supervisors were generally very talkative, perhaps in part because they are used to having conversations because of the nature of their work. Many of them indicated they found it interesting to be on the other side of an interview, since usually they are the ones asking the questions. Most respondents talked very open about the different elements of their work and seemed to enjoy the fact that someone showed interest in how they go about this. The interviews likely further benefitted from the fact that both Dr. de Ridder and myself had been working on this topic for a while and were relatively well informed about the main issues. Moreover, Dr. de Ridder had the added benefit of having experience with the Belgium system regarding punishment and deportation, something departure supervisors were generally very interested in. Finally, as I had been working in the offices of DT&V at JCS for over a year, many departure supervisors there already knew me, resulting in a certain level of rapport and trust.

Interviews with prison officers

Finally, eight semi-structured interviewed were conducted by myself with prison officers working in Ter Apel. These interviews took place over the course of two days in October 2016. The total number of interviews is relatively low, because the prison had to schedule one extra prison officer during the interview days to take over from the officer being interviewed. It was therefore decided to only conduct interviews during two days. Respondents were recruited via the contact person in Ter Apel prison, who deliberately sampled a rather diverse group in terms of age, gender, and years of experience. All respondents received a short letter describing the research project and the interview process.

The interviews took place in one of the meeting rooms inside the part of the prison where the offices of staff members are also located and lasted between forty minutes and almost two hours. Respondents were guaranteed anonymity and confidentiality, although most prison officers indicated this was not important to them. A topic list was used to structure the interviews, but in many cases conversations went beyond the topics on this list. The interviews focussed on the question how the creation of an all-foreign prison influenced their tasks and responsibilities, their day-to-day work activities, and how they experienced working in such a novel institution. Some respondents were particularly talkative and seemed pleased that someone showed interest in their work and have their voice heard.

Data analysis

All interviews with departure supervisors and prison officers have been recorded and subsequently transcribed by a professional transcription service. All interviews with CCNCs were also recorded, except for except for two respondents who preferred not to be recorded. Transcripts of these interviews have been either transcribed by the same professional transcription service or by the interviewers themselves, partly depending on the language of the interview. Interviews in another language than English have been translated by the interviewer, except for interviews in Dutch, where only quotes that have been used in this dissertation have been translated.

All interview transcripts have been analysed and coded according to relevant research themes, this time using the qualitative software program NVivo. The choice of software was the result of my stay as a visiting scholar at Monash University in Melbourne, Australia, where the computers are equipped with NVivo instead of AtlasTi. However, both programmes essentially offer the same services. As with the first case study, a list of different codes was created based on the main research questions and overarching themes of the research. This list was subsequently further amended and expanded during the coding, based on new themes that emerged during this part of the analytical phase. Upon completion of the coding, all the relevant excerpts for specific research questions and topics were extracted, differentiated by the three different groups of respondents: CCNCs, departure supervisors, and prison officers.

Ethical considerations

Like the first case study, all fieldwork and data collection was done in accordance with the 'code of conduct for scientific practice' and the 'code of use of personal data in research' of the Association of Universities in the Netherlands (VSNU). Conducting research on imprisonment and deportation raises a number of ethical concerns, involving both sensitivity (referring to the research area) and vulnerability (referring to the research subjects) (Düvell, Triandafyllidou, & Vollmer, 2009). It is therefore important to not only be aware of these issues, but also to be as transparent as possible about how this might have influenced the research (Düvell et al., 2009). This includes being transparent and accountable about the methodological choices that have been made. The most pressing ethical concerns that rose out of this research project were related to issues of identity and power, informed consent, confidentiality, and accountability (Eastmond, 2007; Hasselberg, 2016; Peutz, 2006). Although some of the ethical issues could be addressed in advance, in other cases they required ongoing sensitivity and reflection in terms of ethical decision-making. In those cases, it was particularly valuable to be able to fall back on advice of more experienced academic colleagues or supervisors.

All research affects their subjects in one way or another, but there are different levels of influence. It is commonly accepted that the researcher is not so much interfering with the data, but rather an integral part of it (Eastmond, 2007). Especially conducting research with individuals who have very limited control over the way their narratives are presented, raises a number of issues regarding researcher identity vis-à-vis the research subjects, power and representation (Düvell et al., 2009; Eastmond, 2007; Jacobsen & Landau, 2003). A common experience among people studying unauthorised migrants is to find that research subjects have certain expectations of the researcher (Düvell et al., 2009; Hasselberg, 2016). This was also the case with some of the respondents of this study, as several of them expressed the hope that their participation would help in making the 'outside world' aware of their situation. One respondent had even smuggled some food to the interview, in order for the researcher to bring this outside the prison and raise public attention about the bad quality of food and overall perceived bad circumstances. Such cases required the researcher to be very clear about what they can – and especially cannot – do for respondents, in order to not raise false hope among respondents. In all these cases, the researcher therefore carefully explained the aim of the research project as well as the expected outputs. He or she also emphasised that for any legal assistance, they could best turn to their lawyer.

No interviews were conducted without explicit written informed consent of the respondent. In practice, this meant all respondents signed an informed consent form before the actual interview started. This form outlined the aim of the research project, stressed that all interview data would be treated anonymous and confidential, and that no information would be shared with authorities or third parties. Respondents were asked to confirm that they understood the study design, had been able to ask questions and these had been satisfactorily answered, agreed to participate, and allowed the interview to be recorded and used for research purposes. The informed consent form was available in six languages, matching the languages of the interviews. All of the information was also discussed verbally to make sure respondents clearly understood everything before the signed the form and started with the interview. Respondents were also informed that they could decide to not answer any questions or withdraw from the interview at any time, which would result in destruction of all collected data. Almost all respondents signed the informed consent form, but some admitted to using a false name, while others refused to sign any document because they were hiding their identity from the authorities. In those cases, verbal consent was the best possible alternative.

Finally, there are questions of representation and a fair and balanced discourse. By focusing the analytical gaze on deportees as a group, researchers can unwittingly become part of the everyday production of individuals as a – highly stigmatised – legal category (De Genova, 2002). This is an important critique of any social science research with people who have been marginalised and rendered powerless by state interventions. Although this is to some extent inevitable, a good example of responding to this critique is provided in Coutin's (2000, p. 23) study of legalisation struggles of Salvadoran migrants in the United States, which she frames as "an ethnography of a legal process rather of a particular group of people." A similar approach could be adopted in a study on deportations, by taking as a starting point the socio-political condition of deportation instead of the legal category of deportee. Avoiding language that contributes to stigmatisation, including victimisation, is important (Düvell et al., 2009).

Because departure supervisors and prison officers are not considered vulnerable respondents, a less stringent protocol was adhered to for the interviews with these actors. For example, no informed consent form was used in these cases, as their agreement to participate in the research was seen as a sufficient indication of their consent. At the beginning of all interviews, respondents were also informed about the aim and methods of the research project, the position and role of the interviewer, and the envisaged outcomes of the research project. All respondents were guaranteed anonymity and confidentially, meaning that none of the information they provided would be traceable to an individual. However, many departure supervisors and prison officer indicated this was not an important issue to them and they would have no problem with information being not anonymous. The interviewer also always stressed the independent nature of the research project, which was not commissioned by DJI or DT&V. Transcripts of the interview would therefore not be shared with the employers of respondents. Before starting the actual interview, as well as at the end of the interview, respondents were always given the opportunity to ask any questions they might have.

Finally, data was handled and stored in a secure manner. This means that all audio files and transcripts, as well as the data file from DT&V with the information on the population of CCNCs, were stored in password protected folder that was only accessible by myself. E-mails containing audio files and transcripts that were sent between the different interviewers were immediately deleted upon sending or receiving them.

In the range of books published by the Meijers Research Institute and Graduate School of Leiden Law School, Leiden University, the following titles were published in 2018, 2019 and 2020

MI-300 N.N. Koster, *Crime victims and the police: Crime victims' evaluations of police behavior, legitimacy, and cooperation: A multi-method study*, (diss. Leiden), Amsterdam: Ipskamp Printing 2018

MI-301 J. Zhu, *Straightjacket: Same-Sex Orientation under Chinese Family Law – Marriage, Parenthood, Eldercare*, (diss. Leiden), Amsterdam: Ipskamp Printing 2018

MI-302 X. Li, *Collective Labour Rights and Collective Labour Relations of China*, (diss. Leiden), Amsterdam: Ipskamp Printing 2018, ISBN 978 94 0280 924 4

MI-303 F. de Paula, *Legislative Policy in Brazil: Limits and Possibilities*, (diss. Leiden), Amsterdam: Ipskamp Printing 2018, ISBN 978 94 028 0957 2

MI-304 C. Achmad, *Children's Rights in International Commercial Surrogacy: Exploring the challenges from a child rights, public international human rights law perspective*, (diss. Leiden), Amsterdam: Ipskamp Printing 2018, ISBN 978 94 028 1061 5

MI-305 E.B. Beenakker, *The implementation of international law in the national legal order – A legislative perspective*, (diss. Leiden), Amsterdam: Ipskamp Printing 2018

MI-306 Linlin Sun, *International Environmental Obligations and Liabilities in Deep Seabed Mining*, (diss. Leiden), Amsterdam: Ipskamp Printing 2018

MI-307 Qiulin Hu, *Perspectives on the Regulation of Working Conditions in Times of Globalization – Challenges & Obstacles Facing Regulatory Intervention*, (diss. Leiden), Amsterdam: Ipskamp Printing 2018, ISBN 978 94 028 1096 7

MI-308 L.M. de Hoog, *De prioriteitsregel in het vermogensrecht*, (diss. Leiden), Vianen: Proefschrift maken.nl 2018

MI-309 E.S. Daalder, *De rechtspraakverzamelingen van Julius Paulus. Recht en rechtvaardigheid in de rechterlijke uitspraken van keizer Septimius Severus*, (diss. Leiden), Den Haag: Boom juridisch 2018, ISBN 978 94 6290 556 6

MI-310 T.H. Sikkema, *Beginsel en begrip van verdeling*, (diss. Leiden), Vianen: Proefschrift maken.nl 2018, ISBN 978 94 9301 997 3

MI-311 L. Kools, *Essays on wealth, health and data collection*, (diss. Leiden), Amsterdam: Ipskamp Printing 2018, ISBN 978 94 0281 168 1

MI-312 S. Voskamp, *Onderwijsovereenkomst. Contractenrechtelijke leerstukken toegepast op de re chtsverhouding tussen school, leerling en ouders in het primair en voortgezet bekostigd onderwijs*, (diss. Leiden), Den Haag: Boom juridisch 2018, ISBN 978 94 6290 585 6

MI-313 S. van der Hof e.a. (red.), *Recht uit het hart*, (liber amicorum W. Hins), Amsterdam: Ipskamp Printing 2018, ISBN 978 94 028 1310 4

MI-314 D. Kong, *Civil Liability for Damage caused by Global Navigation Satellite System*, (diss. Leiden), Amsterdam: Ipskamp Printing 2018

MI-315 T.B.D. van der Wal, *Nemo condicit rem suam. Over de samenloop tussen de rei vindicatio en de condictio*, (diss. Leiden), Den Haag: Boom juridisch 2019

MI-316 R. Zandvliet, *Trade, Investment and Labour: Interactions in International Law*, (diss. Leiden), Amsterdam: Ipskamp Printing 2019

MI-317 M. de Jong-de Kruijf, *Legitimiteit en rechtswaarborgen bij gesloten plaatsingen van kinderen. De externe rechtspositie van kinderen in gesloten jeugdhulp bezien vanuit kinder- en mensenrechten*, (diss. Leiden), Den Haag: Boom juridisch 2019, ISBN 978 94 6290 600 6

MI-318 R.J.W. van Eijk, *Web Privacy Measurement in Real-Time Bidding Systems. A Graph-Based Approach to RTB system classification*, (diss. Leiden), Amsterdam: Ipskamp Printing 2019, ISBN 978 94 028 1323 4

MI-319 M.P. Sombroek-van Doorm, *Medisch beroepsgeheim en de zorgplicht van de arts bij kindermishandeling in de rechtsverhouding tussen arts, kind en ouders*, (diss. Leiden), Den Haag: Boom juridisch 2019, ISBN 978 94 6236 906 1

MI-320 Y. Tan, *The Rome Statute as Evidence of Customary International Law*, (diss. Leiden), Amsterdam: Ipskamp Printing 2019

MI-321 T. van der Linden, *Aanvullend Verrijkingsrecht*, (diss. Leiden), Den Haag: Boom juridisch 2019, ISBN 978 94 6290 678 5, e-ISBN 978 94 6274 544 5

MI-322 L.B. Louwerse, *The EU's Conceptualisation of the Rule of Law in its External Relations. Case studies on development cooperation and enlargement*, (diss. Leiden), Amsterdam: Ipskamp Printing 2019

MI-323 I. Antonaki, *Privatisations and golden shares. Bridging the gap between the State and the market in the area of free movement of capital in the EU*, (diss. Leiden), Amsterdam: Ipskamp Printing 2019

MI-324 E. Cammeraat, *Economic Effects of Social Protection*, (diss. Leiden), Amsterdam: Ipskamp Printing 2019

MI-325 L.B. Esser, *De strafbaarstelling van mensenhandel ontrafeld. Een analyse en heroriëntatie in het licht van rechtsbelangen* (diss. Leiden), Den Haag: Boom juridisch 2019, ISBN 978 94 6290 697 6

MI-326 L.G.A. Janssen, *EU bank resolution framework. A comparative study on the relation with national private law*, (diss. Leiden), Amsterdam: Ipskamp Printing 2019

MI-327 L.Y. d'Hondt, *Addressing Industrial Pollution in Indonesia. The Nexus between Regulation and Redress Seeking* (diss. Leiden) Amsterdam: Ipskamp Printing 2019, ISBN 978 94 028 1697 6

MI-328 L.F. Fiallos Pazmiño, *Legal Perspectives on the Cross Border Operations of Unmanned Aircraft Systems*, (diss. Leiden)

MI-329 M. Lochs, *Contempt of court. Een meerwaarde voor de goede strafrechtspleging in Nederland?* (diss. Leiden), Den Haag: Boom juridisch 2019, ISBN 978 94 6290 714 0

MI-330 M.V. Antonov, *Formalism, Realism and Conservatism in Russian Law*, (diss. Leiden) Amsterdam: Ipskamp Printing 2019

MI-331 P. van Berlo, *Human Rights Elephants in an Era of Globalisation. Commodification, Crimmigration, and Human Rights in Confinement* (diss. Leiden), Nijmegen: Wolf Legal Publishers 2020, ISBN 978 94 6240 565 3

MI-332 M. Wensveen, *Eigen haard is goud waard? Een studie naar de woonsituatie, het verhuisgedrag en recidive van (ex-)gedetineerden* (diss. Leiden), Amsterdam: Ipskamp Printing 2019, ISBN 978 94 0281 780 5

MI-333 J. Brouwer, *Detection, Detention, Deportation. Criminal justice and migration control through the lens of crimmigration* (diss. Leiden), Den Haag: Boom juridisch 2020, ISBN 978 94 6236 988 7

9 789462 369887

Printed by Libri Plureos GmbH in Hamburg,
Germany